The Police Function

Revised First Edition

To MY BROTHER-IN-ARMS STEVE, WITH RESPECT AND LOVE. *A Wiechmann*

Arthur Wiechmann

California State University – Fullerton

cognella® | ACADEMIC PUBLISHING

Bassim Hamadeh, CEO and Publisher
Kassie Graves, Director of Acquisitions and Sales
Jamie Giganti, Senior Managing Editor
Jess Estrella, Senior Graphic Designer
Marissa Applegate, Acquisitions Editor
Kaela Martin, Associate Editor
Natalie Lakosil, Licensing Manager
Berenice Quirino, Associate Editor
Kate Ready, Associate Production Editor

Cover image copyright © 2015 /franckreporter.
Copyright © 2014 iStockphoto LP/Kaybe70.

Printed in the United States of America

ISBN: 978-1-5165-2296-5 (pbk) / 978-1-5165-2297-2 (br)

cognella | ACADEMIC PUBLISHING

TABLE OF CONTENTS

CHAPTER 1

THE PATROL FUNCTION

Topics

- Purpose of Patrol
- Problems and Controversies
- Functions of the Police
- Field Investigations
- Transfer of Evidence Theory
- First-Officer Responsibilities
- Special Situations

INTRODUCTION

To say that the job of law enforcement is unique, physically demanding, mentally challenging, dynamic, exciting, interesting, rewarding, exhilarating, frustrating, demoralizing, dangerous, and stressful is an understatement. Literally, there is no other job in the world like it. Only 1 percent of all police applicants ever achieve the goal of becoming a police officer. For them, there is no other job that they would rather do. For the remainder of the population, there is not enough money for them to do the job, even if they were capable.

This book will address a variety of issues facing police officers. It will address their official responsibilities, how they function, the dynamics that have a profound effect on their ability to do their job, how the job affects their personalities, and their potential to be effective in reaching the goals of preventing and reducing crime.

This chapter appropriately addresses the function of police patrol, which by far is the most dynamic, interesting, dangerous, and volatile area of the law enforcement function. A police officer on patrol, cruising the streets in a black and white, his head on a swivel looking for trouble and danger, is the epitome of determination and fortitude—the thin blue line that separates civilized society from complete anarchy.

A little melodramatic? Not really. Not for cops, because they know the truth. They know that they really make a difference in people's lives. They know that they are part of a noble profession that most people cannot or would not do. No other career requires employees to live on the edge, the edge of society, in which police officers must fight the scum of the earth, playing by the rules against those who have no rules.

So, we start with the patrol function—the most dynamic, interesting, and challenging aspect of the law enforcement profession—to which only the most dedicated and courageous of individuals belong.

THE PURPOSE OF PATROL

The patrol function is the backbone of policing. That is, patrol is the supporting structure and strength of all law enforcement efforts. This is a phrase that you will read in some context or another in every book written on the subject of police activities. Almost everything else that the police do is in response to a patrol action or function.

This is where it begins; this is where it all starts. And this is where *police manpower is the most critical.* If there are not enough police officers to respond to calls for service and to patrol for criminal activity, then none of the other functions of the police will much matter, because the thin blue line is not there to maintain a civilized society.

So, why do the police drive around and patrol their cities, rather than sitting around in the station and waiting for calls like firefighters do? It is because the functions of these two jobs are different in the way that they complete their tasks and fulfill their goals. One of the primary functions of the police is *detection and deterrence.*

> **Example:** Firefighters fight fires and engage in rescue operations. They do not drive around looking for fires and situations requiring rescues. These

incidents are so few and far between that doing so would be a waste of resources. But the focus of the police, which is to fight crime, is much more widespread and frequent.

Another difference between the police and fire service is in the area of how they respond to calls. The fire department receives a call of a fire or rescue, and then responds to the scene. Their response time is not as fast as that of the police because they are at the station and they may be sleeping if it is late at night. In contrast, the police are mobile—they are awake, they are in a moving car, and, because of geographic assignments, they are comparatively very close to the scene of the call. Their response times are generally impressive, which is essential for saving lives and catching violators.

Besides being the first line of defense against crime and public safety, *the patrol function comprises 60 to 70 percent of a police department's workforce,* making it the most expensive and largest unit in any police department.

PROBLEMS AND CONTROVERSIES

Without a doubt, *most of the controversy and problems in policing involve patrol-related incidents.* Rarely does a night go by when the police are not on the evening news, either being involved in a high-speed chase, a shooting, or some other controversial incident that stirs the ire of some people as cops out of control and others as cops losing control over crime.

Certainly there are times when the other primary function of the police (i.e., investigation) is in the media spotlight. Often, drug interdiction units ('narcs'), find themselves involved in shootings when a drug deal goes bad, or detectives attempting to serve a search warrant have to shoot it out with the suspect. But, proportionally speaking, patrol officers are involved in the majority of incidents (good and bad) that draw public attention to law enforcement.

Generally, three categories of incidents create controversy and problems for law enforcement. All of these incidents have life or death consequences or otherwise significantly alter the course of people's lives. And all of them result in emotional responses to two diametrically opposed segments of the population: those who believe the police are henchmen of an over-controlling government, and those who believe they are the handcuffed defenders of a defenseless society.

Use of Force

The use of force against citizens of this country is a unique characteristic of the law enforcement function. On a daily basis, police officers use physical force to detain individuals and arrest offenders. This use of force usually results in physical injury to the suspect, and sometimes the officer. Critics of law enforcement are quick to second-guess the necessity of these tactics, and just as quick to criticize the amount of force used.

It is difficult, if not impossible, for those not experienced in law enforcement to understand the concept of fighting with people as part of their job description, but it never stops them from assuming that they know what it is like.

Police Shootings and Pursuits

Every police officer who has been on the job for more than a few months has been involved in a violent confrontation, requiring the use of physical force in the performance of his duties. Most of these confrontations do not make the news.

But when a police officer must resort to the highest level of force—deadly force—it always makes the papers. And these life-and-death decisions, made in a split second by an officer defending his life or the life of another, are scrutinized in great detail by the media, the public, the courts, and the police administration.

Detentions and Arrests

In a typical workday, the average patrol officer will detain many individuals, and arrest a few of them. This is a lot of people being legally detained and arrested. Among these thousands of individuals, there will certainly be a few who were detained without probable cause, resulting in a violation of their rights. It is these few incidents that create headlines and result in civil litigation and unfavorable court decisions, rather than the thousands that result in arrests of criminals and the preservation of life and property.

A number of Constitutional and liability issues linked with patrol activities make the patrol function *dynamic* and *volatile*. This is true not just at the street level of patrol, but also with police management and supervision, because it is the supervisors and managers that must deal with the aftermath of use-of-force incidents, shootings, pursuits, detentions, and arrests. (When was the last time you saw a police officer on the evening news, explaining why he chose to pursue a suspect that ended up crashing into a family, or why he shot a kid who pulled a gun on him? Never. It is always a supervisor or manager who handles the damage control and attempts to explain the actions of the officer.)

Let's break down the two characteristics that Constitutional and liability issues create for patrol activities that affect the character of the patrol function: *dynamic* and *volatile*.

Dynamic

From the patrol officer's standpoint, the job is interesting and exciting—he or she is doing things that the rest of the world only gets to see on television. To the patrol officer, it can be a really fun job.

From the police supervisor's or manager's standpoint, the activities of patrol officers draw the attention of the public and the media, requiring them to be constantly justifying the activities of their officers, and explaining to the community and its leaders why their officers took the actions that they did.

Volatile

The job of a patrol officer is physically dangerous, and every police officer with any tenable level of experience has suffered personal injury as a result of a violent confrontation with a suspect. This is a subject of grave concern for police supervisors, who are ultimately responsible for the activities, training, and safety of their officers.

From a police management perspective, the job of a patrol officer is volatile in a controversial sense, because there are a lot of people who do not agree with the functions or activities of the police and are quick to criticize when an incident has less than a perfect outcome.

FUNCTIONS OF THE POLICE

One expert refers to the two basic activities of the patrol function as "watching" and "being watched." What this expert is referring to is the primary purpose of patrol—*detection* and *deterrence*.

The function of detection as it relates to the patrol function is maintaining a mobile surveillance of an assigned area to locate suspicious and criminal activity, and to take enforcement action as necessary. The term *watching* is a simplistic term that means the same thing as detection—patrol officers watch out for activity that could be unlawful, and respond to investigate and resolve the incident.

This function of detection (i.e., detecting crime) is not as effective as anyone would like it to be. In all actuality, patrol officers witness very few crimes in progress, contrary to what television shows would lead most people to believe.

Patrol officers make a handful of arrests each month, and can probably count on one hand the number of serious crimes that they have actually witnessed as a result of routine patrol activities. This, of course, does not count the crimes that officers have witnessed because they responded to a report of a crime in progress or suspicious activity that turned out to be a crime in progress.

Being watched is also a simplistic term for the patrol purpose and function of deterrence, which is the foundation of preventive patrol functions—making a visible presence—by way of distinctively marked police units and spiffy uniforms, to deter would-be criminals from committing crimes for fear of being caught by these vigilant guardians of society.

However, the patrol efforts of deterrence (being watched) are difficult to measure, because it is not possible to measure something that did not occur. This is one of the reasons that there is a lot of controversy over the effectiveness of police efforts at deterrence, because we cannot measure something that was prevented before it happened.

> **Example:** A patrol officer drives through the parking lot of a convenience store as part of his routine patrol duties. Because of this, a potential robber, who was hiding in the shadows, decides not to rob the store. The patrol officer prevented a serious crime from occurring, but this effort cannot be measured.

The police can measure the effectiveness of their investigators through their clearance rates, but they cannot measure the effectiveness of patrol activities. This begs the question of the patrol function: do visible patrols prevent people from committing crimes?

The effectiveness of police patrols cannot be properly measured, because we cannot measure things that did not happen because of patrol activities. An assessment of effectiveness is based on more of a commonsense approach rather than on quantifiable data; it is just common sense that if a police car is around people do not commit crimes.

> **Example:** Even the most conscientious driver, one who always obeys the traffic laws, will be a little disconcerted when a police car is right behind them. All of us slow down and are more careful of our driving when the police are around.

This is the reason that patrol officers wear uniforms and drive such distinctively marked cars. It is these uniforms and marked cars that, in theory, prevent crime.

This whole idea of deterrence has to do with the *doctrine of preventive patrol*; that is, creating the illusion that the police are everywhere, so you better behave. Many studies have been conducted to explore the most effective use of patrol resources, but there is no clear answer.

In 1971, the Kansas City Police Department conducted a two-year experiment to determine if random patrol had an effect on crime. The results had a major impact on how the police viewed their activities. We will examine this study in chapter 3, community-oriented policing.

Police Image

Besides the important functions of detection and deterrence, patrol officers have more impact on *the image of the police* than in any other assignment in a police department.

Imagine that you are a police officer, in uniform, driving a police car. You pull someone over for speeding or for looking suspicious in an alley, or you arrive at the scene of an accident, or you meet with someone whose home was burglarized. This is probably the first time that this individual has had contact with a police officer in a long time. It may have been months, or more likely, years since they have even talked to a police officer, if ever. So imagine the tremendous impact that you have on them— not just on their lives because of this important contact they are having with you, but also because of the impression they have about the police based on your behavior, attitude, and effort.

So, the way an officer deals with a citizen's problem or conducts a field investigation has a tremendous effect on the police image, and on the *potential for solving the crime*.

Uniformed police officers are out on patrol for three reasons:

- Detection and deterrence
- Responding to calls for service
- Conducting field investigations

FIELD INVESTIGATIONS

There is a big difference between taking a report and conducting an investigation. Anyone with average intelligence and skills can take information from a witness or victim and write a report. What police officers are expected to do, however, is to conduct a *field investigation*, which is much more involved and complex than just writing down facts.

Many police departments create civilian positions to handle routine duties, and sometimes these duties include taking reports. These civilians are not trained to conduct investigations as police officers are, so generally speaking, the more serious investigations are (or should) be conducted by police officers rather than civilians. (This observation is not meant as a slight against civilian police employees. Experienced civilians are very capable in obtaining all necessary information for a follow-up investigation. But when suspects are at the scene and need to be interrogated, or witnesses are reluctant or uncooperative, a sworn police officer should conduct the field investigation.)

Not every call that a police officer responds to is actually a crime. Police officers handle disturbances, suspicious activity, a variety of disputes, and many other types of incidents that turn out not to be crimes. However, police officers should handle each incident as a potential crime and investigate it as such until they determine that no crime has occurred.

By taking this approach, many incidents initially thought not to be crimes can be uncovered, resulting in a higher level of effectiveness. And, more important, conducting an investigation rather than just taking a report *greatly increases the potential for solving the crime.*

The field investigation is the initial inquiry by officers to *establish facts* and the circumstances of a suspected crime and to *preserve evidence* related to that crime. The objective is to identify and apprehend the offender by gathering evidence.

So, the two parts of the field investigation are *obtaining facts*, usually through statements, and *obtaining evidence*, usually physical evidence, but it may also include statements. (Yes, statements establish facts, and they can also be evidence, but not all statements are evidence.)

> **Example:** Witness A established facts that a business was locked up the night before and everything was normal at the time. This is not considered evidence. Witness B saw a vehicle pull up to the business late at night and witnessed a suspect break out a window and go inside. This statement is evidence.

When we refer to evidence, we are referring to all types of evidence. *The most common kind of evidence that will be found at most crime scenes will be statements by victims and witnesses.* And if the police luck out, there may be physical evidence at the scene.

Officers must be aware that the crime scene is a major source of physical evidence. Because of this, *protection of the scene*, especially in major crimes, will be the responsibility of the investigator conducting the preliminary investigation—the patrol officer. The role of evidence at the crime scene can be critical for successfully solving a crime.

Role of Evidence at the Crime Scene

The patrol officer must protect a crime scene to prevent contamination, prevent loss of evidence, and prevent movement of evidence. This refers to physical evidence as well as witness and victim statements.

- **Contamination:** This occurs when evidence is mixed with something else, such as touching an object that has fingerprints on it.
- **Loss:** Sometimes evidence can be lost or taken away from the scene, accidentally or on purpose. Bullet casings at a crime scene are actually taken by bystanders as souvenirs.
- **Movement:** Items of evidential value should never be moved until the items have been photographed. Showing the exact location of items could later be critical, and officers must protect these items from being moved prior to photographing. Note that if an item has to be moved (such as a loaded gun on a sidewalk) the item should not be placed back in its original position to be photographed. This would be nothing more than a "reenactment" photo, which would have no evidential value.

Some types of evidence are more susceptible to loss than others because they have a shorter lifespan than others. When officers arrive at a scene, they should immediately take note of evidence that has a short life, such as odors (perfume, smoke, and gunpowder), wet footprints on cement, a burning cigarette, and any other evidence that can change form in a short period of time.

As mentioned earlier, contamination, loss, and movement also includes witnesses and victims. When there are several witnesses to a crime, *they should never be placed together while waiting to be interviewed.* What naturally happens is that they will talk among themselves, and pretty soon everyone has the same version of the incident, even if they did not see all of it. This *contamination* of statements will prevent any of these statements from being admissible in court.

Additionally, *many witnesses can be lost* if the officers do not take steps to keep them at the scene. At major incidents, officers cannot always start questioning witnesses right away. But before they just leave a witness standing and waiting, *they should ask for the witness's identification.* If the officer has this in his possession, the witness is less likely to leave without it. And if he does, at least the police know who the witness is, which will make it easier to find him later.

This whole concept of contamination at crime scenes falls under the *transfer of evidence theory.*

TRANSFER OF EVIDENCE THEORY

Contamination occurs when it is mixed with other evidence or altered from its original condition.

- **Theory:** When two objects come into contact with each other, there is an exchange between the two objects.
- **Example:** A suspect may leave hair, blood, bodily fluids, fingerprints, clothing fibers, and footprints at the crime scene.
- **Example:** The suspect may carry away with him carpet fibers from the scene, shards of glass from a window he broke to get in, or hairs and other sources of DNA from a victim.

The crime scene must be protected from everyone. This includes other officers as well as bystanders. The transfer of evidence theory applies when investigators, rescue personnel, and other officers walk through the scene, and that transfer must be considered, with efforts made to reduce the transfer:

- **Only those personnel who have a legitimate reason to be in the scene should be allowed in.** To control this, at major scenes such as homicides, a crime scene log must be completed by personnel as they enter and exit the scene. (In the past, nosy administrators would come in to the scene to look around. Lately, this has not been as much of a problem because the role of trace evidence has become more prominent.)
- **The first officer entering the scene should take an indirect route.** That is, the officer should choose a path that the suspect probably did not take. Everyone else who enters the scene should take the same indirect route.
- **At major crimes scenes, the shoe soles of all personnel (i.e., paramedics, officers, investigators, and coroner) must be photographed because of the inherent contamination that occurs.** This inherent contamination is the fact that these personnel will leave footprints at the scene. It is impossible not to. But there must not be any unexplained footprints at the scene; if there are unexplained footprints it will open the door for the suspect to make a "second suspect" defense that the prosecution would not be able to refute.

Example: A suspect is interrogated about a murder. There is physical evidence that links him to the scene. But there are unexplained footprints, because the police did not photograph the shoe soles of all the personnel. The suspect says that he was at the scene, but he was with a second suspect who actually committed the crime.

Without photographs of the shoe soles of all the personnel, coupled with verification that there are no unaccounted for shoe prints, this defense cannot be very successfully refuted.

A lot of contamination occurs with *trace evidence,* which is minute or microscopic evidence, such as hairs or fibers that are not immediately detectable without special equipment. It is fairly simple to avoid touching an object that the suspect may have touched, but it is far more difficult to avoid stepping where there may be a suspect hair or fiber.

Efforts to locate and collect trace evidence are usually reserved for major crimes, such as homicides and sex crimes. A lot of these types of crimes are solved because of trace evidence that connects the suspect to the crime scene. Seldom are there witnesses to these crimes, which make the protection, preservation, and collection of physical evidence so important.

FIRST-OFFICER RESPONSIBILITIES

The first officer who arrives at the scene of a major crime has many important responsibilities, most of which occur simultaneously, or at the very least, occur in rapid succession. A lot of responsibility is placed on the shoulders of that first officer, and he needs to be able to delegate some of these tasks as other officers arrive. He must understand that he is in charge of the scene, and must coordinate the activities of responding officers on top of everything else.

Responding to the Scene

The first officers who respond to a major crime scene must focus on the *potential escape routes* that the suspect may take, rather than all the officers quickly reaching the scene. For instance, when there is freeway access in a particular city, officers should respond to the freeway to watch for the suspect vehicle attempting to get out of the area. *A majority of crimes occur within close proximity to freeways,* because it provides suspects with an easy way to get out of the area quickly.

Usually, the responding officers will ask the dispatcher for the *time delay*. They want to know how much time has passed from the crime occurring to the officers being dispatched to it. This provides the officers with information that will help them decide how wide their search pattern should be. They then factor in the amount of traffic to determine how far away the suspect could be and watch for potential suspect vehicles many miles prior to arriving at the scene.

Keep in the mind that not all officers in the area will respond to the scene at all. Many of them will search the immediate and outlying areas until it is apparent that the suspect has slipped out of the area.

Once the officers arrive and begin to take statements from witnesses for suspect descriptions, *they need to consider how poor these descriptions can be.* These people are being asked a lot of questions after witnessing something they are not used to, and this becomes a stressful situation for them. (Convenience stores even have a device to help clerks with their descriptions of suspects. On the inside of the entrance, there is usually a measuring tape running up one side of the door frame so that the clerk can see how tall the suspect is as he is leaving.)

Officers must realize that the descriptions initially given by witnesses can change dramatically once they are able to calm down and think for a minute. The first description of a suspect is usually obtained by the police dispatcher, which is done quickly, and just after the crime has occurred. Once an officer arrives at the scene and gets everyone calm, he obtains an *updated description*, which is a more accurate and detailed description than the first.

What this means is that officers searching for suspects and suspect vehicles must keep an open mind—the initial descriptions may very likely be inaccurate. For instance, if the initial description of a suspect vehicle is a brown van, the officers should not discount a suspicious black truck leaving the area.

Identification and Separation of Witnesses

Witnesses must be distinguished from onlookers, and as mentioned earlier, separated from each other to prevent contamination. Sometimes, who the police think are witnesses turn out to be suspects or accomplices. Because of this, it is important that when officers initially talk to witnesses, their statements must be accurately recalled.

> **Example:** Police officers respond to a gang fight involving several suspects armed with guns, knives, and bats. As the officers go through the crowd of bystanders in search of witnesses, an individual says he did not see anything, he had just come out of his house to see what was going on.

As officers get information from other witnesses, they discover that this individual does not live at the house. The officer questions him again, and when confronted with his initial statement that he had just come out of his house, the individual says the officer is mistaken, he never said that. If the officer did not write down or specifically recall the first brief interview (perhaps because he had talked to so many people and now cannot be sure), this would create a real problem in showing that the individual is lying.

These days, many officers carry digital audio recorders with them, which could prevent problems such as the one described above.

Sometimes suspects mingle in with the bystanders, and some arsonists want to stay to admire their work. But other suspects may be unable to get out of the area before the police arrive and set up a perimeter. Now they are stuck there, and try to blend in with the crowd until the police leave.

So, officers must consider this when talking to bystanders and potential witnesses. They should try to verify that the bystander lives there, or, if this not occurring in a residential area, verify their activity in the area.

> **Example:** Police respond to a home invasion robbery in progress. Five suspects flee in different directions when the officers arrive. Officers set up a perimeter and conduct yard-to-yard searches, but capture only four of the five suspects. When the fifth suspect was apprehended by investigators at a later date, he explained that he had been hiding in a back yard, but knew the yard was going to be searched.

The suspect stripped down to his boxer shorts and walked out of the yard and mingled with the substantially large crowd. After the police left, he called a friend to come and pick him up.

If the officers had considered this possibility, they could have contacted each bystander and verified where they lived. The suspect would have quickly been singled out as not being a resident.

Determine the Size of the Crime Scene

The biggest mistake in determining the size of the crime scene is that officers usually make the scene too small. Officers briefly evaluate what has occurred and cordon off the immediate area to protect physical evidence. But too often, officers underestimate how large the scene actually is. Once they realize that there is evidence outside the scene, officers expand it, but by that time the potential for contamination, loss, or movement of evidence is much higher.

This common mistake is often the case when guns are involved. When there has been a shooting, the crime scene must be very large, and can be reduced as officers verify that there are no bullet holes, bullets, or victims in the vicinity.

Also, officers should consider that suspects often discard weapons or clothing as they flee the area. These items may be a considerable distance from the actual scene. If the police do not consider this possibility when cordoning off the crime scene, they will likely never find this valuable evidence.

Suspect Descriptions

When police officers arrive at the scene of a crime that has just occurred, they are anxious to get an updated description of the suspect that they can then broadcast to other officers who are searching for the suspect. In their quest for gathering accurate information very quickly, officers can unintentionally add to the witness's stress level by pushing the person too hard for information.

This is a critical time, which requires a tactful, yet firm, approach by the officers.

So, officers must realize that witnessing crimes and giving suspect descriptions is not something that people are used to doing. They probably have no idea what information the officer wants, and may not have gotten as good a look at the suspect as they would like. Even if the suspect was very close to a witness, the witness may not be able to give many descriptive details, usually because the incident happened so quickly, and the witness is in shock from witnessing the crime.

Officers should ask the witnesses specific questions, rather than general ones. Specific questions force witnesses to decide what they think the officer wants to know.

> **Example:** An officer asks a witness a general question, "What did he look like?" Well, not having any idea what the officer needs for his broadcast, she replies, "He was a big guy, and had very sad eyes."

Obviously the descriptor of "big" differs from one witness to another. What a 100-pound female would view as "big" is different from what a 300-pound male would think. And, of course, the subjective observation about the suspect's eyes has little value to the officer.

The officer should specifically ask the witness to tell him the race, age, and gender of the suspect. Then he will ask the height and weight of the suspect, followed by a clothing description and anything unusual, such as hair length, glasses, facial hair, tattoos, among other things. (Some physical oddities can be traced to suspects through a computer check.) Many people have a difficult time judging the age, height, and weight of other people. When this is the case, the officer can *ask the witness to make a comparison,* such as "Was the suspect taller than me or shorter than me?"

As mentioned earlier in this section, the officer should not press the witness too hard for descriptive information. If an officer tries to force a witness to give a description that he cannot provide, it may pressure the witness to guess, which will make the situation much worse.

> **Example:** An officer is trying to get a witness to give a clothing description of a suspect, but the witness just does not remember the color of the suspect's pants. Frustrated, the officer asks if perhaps the suspect was wearing blue jeans. Equally frustrated, the witness says that it is possible. The officer puts a broadcast out to other officers, but since the suspect was wearing khakis, the officers never detain the suspect, who walks right out of the area.

But let's say an astute officer who is open-minded about initial descriptions does stop the suspect, and he is ultimately arrested. When the witness is questioned by the defense at trial, the issue about the conflicting clothing description will be raised, which will reduce the witness's credibility in court.

SPECIAL SITUATIONS

Dead Bodies

When there is a dead body at a crime scene, the obvious first step is to determine the apparent cause of death. Officers will look for wounds on the body, which will give them clues about what type of weapon was involved. Obviously, if the body has gunshot wounds, the officers know to look for bullet holes in the area, as well as possible bullet casings. If there are no casings, the officers will know that the firearm was a revolver, as opposed to a semi-automatic pistol.

Officers will also immediately check for signs of death. Paramedics routinely respond to these calls, but as part of the preliminary investigation the first officers on scene will want to establish if they are dealing with a homicide or an attempt.

- **Decomposition**: If the crime is old, the body may be in a state of decomposition, in which it has started to rot. The signs of decomposition are obvious; there is generally a foul odor, discoloration beginning at the extremities, and possible bloating caused by the buildup of gases.
- **Rigor mortis**: Upon death, chemical changes occur in the muscles of body that cause the body to stiffen. Rigor mortis occurs over a 36-hour period (depending on environmental factors) and then the body begins to relax. Based on the amount of muscle contraction due

to rigor mortis, officers and medical examiners can determine the approximate time of death.

- **Post-mortem lividity:** When the heart stops beating, blood in the body is no longer pushed through the body. Gravity takes over and blood slowly travels to the lowest portion of the body. This pooling of the blood gives the appearance of bruising. The presence of lividity also gives clues about the time of death. The location of lividity can also tell officers and medical examiners if the body was moved after death.

    Example: A body is found in an isolated area, and post-mortem lividity is present along the back of the body. However, the body is lying face down. This tells investigators that the victim died while lying on his back, but was moved and ended up face down. Investigators will be able to surmise that the death occurred elsewhere and the body was moved to its present location.

As mentioned above, paramedics usually respond to death scenes to confirm the death. This adds to the problem of contamination. The body will generally be moved, clothing will also be removed, and there will be enormous amounts of transfer within the most critical area of the scene—the immediate area around the body.

Paramedics usually remove clothing by cutting it off. Officers routinely request that they cut the clothing in areas where there are no bullet or knife holes, so as to minimize contamination.

Medical Examiner Notification

Whenever there is a homicide, suicide, or accidental death or a natural death in which the victim was not being treated by a physician, an investigation will be conducted to *determine the cause of death*. This is the responsibility of a *medical examiner*, and is separate from any police investigation. Medical examiners are also referred to as *coroners*, a term usually reserved for when it is an elected position (and is usually under the office of the county sheriff, which is the elected position).

The medical examiner must determine the *cause* of death, such as *exsanguinations* (bleeding to death, which can be a result of many types of injuries), *asphyxiation, electrocution*, and many other causes. They also determine the *means* of death, which fall into one of four categories; *homicide, suicide, accidental*, or *natural*.

It is the responsibility of the police to notify the medical examiner of the death. Once the medical examiner arrives, he has full control over the scene. Because of this, the police usually wait until they have completed their crime scene investigation before notifying the medical examiner.

Additionally, the coroner or medical examiner is also the only person who has the authority to remove personal property from a dead body, even identification. If for some reason the police need to immediately know the identification of a victim, they may notify the coroner sooner.

> **Example:** Just before a suspect kills the victim, witnesses hear the suspect say, "After I kill you, I'm going to kill your

family." Obviously, the police would like to know who the victim is right away so that they can protect the family.

Personal observation: In reality, in such a critical situation as the one described above, the police would probably make a decision to remove the identification from the body since other lives would be at stake, and then face the music later regarding this violation of law.

Firearms

As previously presented, when firearms are used at a crime scene the investigators must consider the size of the scene. Not only will the scene have to be larger than normal because of the potential of bullet holes some distance away from the immediate scene, but there will be the possibility of other injured parties.

Especially important at these scenes is the possibility of shell casings being left at the scene. When a semi-automatic firearm is used, expended shell casings from fired rounds will be scattered about. Collection of these casings as well as recording the exact location of each casing is of critical importance to the case.

The location and direction of the casings can determine the direction that the weapon was fired from. All too often, bystanders take unnoticed casings as souvenirs. The casings themselves tell what caliber the gun is, have markings that can be linked to the gun it was fired from, and can even have fingerprints of the suspect on them.

Another very important consideration for officers when dealing with firearm-related incidents is the presence of *gunshot residue* (GSR). When someone fires a handgun, gunpowder residue from the discharge gets on their hands, and can remain on their hands for several hours. If the suspect can be located within a few hours of the shooting, a swabbing of his hands can be done to test for the presence of gunshot residue. So, when a shooting suspect is detained in a timely manner, his hands must be bagged to prevent the loss of the residue until the GSR test can be conducted.

Contacting Neighbors

A neighborhood canvass may also be in order during the early stages of a major investigation. In major crimes such as homicides, every resident within a certain proximity to the crime will be contacted and interviewed. Often, attentive neighbors will be able to provide the police with excellent leads and clues.

This function can be performed by follow-up investigators who respond to the scene, but the first officer on the scene may be directed to conduct the canvass or may be required to direct other officers to do so.

This tactic applies not only to residential areas; it could also be used in commercial and business areas— anywhere where there are potential witnesses who have been in the area for an extended period. This would include store employees, delivery people, mail carriers (who really know the area and know who belongs in an area and who does not).

In addition, officers should make it a habit of conducting a limited canvass with all their investigations. If a police officer does this in his routine investigations, it will demonstrate his tenacity, initiative, and thoroughness. This will undoubtedly result in more successful investigations, and concomitantly, improve the image of the police as well as provide greater service to the community.

CHAPTER 2

INVESTIGATION FUNCTION

Topics

- Role of the Investigator
- Specialists versus Generalists
- Phases of the Investigation
- Sources of Information
- Basic Investigative Leads

ROLE OF THE INVESTIGATOR

An investigator is the after-the-fact gatherer of information related to an active criminal investigation. This function is done after the field officer has completed the field investigation. Rarely does a follow-up investigator respond to the scene of the crime, except in major cases such as homicides. (In other instances, investigators may

31

be called in from home when a major crime occurs after business hours and there are active leads that need to be followed right away. The field officers are needed for calls for service and usually cannot be taken out of the field for the time required to follow the leads.)

Most experts in the field of criminal justice agree that crime rates would decline if the criminal justice system worked at peak performance. *Investigators are in a position to reduce crime* by investigating cases so that they result in convictions, making the criminal justice system more efficient.

Investigators are the link between the efforts of law enforcement and the efforts of the court system. It is the quality of their work that determines which cases make it to court. A skilled and experienced investigator knows what details and elements the district attorney will need to file charges. He will also have the skills to obtain confessions and detailed witness statements to help the prosecutor get a conviction.

If criminal cases are poorly investigated, the result is that the district attorney will not file charges or, if he does, he will be inclined to accept plea bargains rather than risk taking a weak case to trial. When this happens, offenders receive little or no time in jail or prison. If this occurs often enough, offenders are out of jail instead of in.

Offenders in jail do not commit more crimes, and the crime rate stays down. If cases are poorly investigated and offenders are running amok, crime rates go up, and the criminal justice system has failed again. Much if this responsibility lies with the investigator; the district attorney can only work with what is given to him by the police.

There are many ways that a criminal investigation can evolve from a potentially strong case to a marginal or weak case that a prosecutor does not want any part of:

- **Improper evidence collection**: If the agency has to go back to a crime scene to collect evidence that should have been collected during the initial crime scene investigation, then there is a lack of continuity and control, which breaks the chain of control. Many major cases, such as homicides and sexual assaults, rely on physical evidence to bolster the inherent circumstantial evidence that accompanies these types of crimes.
- **Violation of civil rights**: If a confession is obtained without a *Miranda* advisement or a search is conducted without probable cause, a warrant, or consent, any evidence will not be admissible. It is critical that an investigator review each case to make sure that all the evidence that is obtained, including statements and physical evidence, will stand up to scrutiny in court.
- **Less than thorough investigations**: As opposed to what people see on television, investigators do not have the luxury of working only one case at a time. Investigators have a caseload which can be anywhere from 20 to 50 cases or more, depending upon their specialty and the staffing levels of the bureau.

If investigators get buried in their caseload, it is easier to justify taking shortcuts to get cases off their desks. Rather than scrutinizing all aspects of a police report to make sure it is solid, it can be really easy to just take what a patrol officer did and take it to the district attorney for filing.

If the district attorney refuses to file a case because there was insufficient evidence (since the investigator did not do his job), it is too easy for the investigator to blame the patrol officer or the district attorney, rather than where the true responsibility lies—with the person who is the link between the efforts of the police, and the efforts of the courts, the investigator himself.

SPECIALISTS VERSUS GENERALISTS

Depending on how an investigation division in a police department is organized, the detectives (or investigators) are considered either specialists or generalists. This distinction will depend on the individual needs and work activities of the agency.

In very small police departments, where there is not enough crime to justify a separate detective bureau, or not enough personnel to properly staff a detective bureau, patrol officers are also the follow-up investigators to the crimes that occur.

However, medium and large police departments often have a distinct division or bureau of investigators who exclusively follow up on crimes initiated by patrol operations. These investigation bureaus are structured depending on variables such as the agency's size, philosophy, and unique needs.

Cases are assigned to investigators based on the type of crime it is or on a geographic area, which classifies them as either a specialist or a generalist.

Specialists

If case assignment is based on the type of crime, then a case is assigned to an investigator who *specializes* in the particular type of crime that the case involves. When this is the situation, the investigator is considered a *specialist*. An advantage to this type of case assignment and organizational structure is that the investigator *develops a certain level of expertise* over a period of time.

The larger the police department, the better suited it is for a specialist type of structure, because there are enough personnel and enough cases to justify and keep specialized units busy. When a police agency has a large number of specialists (who are pretty much experts in their area of specialization), the organization and community benefit greatly by having an agency full of experts who are able to investigate cases quickly and with a higher level of knowledge and expertise than nonspecialists, resulting in a greater number of successfully concluded investigations.

Another advantage to a specialist type of structure is the fact that *specialists tend to be more effective at developing professional networks* for efficient gathering of information than nonspecialists.

Specialists in law enforcement have the opportunity to join various associations that are specifically designed to facilitate the exchange of information to improve the ability of everyone involved to solve crimes. These specialized investigative associations meet on a regular basis to exchange information about suspects they are looking at, suspects they are looking for, and cases they need help with. Because criminal activity does not consider city boundaries, this type of interaction is critical for the successful resolution of many cases.

A potential problem or drawback with the specialist approach is that investigators do not get experience in other areas of the job because they work strictly with one specific area of crime. However, if investigators are rotated through various specialized areas over a period of years, this problem can be alleviated.

However, in most agencies investigators work their way up from more routine assignments to more specialized areas. This allows them to get experience in other areas of investigation on their way up to the more specialized and technical areas of investigation.

> **Example:** A detective does not start out in homicide. He starts off in a lower-grade crime area, such as thefts, and then works his way up to a more high-status detail, such as assaults or robbery. From there he will be assigned to the most elite details: sexual assault or homicide.

But, if that is not the case, *if somehow a police officer is assigned directly into a highly specialized area, he will have limited experience* if his work is focused in only one specialized area.

Generalists

When case assignment is based on either the *geographic* responsibility of an investigator or on a *rotation* basis, with no consideration given to the type of crime, the investigator is considered a *generalist*.

Geographic Responsibility

In a generalist type of work structure, a group of investigators are responsible for a *specific area of their jurisdiction* and investigate all crimes that occur in this area. This type of structure is designed to promote *proactive investigations and personal accountability* for all the crimes in the particular area.

The theory behind this approach is that if investigators deal with all the crimes that occur in a specific area, rather than focusing solely on one particular type of crime, they will develop a better understanding of crime patterns, crime trends, and possible links between various criminals and crimes in that area. Armed with this information, the investigators can do more than simply react to crimes that have already occurred, which have a very low clearance rate.

If investigators take a proactive approach to the investigation process, such as developing informants, conducting surveillances, and building intelligence networks, they will be much more successful in reducing crime than the traditional approach of follow up investigation.

Rotation

Case assignment based on rotation has no bearing on specific areas of geographic responsibility. Rotation refers to a simple process of *assigning cases to investigators because it is their turn.* The assignments are rotated from one investigator to the next, so that each investigator is assigned the same number of cases. (Note that consideration must be given by the assigning supervisor regarding the *complexity* of the cases assigned.)

> **Example:** If a detective is assigned a complex child sexual assault case, the other detectives should be assigned a higher number of less cumbersome cases, so that the *workload* between the investigators is equal.

A rotation type of system is generally used in agencies that have a comparatively small investigation unit, which does not have the staffing to support a specialist structure or geographic responsibility approach. If a detective bureau consists of only three or four detectives, the rotation structure would most likely be the most efficient.

A disadvantage to the generalist approach of case assignment either by geographic responsibility or rotation is that there is a *lack of opportunity for the investigator to develop expertise* in one particular area.

> **Example:** A generalist who is assigned a child abuse investigation does not develop the same level of skill in interviewing a young victim of sexual assault, which is delicate and tedious to say the least. This is because the generalist

simply does not investigate enough of these cases to get really good at them.

In some types of crimes, such as sexual assault, homicide, and auto theft, a great deal of technical knowledge is required and, coupled with extensive experience in the area, it provides the detective with sufficient skill to be effective in investigating these particular crimes.

Many agencies that use the generalist approach still have one or two specialized work units. For instance, all detectives are generalists except for one specialized unit that investigates homicides and sexual assault cases. The generalists are responsible for all crimes in their specific area except for homicides and sexual assaults.

Another potential problem with the generalist approach is that usually there will be *less opportunity for the detectives to effectively network with investigators of neighboring agencies.* This is because there are professional investigation associations for specialists that meet on a monthly basis and share intelligence and other information. Generalists would not be excluded from attending these meetings, but it is unlikely that they would attend, and if they did, it certainly would not be on as consistent a basis that a specialist would attend.

Additionally, when neighboring agencies have specialists, and a specialist attempts to contact a specialist in another agency that only has generalists, there can be great difficulty in exchanging information.

> **Example:** A robbery detective has important information about a bank robbery case, which he needs to share with neighboring agencies. He calls a

neighboring agency and asks to speak to a robbery detective. But because there is no such thing, he and whoever is on the telephone go back and forth about the crime and who they should be talking to. Needless to say, the difference in investigative structures can be less than optimal for successful networking.

An advantage to the generalist approach is that it *provides investigators with a wide variety of experience* investigating different types of crimes. This gives detectives a well-rounded experience base, rather than expertise in only one particular area. Additionally, this job variety is effective in improving workplace motivation by *increasing job satisfaction levels* of the investigators because of the inherent attraction associated with variations in the work.

And, as previously mentioned, another advantage to the generalist approach is that it *promotes an awareness of problem areas* that require special attention by the investigators. Rather than being responsible strictly for the cases they are assigned, they are accountable for all the crime that occurs in their area of geographic responsibility.

PHASES OF THE INVESTIGATION

The criminal investigation process is very complex and demanding, and no two crimes or the ensuing investigations are the same. The investigation process is a team effort, involving patrol officers, forensic specialists, detectives, crime lab technicians, prosecutors, and many peripheral law enforcement and court personnel.

Obviously, the efforts of all of these dedicated individuals must be coordinated and organized. Most (if not all) law enforcement agencies are bureaucratic structures, in which there are specialized units that have a limited area of responsibility. This separation of work activities enhances the coordination of the work and improves the efficiency of the agency.

To maintain a high level of efficiency and effectiveness in the investigation process, *most criminal investigations are divided into three general phases*: the preliminary investigation, the in-depth (or follow-up) investigation, and the concluding investigation.

Preliminary Investigation

The preliminary investigation is the first exposure that law enforcement has to the crime, and it is the beginning of the investigative process. As the first step in the process, the preliminary investigation is critical. *It serves as the foundation to the entire investigation.* If this part of the process is conducted improperly, it can have a negative effect on the entire case. (If physical evidence was not collected, or bystanders were not questioned to determine if they witnessed the crime, investigators cannot simply return to the scene and collect the evidence. And certainly, the bystanders will not be available for questioning. Any physical evidence that is collected after the fact will very likely not stand up to scrutiny in court as being uncontaminated.)

As was presented in chapter 1, *this phase of the investigation is the field investigation,* in which patrol officers obtain statements from all the involved parties. They also collect physical evidence during this phase. The goal of the patrol officers during this phase of the investigation is to *determine if a crime occurred*, discover *who committed it*, and to *arrest the offender*.

- **Did a crime occur?** Most calls for service to the police turn out not to be crimes. Many of the calls are for incidents that may be crimes, but cannot be fully determined until the police fully investigate the incident. So, the first thing that an officer will do when he arrives at a scene is to gather sufficient information to determine if a crime has occurred, because this will determine how he handles the scene. Regardless of whether it is a crime, the officer will take steps to resolve the incident, but when the incident does not rise to criminal activity, there are many procedures and considerations that do not have to take place, such as protecting a crime scene, locating witnesses, and searching for suspects.
- **Who committed the crime?** When the patrol officers determine that a crime has occurred, they take statements from the victims, witnesses, and suspects. They also collect physical evidence to connect the suspect to the crime.
- **Arrest the offender.** If the suspect is at the scene or can be located by patrol officers, officers will make an arrest if there is probable cause linking the suspect to the crime. (If the suspect is not in the area, and it may take hours to track him down, patrol officers generally will not handle this task themselves, because they are responsible for handling calls for service. And,

especially if the officers need to leave their jurisdiction, they will likely hand this responsibility off to detectives.)

In-depth Investigation

This phase is the follow-up investigation, which occurs after a preliminary report has been completed by the patrol officer conducting the field investigation and it has been routed to the detective bureau. Whether this field investigation report is forwarded for additional investigation depends on what are called *solvability factors*.

Solvability Factors

If a detective is assigned a case for investigation, *there should be some tangible leads for him to pursue*. If there are no leads, it is pointless for the case to be assigned. The detective is not a magician; he cannot pull leads out of the air. So to ensure that detectives are only assigned cases worthy of their attention, crime reports must go through a *screening process* of sorts before it reaches an investigator.

The screening process entails the supervisor, who reviews the completed report to *assign a point value based on certain variables* that are present, which can increase the potential for solving the crime.

The following are some of the variables to be considered:

- There is a witness to the crime.
- There is a suspect description.
- There is a named suspect.

- There is complete or partial suspect vehicle license number.
- There is significant physical evidence.
- Additional witnesses need to be contacted.

A combination of one, two, or three of the variables would result in a point score that would require the case to be assigned to an investigator. Some variables, such as "there is a named suspect," have a higher point value than "there is a suspect description."

Because patrol officers are assigned geographic areas for patrolling and responding to calls for service, *this phase of the investigation process is better suited to a nonuniformed investigator* who is not constrained to a geographic area or manpower deployment requirements.

Note that patrol officers must be available for calls for service, especially emergency calls. If patrol officers had to take on the responsibility of conducting the in-depth phase of all their field investigations, there would be no patrol officers left for the critical task of responding to calls for service. Additionally, many of these in-depth investigations take the investigator out of the city or county, making the patrol officer even less available. On top of that, a patrol officer's presence is much more noticeable than that of a non-uniformed investigator. In-depth investigations often require subtlety and a low profile, rather than drawing attention to themselves and their activities.

Satisfying the Corpus of the Crime

The investigator will evaluate the preliminary investigation to determine what additional information is needed to get a criminal filing from the district attorney. The investigator is basically "filling in the gaps" that are missing, making sure that the corpus delecti of the case is satisfied. The corpus of any crime has four components: the elements of the crime, the location of the crime, the time of the crime, and the nexus of the suspect to the crime.

Elements of the crime

All crimes consist of elements that must be present before an event can be considered to be a crime. Lack of one element may cause a burglary to be only a minor theft, so the detective must satisfy that element.

> **Example:** A patrol officer arrests a shoplifter at a store and charges the suspect with burglary because the suspect's actions lead the officer to believe that the suspect entered the store with the intent to commit a theft. One of the elements of burglary is that the suspect entered a structure with the specific intent to commit a theft or a felony.

The detective believes that this element has not been satisfied, and doubts that the district attorney will file anything more than petty theft, based on the evidence. So the detective conducts an interrogation of the suspect and obtains a confession from him that he did enter the store with the intent to commit the theft. The detective has satisfied the elements for burglary, and will likely get the criminal filing he is seeking.

Not only does the investigator ensure that all the elements of the crime are present, he must also make sure that all of the elements of the corpus were obtained in a legally prescribed manner.

> **Example:** After reviewing the preliminary investigation, he discovers that the suspect confessed to the patrol officer. However, at the time of the confession, the suspect was already arrested, and the patrol officer had not yet read the suspect his rights. Therefore, the detective must contact the suspect, inform him of his rights, and attempt to gain another confession from him.

Location of the crime

Determining the location of the crime is usually pretty easy. In the above example it would not even be an issue that the investigator needs to address. But with some cases, in which the crime occurred some time ago and is just now being reported, *the location must be clarified because of potential jurisdictional problems* that could occur if the investigator attempts to obtain a criminal filing in the wrong county or state.

> **Example:** A victim of child abuse reveals to investigators that she was abused over a long period of time by a relative in her home. During this period of time, the family has moved a few times. These different locations must be clarified, so that each offense is filed in the appropriate jurisdiction.

Time of the crime

This factor is also not usually an issue that an investigator needs to concern himself with. But again, as in the above example with the child abuse victim, when there have been a series of crimes committed over a long period of time *the statute of limitations (in which certain crimes must be charged within certain time frames) can become a critical factor.*

> **Example (continued):** With the victim of child abuse, the investigators must do their best to determine when each of the alleged crimes took place. Unfortunately, children's perception of time is not well-developed. For a child victim to accurately provide the date of an offense that occurred years ago will be a challenge for the investigators.

The investigators use several tactics and procedures to help the victim to provide a more accurate time table of events, such as associating the time of an offense with a date or event significant to the victim, such as the time proximity of the offense in relationship to his birthday, the beginning of school, the start of summer vacation, or after a soccer game.

Nexus of the suspect to the crime

This is obviously the most challenging and difficult part of an investigator's job, which takes most of his time — *proving that the suspect committed the crime.* This can be done in various ways, such as witness identification of the suspect as the person who committed the crime, confessions by the suspect obtained by the investigator or patrol officer, and physical evidence at the scene and/or on the suspect that connects him to the crime.

Process evidence

Physical evidence that is collected at a crime scene does not get processed by itself. It is not the responsibility of the forensic specialists who collect the evidence to process it, because they are not involved in the in-depth investigation (contrary to what many current television shows would have you believe).

It is the responsibility of the follow-up investigator to determine what, if any, physical evidence is processed.

> **Example:** In a rape case, semen from the suspect was collected. But until the investigators have a potential suspect and a sample of his DNA, processing the physical evidence would be pointless, especially because the evidence requires a sample from the suspect to compare it to.

> **Example:** Fingerprints are lifted at a crime scene. The detective would automatically request a computer analysis of the prints to determine who they belong to. Footprints are also located and photographed at the crime scene. But the investigator must first find the suspect, and then obtain a search warrant to seize the suspect's shoes, and only then request a forensic comparison of the photographs to the suspect's shoes.

Locate and interview witnesses and victims

Sometimes when a patrol officer conducts his preliminary investigation potential witnesses have already left the scene. Their information is placed in the preliminary investigation report, and it becomes the responsibility of the follow-up investigator to locate and interview these witnesses.

Oftentimes, victims themselves are not available or the patrol officer is not able to conduct an interview, perhaps because the victim was too traumatized or too injured.

Reinterview witnesses, victims, and suspects at more depth

In major crimes, such as homicides, all witnesses will be reinterviewed in depth, and usually these interviews are videotaped.

In sexual assault cases, the patrol officer will usually attempt to obtain enough information from the victim to establish the crime, but will not go into the amount of detail that will be necessary later. This would be done by a detective who is trained and experienced in the field of sexual assault investigation.

Additionally, when the victim of a crime is a young child, the patrol officer should limit the interview, because the interview process for children is very complex and should be handled by an expert in the field.

Sometimes a patrol officer will attempt to interrogate a suspect, but it is usually best that the officer leave it to the investigator to conduct the interrogation. The interrogation process is very complex and time consuming, and if the patrol officer does not have the skills necessary for a proper interrogation, or simply does not have the time to devote to it, a less-than-stellar attempt could jeopardize the case.

Even if the patrol officer does obtain a confession, the detective will likely need to obtain additional information from the suspect, depending upon the complexity of the investigation, which would require him to reinterrogate the suspect.

Concluding the Investigation

Sadly, *most follow-up investigations are unsuccessful.* "Crimes against persons" cases are the most successful, with success rates of 20 to 30 percent. This success rate is simply because there is a witness the crime—the victim. Unwitnessed "crimes against property" have about a 10 percent success rate.

There comes a time when the investigator must close out the case, simply because no new information has been developed to help in identifying the suspect, and so there is no reason to keep working on it.

The small percentage of cases that do reach a successful conclusion are taken to the prosecutor during this stage. The prosecutor (district attorney) evaluates the evidence, and then decides whether to issue a criminal complaint.

Once that decision had been made by the prosecutor, *the case is closed by the investigator.* Law enforcement does not wait to see if the prosecutor gets a conviction, because that part of the criminal justice system is out of their hands. And even if the defendant is found not guilty by a jury, it does not mean that he did not commit the crime; it just meant that this fact could not be proven beyond a reasonable doubt.

In some instances, however, the investigator continues to work on a case after the criminal filing has been obtained. This is because when a suspect is in custody the investigator has only two or three days to get the case filed with the prosecutor or the suspect must be released from custody. So, rather than releasing a dangerous suspect, the prosecutor files the charges, sometimes without even a completed police report. The prosecutor does this with the understanding that the police will complete their investigation.

> **Example:** A suspect commits a murder and is arrested at the scene by patrol officers. The homicide investigation will take weeks to complete, but the suspect must be formally charged in a few days or be released into society. To prevent this from happening, the charges are filed, but the work has not been completed.

This is why investigators are not in a hurry to make an arrest when dealing with a complex case, such as a homicide. They want to take their time and do it right. When all the information is collected, they obtain an arrest warrant and make the arrest.

> **Example:** In the Scott Peterson murder case, the investigators knew he had killed his wife, but because the case was circumstantial (which many murder cases are) they were busy obtaining additional evidence. But when Peterson headed for

the Mexican border, they had no choice but to arrest him early. Their investigation continued after he was in custody.

SOURCES OF INFORMATION

Being able to obtain information is vital to criminal investigations. Investigators must be aware of all of the sources of information that they have at their disposal. Thousands of public and private sources of information are available, some of which investigators have full access to and others that they have limited access to.

The Internet has provided the police with a plethora of channels of information that were not available a few years ago. Locating a suspect or at least finding leads to where a suspect may be living is much easier and faster than in the past.

> **Example:** An investigator looking for where a suspect may be hiding out gets on a website that shows the suspect's house information, including who holds the mortgage to the house. The investigator contacts the company, who provides him with a copy of the loan application. The "emergency contact" information is not really for "emergencies"—it is for the mortgage company to track down a deadbeat for payment by having information on a close friend. This can be a solid lead for the investigator's attempt to locate the suspect.

Investigators must determine early on what information they have access to and what information they have limited access to. Investigators have pretty much full access to public records but limited access to private records, such as those held by private companies and utilities.

> **Example:** If an investigator wants to get a suspect's address from a telephone company, and the telephone number is unlisted, the investigator will have to obtain a search warrant for the telephone company records. The telephone company is not required by law to withhold the records, but it is their policy not to voluntarily turn over the records because of client privacy concerns.

Investigators should also be cognizant of information that they have right around them. Oftentimes, fellow investigators, because of their specialized assignments, may have information that others do not have, and do not know how to go about getting it.

> **Example:** A narcotics detective (*drug interdiction investigator* is a more accurate term) is trying to track the assets of a drug dealer. He needs to find out what the drug dealer's reported income was for the previous year, but does not know how to go about it, and does not know who he should call to get the information. (Making a telephone call to the Internal Revenue Service will likely take hours to

get to a person who can give him the
information he is looking for.)

However, a fraud detective who works in the same office
will likely have personal contacts at the IRS and can help
route him to the right person, saving valuable time and
preventing much frustration.

An investigator will be much more successful when he
has developed good sources of information. He should
start this practice early in his career by *cultivating his
contacts and informants.* By not blowing people off, by
giving people his time and his business card, with offers
to help them with any problems, patrol officers and
investigators alike will get information from people now
and in the future.

The people that the police get valuable information from
that should be potential targets as informants are street
people (homeless), arrestees, teachers and school
administrators, and businesspeople, among others. These
people are in positions to know much about what is going
on around them; much more than the police can find out
on their own.

The most successful investigators are those who have
developed a wide range of personal contacts over the
years. This is one reason that an experienced investigator
is more efficient and effective than a new investigator—
they have developed networks and shortcuts, as well as
contacts and informants.

> **Example:** An experienced investigator
> who has a lot of informants (because he
> treats people well, even people he has
> arrested) is working a string of armed

robberies. One of his informants calls him,
and since he owes the investigator a favor,
tells him who is pulling the robberies.

This is an extraordinary shortcut, and the savings of
hundreds of man hours, not to mention getting
dangerous criminals behind bars, all because the
investigator knows how to work with people for his
benefit and the benefit of the organization.

Even if an investigator has no legal right to some records
without a subpoena, (usually private records), a friend in
the right place, or a person in the right place who is
cultivated as a friend, can get the investigator the
information that no one else would be able to get.

Example: During the course of many
investigations, a detective has occasion to
deal with a security agent with the
telephone company. Over time, the
detective takes more time to talk and be
friendly with the agent, and turns the
acquaintance into a casual friendship.

Eventually, when the detective needs an address for an
unlisted number, he can call his friend and get what he
needs, without wasting half his day getting a subpoena,
then another half day serving it on the company—all just
to get an address of a suspect or witness that may or may
not do him any good.

And although private records can be subpoenaed, it is not
an automatic process of just completing paperwork for
the court and getting the court order for the records. The
investigator must articulate in his affidavit that the
information he is requesting is directly related to his

criminal investigation and must also explain the necessity for the information.

The problem is that the investigator often will not know if the information will be important unless he sees it. And he cannot see the information with explaining why he needs it. It can become a vicious cycle of not getting what he wants, without explaining why he needs it, but cannot explain why he needs it without seeing the information first.

> **Example:** During a homicide investigation, a nurse lets it slip to the detective that the suspect's medical records have some interesting information in them, but she is not allowed to show him the records. The detective cannot request a subpoena for the records, because he does not know why he needs to see them. So a loyal contact in the right place can not only streamline the detective's work, but be instrumental in putting dangerous criminals away.

Informants

As already mentioned, informants are a great source of information for investigators. But *people have different reasons and motives* for giving information, and the investigator may not always be aware of the motive. Consequently, *he must look at information from people with a critical eye* and be suspicious of its accuracy.

More important, these sources of information must be kept *confidential* unless there are urgent circumstances that require the identity of an informant be revealed:

- A contact that breaches his company's policy to provide information to an investigator could lose his job.
- Informants have been killed when the investigator did not protect the identity of the source of his information.

If an investigator promises to keep the source of information confidential, then he must, even if it means losing the case. There will always be other cases to pursue, but a valuable informant is hard to come by, and can be responsible for helping the investigator with many other cases in the future. (But if there is some very compelling reason that causes an investigator to reveal the informant's identity, such as being ordered to by the court, the agency will have to consider a witness protection program, which is usually reserved for federal criminal cases.)

Voluntary Informants

For many people, the term *informant* usually has a negative connotation. The term is often equated with the even more negative term of *snitch*, which conjures up an image of some sort of nefarious individual trading information for improper favors. But most people in this voluntary category do not fit this description, nor do these people consider themselves to be informants, but rather good citizens (regardless of their criminal history) who are *providing information to the police, **including their identity**, without an ulterior motive or payment.*

Investigators can get voluntary information in three ways: personal cultivation, departmental reference, and unsolicited contacts.

Personal cultivation

As mentioned earlier in this chapter, investigators should develop positive contacts and interactions with a variety of people that they come into contact with in the course of their investigations. When they are able to do this, the investigators have opportunities to turn these people into informants. These people range from business owners that the investigator has helped to criminals that the investigator either put away (but treated him well) or gave the impression that he did a favor that needs to be repaid.

> **Example:** A detective conducts an investigation involving a particular suspect. The case against the suspect is not very strong, and the detective also knows that this individual has a lot of contacts in the crime world. When the district attorney fails to file charges, the detective insinuates to the suspect that he talked the DA out of filing charges and makes the suspect feel that he must repay this kindness by informing him of other crimes being committed by people he knows.

A network of past suspects who have been turned into informants can be a gold mine for investigators. If an investigator treats his suspects well, showing them respect and not lying to them, a surprising number of suspects can be cultivated for future use.

If you think about it, some criminals do not have much opportunity to interact with decent and normal people, much less a police detective. These investigator–informant relationships have the appearance of friendships at times, which can be an ego boost to a criminal, whose only friends are other losers just like him. They also like the idea that by giving information to a detective, the detective will owe them a favor, which can come in handy the next time they get arrested.

Departmental reference

Sometimes an investigator can develop informants by contacting former friends and acquaintances of suspects, because people who commit crimes also cheat and steal from their friends, and certainly from their acquaintances, often making them prime candidates for informants.

Investigators can find these people through computer cross-checks, based on prior police reports or contact cards (field interview cards) completed by patrol officers.

> **Example:** When a patrol officer stops a bunch of parolee types, he completes contact cards on all of them, which are then entered into a computer. When the suspect's name is run through, these other subjects' names show up also. This provides the investigator with a lot of potential informants. (Ex-wives and girlfriends can be an especially good

source of information, especially if the relationships did not end well.)

Unsolicited contacts

These are people who initiate contact with the police by giving an *anonymous tip*, as opposed to voluntary informants who provide their identity. This information can be useful to investigators, but any ensuing investigation must stand on its own merit. This is because there is no witness available to be a starting point for the investigation.

> **Example:** The police get a tip of drug dealing at a house. If they had an identified informant, they could possibly use this statement (the tip) in an affidavit to get a search warrant. But since they do not, they have to start from scratch— surveillances, detaining suspects leaving the location, whatever else—until they develop enough information for their warrant.

Nonvoluntary Informants

This category of informant *has an ulterior motive* for giving information to the police. But this nonvoluntary denotation suggests that the police are beating information out of people, rather than *individuals who are questionable* as to why they are helping, and what they are trying to get out of it.

A lot of people have self-serving reasons to give information about other people to the police. Some are seeking revenge for a variety of reasons, some criminals are seeking a reduced sentence in return for information, and sometimes drug dealers give information about other drug dealers so the police will eliminate their competition.

Because of the hidden agenda that most of these nonvoluntary informants have, *the information that the police receive from these individuals is very questionable.* So the investigator receiving this information must be very skeptical of its accuracy. But generally, the information is worth checking out, because it is usually reliable.

Paid Informants

Informants who are paid by the police for the information they provide are usually involved in crime themselves, or are at least very closely associated with it. For instance, a girlfriend of a mobster hears valuable information and sells it to the police. Or a lower-level member of a drug cartel makes money on both sides: he is paid for his part in the drug dealing operation, and he is paid by the police for the information that he sells them about the operation.

Most of the time, people are paid for information that would never be discovered through conventional investigative practices. The use of undercover police officers has limited use; they cannot infiltrate the Columbian drug cartels, and they cannot get into the Mafia unless they are born into it. Therefore, they rely on individuals who are already in these organizations to sell information to them.

Some of these high-level informants can earn enough money to make a living at it, but the risk is extremely high. If an individual is identified by his coconspirators as a police informant, he will surely be killed. Law enforcement probably would not like the idea of their own people infiltrating such dangerous organizations anyway, because of the inherent risk of detection, which would result in the murder of their personnel.

Most paid informants are the result of consensual crimes, such as drugs, prostitution and gambling, in which there is no tangible victim. When there is a tangible victim, the police are notified of the crime. But with what some have called a *victimless crime*, often the police can only find out about the illegal activity from these paid informants.

BASIC INVESTIGATIVE LEADS

When an investigator is assigned a case to solve, there is no magic involved; there is no crystal ball, just a commonsense approach of searching for anything that will provide information about the identity of the suspect. As mentioned earlier in the chapter, ensuring that the corpus of the crime is satisfied is often the best starting point. But when the identity of the suspect is not known, the investigator must turn to a process of seeking basic investigative leads.

The four basic investigative leads that give investigators a good starting point at which to begin the task of seeking the identity of a suspect are the victim's background and knowledge of who might benefit from the crime, who has the opportunity to commit the crime, and who has knowledge of the crime.

Victim's Background

With many crimes, the victim is not randomly chosen. With many property crimes, as well as crimes of violence, the victim was chosen for a reason. Although property crimes are more often the result of opportunists than are violent crimes, sometimes a victim of a property crime is targeted because of a variable that, if identified by the investigator, could lead to the identity of the suspect.

> **Example:** A woman is a victim of an auto theft. By spending time interviewing the victim at depth, the investigator discovers that she had recently broken up with her boyfriend, who had been helping her with her car payments. The breakup had not been amicable, and he had demanded money for his help with her car payments. Obviously, the investigator will entertain the possibility that the ex-boyfriend is the thief.

With many violent crimes, depending on the circumstances, the victim may know the suspect but pretend not to. When a patrol officer or investigator is dealing with a reluctant witness (such as an injured victim who goes to the hospital and then the hospital calls the police), they do not always get the full story.

> **Example:** A victim of domestic violence is so badly assaulted that she has to go to the hospital. When the police arrive and question her, she claims that she fell down the stairs or that she was attacked by a stranger, because she does not want to get

her husband in trouble (which is a typical symptom of domestic violence syndrome).

If the officer looks into the background of the victim, he may discover past cases of domestic violence. He can then confront her with this to get the truth about what happened, and then focus on the husband as a possible suspect.

> **Example:** A rape victim goes to the hospital and the hospital calls the police. The victim does not want to talk to the police, but the officer is persistent, and the victim only tells him that someone jumped out of some bushes and attacked her. When an investigator gets the case, he looks into the victim's background. He talks to friends and family and finds out that she had been on a date the evening of the attack. Eventually, the investigator uncovers that the incident was a date rape, and the victim did not want to get the suspect in trouble.

Statistically, *in half of all homicide cases, the victim and suspect are acquainted.* So, if a homicide investigator is able to get names of everyone the victim knows, there is a 50 percent chance that the killer is on that list.

So, especially in major cases, an investigator should find out a little about the victim's past, including previous acts of violence against the victim, love interests of a homicide victim, and recent business disputes involving the victim.

Benefit

The question of who might benefit from a particular crime can be a good focus for the investigation. But the focus of benefit is not always a beneficial route. In more routine crimes, such as thefts, the benefit question does not really help in identifying the suspect, because the benefit of theft is monetary gain, which does little to narrow down the field of suspects.

But in more complex cases, such as homicides, the question of benefit requires that the investigators focus on motive, which is of paramount importance in identifying a suspect.

> **Example:** When a married person is murdered, the spouse of the victim is usually a prime suspect. This is because of the obvious benefit of insurance benefits, or to eliminate the undesirable third party to a love triangle, or to prevent a costly divorce.

> **Example:** In arson cases, the property owner is generally a prime suspect. The investigators will automatically delve into the financial records of the business to see if the arson was committed to get insurance money from a failing business. They will also find out if the owner made any recent changes in his insurance benefits.

Opportunity

One thing that investigators must make sure of in any investigation is *determining that a particular suspect was present at the scene of the crime*, at the time that the crime was committed. This is important for determining opportunity for committing the crime. Obviously, if it is clearly established that the suspect was not present, he can be eliminated as a suspect. Because of this, *alibis must be very thoroughly investigated, and must be investigated very quickly*.

> **Example:** Investigators question a suspect about his whereabouts when a certain crime occurred. He tells them that he had been at his girlfriend's house at the time. The investigators must be able to contact the girlfriend immediately, because obviously the suspect will contact her and tell her what to say to the police.

Knowledge

There are many crimes that are committed in which it is obvious that the suspect had special knowledge needed to commit the crime. For instance, a robbery is committed at a business right after a money delivery or a specific item is taken from a hidden location, with nothing else disturbed. And sometimes it is apparent that the suspect knows how the victim operates.

> **Example:** During a bank robbery, one of the masked suspects orders a teller to get the "COW." The teller explains to the officer that this means "cash on wheels," a

cart with money in it, which is common terminology for bank employees. Armed with this revelation, the officer asks about any recently terminated employees, which leads him to one of the robbers.

Example: A burglary occurs at a home in which the only thing that was taken was an envelope with money, which had been hidden in a sock drawer. Nothing else in the house was disturbed. Obviously, the investigator should question the victim about everyone she told about the money and where it was hidden. This would create a list of suspects for the investigator to pursue.

Many of these crimes in which special knowledge is required are committed by ex-employees or friends of employees. And some of these crimes require a special skill or expertise, such as safe-cracking.

Example: Safe-cracking is a very specialized area, with personalized variations in which individual suspects leave their particular method as their trademark. Because it is so specialized and individual, the field of possible suspects is narrow.

A simple step to get names of these "artists" is to contact probation and parole agents and ask if they have any recently released safe-crackers assigned to agents in the area. These agents will have this information and can hand over the name of their most likely suspect.

CHAPTER 3

COMMUNITY-ORIENTED POLICING

Topics

- Goal and Components of Community Policing
- Traditional versus Community Policing
- SARA Model
- Three-Step Problem-Solving Process
- Effectiveness of Patrol Efforts
- Problem-Solving Considerations
- Management Changes

INTRODUCTION

Until the 1970s, American law enforcement was very much a *closed system,* in which the police did not seek a great deal of interaction, assistance, or cooperation from the public. This was intentional as it provided a means for avoiding corruption and political control. Prior to this period, law enforcement was a very open system—open to corruption, bribery, and political influence. *In an effort to professionalize the field of law enforcement, police administrators separated their organizations from public influence.*

This closed-system approach worked fine until the 1960s, which is when the *social environment of the country changed dramatically.* Crime was on the rise, law enforcement responsibilities were becoming more complex, and there was a great amount of civil unrest. Much of this unrest was focused on the police themselves, and the police found that they did not have support, understanding, or cooperation from the public; this meant that they ended up fighting a war in which they were badly outnumbered.

This was when the *community policing era* evolved. Police work became more than just fighting crime, and law enforcement had to become more of an open system in order to gain public support in helping them to deal with a much more complex society. Additionally, with crime on the increase, the police realized that they could not do it alone; they needed the public's help. They also had to figure out a way to be more efficient.

Many requests for police service were repeat requests, which was draining manpower. With a weaker economy than in the past, police resources were at an all-time low. Something had to be done to reduce the cycle of calls. So, what the police needed to do to reduce these cycles of calls, which reduce resources, was to look at ways to *eliminate the source of the problem.*

The police had to ask themselves, "Can traditional, reactive policing really put enough people in jail and keep them there so as to effectively reduce crime and the fear of crime?" The answer was "no," there will always be another criminal to take their place, and criminals will always outnumber cops, so the war will always be in favor of the criminals.

But one of the things they realized they had to do was to even the odds a little. This did not mean hiring tens of thousands of cops; that would never happen. It meant that they had to enlist the help of volunteers—the public. They needed to gain back the support, understanding, and cooperation they had in a previous era. With that support of the public regained, perhaps the police would be able to get a handle on the war.

So now, because of the changes in society, resulting in increased responsibilities given to law enforcement, the police have to view themselves as *agents of social change.* They are in an excellent position to improve the quality of life in their communities, in fact more so than any other criminal justice occupation.

One of the reasons for this is because the police are considered the *agency of last resort*, in which they are available 24/7. There is virtually no other public service agency in which someone can call the agency at any time of the day or night and speak to a member of that profession and have a member of that profession respond to their location and handle their problem.

And with this unique characteristic of the profession, police officers end up handling situations that are not really crimes. This is the primary reason that police work has evolved into more than just law enforcement.

GOAL AND COMPONENTS OF COMMUNITY POLICING

The goal of the police, when using a community policing approach, is to develop a cooperative effort between the police and the community to achieve three things: repress crime, reduce fear of crime, and maintain public order.

Repress Crime

This will always be a goal of law enforcement, no matter what philosophy, style, or strategy the police are using. Repressing crime usually involves the use of *traditional policing strategies,* such as making arrests and maintaining heavy patrols in problem areas. This approach is often be the best way to solve a problem and is often used in a community policing approach.

Reduce Citizen Fear of Crime

In the community policing approach, the police make a concerted effort to reduce fear of crime. This is because studies have shown that people are more concerned about their fear of crime than they are concerned about crime itself. (Perhaps because the fear of crime directly affects more people than actual crime.)

There can be an *ethical dilemma* if the police attempt to reduce the fear of crime without also attempting to reduce crime at the same time. Because if the police make physical changes in the environment that cause a reduction in the fear of crime, but they have not actually reduced crime in the process, it can create a *false sense of security* with the people who live in the area, and this can make people more vulnerable to criminal activity.

> **Example:** In a particular neighborhood, the residents are afraid to go out at night because of the roving gangs. New graffiti shows up every morning, signaling the ongoing presence of the gangs. The police take action: as part of their community policing strategy, they start a graffiti removal program, in which graffiti is removed within 24 hours of it appearing. Soon, all the graffiti is gone, and to the residents, it gives the appearance that the police have run the gangs out of the area.

With this newfound security, residents then venture out at night. The problem is, the gangs never left, and the residents become victims of gang crimes. So, if the police are going to take steps to reduce fear, they must also take steps to reduce the crime associated with it.

Maintain Public Order

Maintaining public order becomes an important issue when it comes to what is called *marginal criminal activity*, which experts also describe as "disorder," which is a breeding ground for serious crime. This is because when there is continual disorderly activity in a particular area it sends a signal that the residents have lost control over their neighborhood.

The two components to the public order issue are deterioration and disorder. *Deterioration* refers to the physical appearance and decay of areas, which sends a signal to outsiders (including potential criminals) that the people who live there are apathetic about their surroundings and do not care about what goes on around them.

> **Example:** If an apartment complex needs painting, the landscaping has been neglected, graffiti adorns the walls, and there are other maintenance issues, it looks like anyone can do just about anything there and get away with it, because, obviously, no one who lives there cares about anything either.

Disorder is the marginal criminal activity that, if left uncontrolled, can lead to more serious crime.

> **Example:** If kids are allowed to loiter, drunks are left alone in the alleys, impromptu parties are allowed to spring up, and a variety of noise issues are left unresolved, it creates a potential breeding ground for serious criminal activity.

The individuals causing these problems or others who observe the lack of social control, or both, evolve this nuisance behavior into crimes—it is just human nature; borderline deviates turn into full-time deviates, petty criminals turn into serious criminals.

In the past, the police did not really concern themselves much with disorder issues, and certainly not with deterioration issues. These issues only became important to law enforcement when studies showed the connection of these two issues to serious criminal activity.

The California Attorney General's Office identifies three components that make up the concepts of community-oriented policing:

> **1. Community policing is a change in philosophy.** Rather than trying to constantly play catch up all the time by always reacting to things that have already happened, *the police must work smarter* than before. They can save time by doing their job right the first time that they respond to an incident (or when they discover a cycle of repeated calls) by eliminating the problem, rather than allowing a continuing strain on their limited manpower.

> Another part of the philosophy involves *a cooperative effort between the police and the community.* By taking an open systems approach, the police embrace community input and interest in law enforcement activities, rather than keeping the public at arm's length.

> This cooperative effort extends beyond community members; it also involves a cooperative effort with other resources. Part of the community policing

philosophy necessitates that the police make *maximum use of both internal and external resources* to help them in their problem-solving efforts.

Rather than trying to do everything themselves, the police should call upon other city departments and public agencies for tasks that the police are unable to do, such as the health department, probation and parole agencies, social services, and code enforcement, just to name a few. Because of this interaction and involvement of outside resources, much of the time that an officer spends on problem-solving projects involves lengthy coordination of activities with these other agencies.

2. Community policing is a change in management style. Law enforcement organizations have traditionally used an *autocratic management style*, which is very task oriented, with little consideration given to the personal needs of employees and void of line-level input in the management decision-making process.

This power-oriented style of leadership has been necessary for the type of work activities that the police are traditionally involved in. *Strict control* is often necessary because of the dynamic and volatile nature of police work, which is provided with this leadership style.

Additionally, *quick decision making*, which is a defining characteristic of autocratic management, is often necessary in the life-and-death situations that law enforcement constantly face.

When employees are armed with guns and have an enormous amount of power and responsibility, a controlling environment is often required.

When officers are involved in crisis situations, which is commonplace, time is of the essence to save lives and protect property. Therefore, it is of paramount importance that decisions be made quickly for immediate action.

But, community policing activities require autonomy at the line level, which makes an autocratic management style a less-than-optimal choice. A *democratic (or participative) style of leadership* must be used as much as is feasible for effective community policing activities.

This preferred style of leadership is people oriented. That is, leaders of the organization are concerned with involving the officers in important decisions that affect them. *This style is characterized by power sharing and participation in the decision-making process, which provides for the line-level autonomy necessary for community policing to be successful.*

Community policing places more responsibility on officers, so the management style must relinquish some power to them, because *management must give authority when they are increasing responsibilities.*

A basic tenet of participative leadership is that when a subordinate is given added responsibility, the authority that accompanies that responsibility must also be relinquished. To withhold the power but still make the employee accountable for the results is manipulation and coercion thinly disguised as delegation.

3. Community policing is a change in organizational strategy. Two of these changes are decentralization and despecialization.

Decentralization refers to a *decentralization of power* throughout the organization. Generally, in a typical autocratic structure, most of the formal power in the organization is "centralized" at the top of the organizational chart; that is, the upper managers have most of the power, with less and less power making its way down the hierarchy to the officers.

When power is decentralized, it is disbursed to others in the organization, usually to the lower levels of the agency. This is the concept of power sharing.

As explained in chapter 2, one police organizational strategy is to make investigators accountable for specific geographic locations rather than a specific type of crime. With despecialization, specialists become generalists and work all types of crime in a particular area rather than only one type of crime throughout the city.

So, these generalist work groups are designed for geographic responsibility, which is believed to improve problem-solving efforts, rather than only having a sense of responsibility for a specific block of time (patrol officers) or a specific type of crime (investigators).

TRADITIONAL VERSUS COMMUNITY POLICING

The most important thing to realize when analyzing the differences between traditional policing and community policing is that it is not a choice between one and the other. Traditional police work, which is making arrests, responding to calls, and handling disputes and problems, will always be a critically important role in law enforcement, serving as the foundation of everything that the police do to protect their communities.

As long as there are people who do not conform to a peaceful and homogenous society, or are unable or unwilling to resolve differences in a civilized and mature manner (which will likely run concurrent with the existence of the human race), these work activities will always be a part of police work.

But there are distinct differences between the two ways of doing the job, and by understanding the differences, we can embrace them and realize that a combination of these two approaches can create a synergistic effect of sorts, in which the best of both worlds are combined to (hopefully) reduce crime to levels that would not be possible by using a singular approach to crime control and prevention.

Traditional Policing

The traditional policing approach is very *incident driven*, which means that the police leap into action only after something has already happened. In this regard, the police are very much like firefighters—they run all over town putting out fires (but in a figurative sense). By dealing with problems after they have already occurred, it is always a game of catch up, in which the police try to resolve a problem that has already happened, rather than preventing the problem from occurring in the first place.

By being a *reactionary force,* the police are limited by previous events, events that have injured or killed people, events that have resulted in damaged or stolen property, and events that have forever changed the courses of people's lives. In always trying to perform damage control, the police, at best, will be able to stem the tide against the tidal wave of man's inhumanity against man—a battle that can never be won. When winning means placing a sizable percentage of the population in cages for a long period of time, winning becomes a shallow victory—one that is neither morally satisfying, nor practically productive.

In their traditional role, the police are handcuffed (okay, a cheap and easy analogy). They can only take action after something has happened, often at great expense to others. Quite literally, if someone were to call the police and explain that someone was trying to kill them, the only response that the police would be able to provide would be, "Well, call us back when he kills you." As sad and pathetic as this example is, it is all too real. The way the law is written a crime must occur before the police can take action against it. What community-oriented policing attempts to do is to prevent some crimes from occurring in the first place.

And this is what traditional policing lacks. With traditional policing, officers are constantly trying to fix things, some of which cannot be fixed because they have already happened; it is like trying to put a spilled glass of water back into the glass, it just is not going to happen, no matter how dedicated and willing the participants are.

This is the primary impediment for efficiency in law enforcement: all of their activity (in a traditional role) is reactionary, which means it is little more than damage control. And damage control is little more than fixing things that are already broken—some of the things can be fixed, and some cannot. Stolen property can be recovered, but someone who has been murdered cannot be brought back. It is a sad state of affairs when a society is at the mercy of its laws, rather than the laws providing society with guidelines that are there to protect and strengthen it.

With the traditional approach to law enforcement, police agencies are closed to the public; that is, they do not seek input or support from citizens, because they know what they are doing and do not need help from outside. *Under the closed system approach*, the police view their activities as battles that they must face alone, because they have no allies. They have no reserves, no comrades who will muster their courage and resolve to take on the daunting task of reducing crime and the fear of crime in their community.

With the traditional approach, the police seek little input or assistance from the community. However, *the goal of both the traditional approach and community policing are the same — to reduce crime.*

Community Policing

The primary focus of this modern approach to police work is in addressing the underlying problems that cause crime. Rather than simply reacting to past events, the police analyze patterns of crime and use an evaluation process to attempt to identify *the root problem* of the crime pattern, rather than just addressing the symptom, which is the traditional approach.

> **Example:** A large apartment complex suddenly experiences a rash of auto burglaries. Using a traditional approach, the police would increase their presence in the area and possibly conduct surveillances in hopes of catching a suspect in the act.

With the community-oriented approach, the officers who work that area spend a lot of their time talking to residents and apartment managers when they are walking around, as opposed to strictly patrolling by car. The learn from the manager that there is a rumor that a new tenant is selling drugs from his apartment, and that he takes stolen property as well as money in exchange for drugs.

The officers notify the narcotics unit and, working together, develop a case against the drug dealer. A warrant is issued, and when the drug dealer is arrested the auto burglaries stop, because it was the dealer's customers committing the thefts to trade for drugs.

With the community-oriented approach, police departments rely on *the expertise of the police officers* to develop tactics and methods to solve problems. In addition to efforts of the police to identify root causes of problems, another important characteristic of the community-oriented policing approach is *involving the public* in the law enforcement effort. Police officers develop relationships with community members with the goal of the public taking responsibility for what happens in their neighborhoods.

It is important that the police be able to get the public to take on at least some of the law enforcement responsibilities, because the police cannot do it alone. Taking on responsibility does *not* mean that the police expect citizens to patrol their streets and confront suspicious characters, but it does mean paying attention to what is going on around them and calling the police when they see something that needs police attention.

When the police initiate a major community policing project, they commit a large number of officers. The officers saturate the area around the clock in order to learn what the problems are and who the troublemakers are, to introduce themselves to community members, to attend neighborhood meetings, to conduct foot patrols, and to perform a number of other activities that are designed to improve the level of trust between the police and the community members to prod them into taking on some responsibility.

But the police cannot do this for a long period of time. This type of activity is manpower intensive and is too expensive to maintain for a long period of time. Also, the police need the officers for other activities; most police departments do not have the luxury of having enough police officers to maintain a high presence in one area for an extended time. The strategy here is to get the community to take on some responsibility, then to quietly back of out the area and let the community to take over some responsibility for their own neighborhood.

The *goal of community policing* will always include the ever-present goal of reducing crime, but it is taken one step further—to *reduce the fear of crime*. As mentioned earlier in this chapter, studies have demonstrated that people are as concerned about their fear of crime as they are about crime itself.

Differences between COP and POP

In addition to the community-oriented policing approach, there is a companion approach known as *problem-oriented policing*, or POP. Both of these approaches to law enforcement evolved at roughly the same time. Different experts in the field of criminology have variations in their theories as to how the police should modify their work activities. Along with these differences came differences in what the approach was called.

The approach discussed so far in this chapter has been community-oriented policing, or COP. But the other popular approach—problem-oriented policing—is equally important as a modern law enforcement approach. Very often, these two terms are used interchangeably, and over a period of time many lay people fail to realize that there is a difference between the two approaches.

COP is generally identified as a *philosophy*, whereas POP is generally identified as a *strategy*. The philosophy, which was described earlier in this chapter, has more to do with the attitude and general outlook that the police have about how they accomplish their goals. The strategy is much more specific, in that police officers follow prescribed tactics and procedures to address tangible law enforcement problems.

The COP approach generally uses the POP approach (i.e., problem solving), but the POP approach does not always subscribe to community policing. The choice of which approach to use depends on the needs of the individual police department and the problems of each community.

Community-Oriented Policing

The primary component of COP is the concept of *shared responsibility* between the police and the community. This sharing of responsibility ideally should evolve to the point that these two entities develop a *partnership* in which the community does not rely on the police to do everything by themselves.

What everyone must realize is that for this to occur *there must be a great deal of commitment by community members.* This will likely only occur if the police instill this feeling of commitment into community members, which is a daunting challenge, to say the least. Police officers are generally very committed to their job; this is the easy part of developing a partnership. The difficult part is getting ambivalent citizens as energized as the police are.

Another significant component of community policing focuses on *community priorities.* That is, the police focus their law enforcement efforts and activities on what the community believes is important.

> **Example:** If the police think that the priority is to locate a serial killer in a community, but the community members think that the priority is a parking problem (which is very likely, because the parking problem affects more of the residents than a serial killer), then the police should focus on the parking problem.

Obviously, this can lead to problems, especially with the relationship of trust and respect that the police and the community have managed to develop over a long period of time. This is because often the police think that they are in a better position (and are more objective) about what the focus of their activities should be.

The final significant component of COP focuses on what has been previously presented in this chapter— deterioration and disorder. This focus has more to do with crime prevention than fighting crime, in the traditional sense.

Problem-Oriented Policing

The primary focus of POP is successfully identifying the *underlying root cause* of the problem rather than a symptom of a problem. This requires the police to have an in-depth understanding of crime causes, as well as an equally deep understanding of crime patterns and activities in the location being evaluated.

> **Example:** If a particular area or location is a constant target for crime, rather than just beefing up patrols and taking reports the police take steps to evaluate what it is about the area or location that makes it more susceptible to being victimized. They may take a target-hardening approach, perhaps with a community watch program.
>
> Using the POP approach, the police take a proactive stance toward their responsibilities. Rather than just using the traditional, reactive approach to policing, police activities also include efforts that

prevent crimes or apprehend suspects before additional crimes are committed.

Example: Officers stake out locations where a pattern of crimes are being committed so that they can catch the suspect in the act, or before he is about to commit a crime, rather than the traditional approach of taking a report and having detectives investigate the case and identify the suspect.

Example: Sometimes, using a proactive approach, the police can actually arrest someone before they commit a crime. For instance, the police receive information from an informant that a certain person, who is on parole, is planning a major crime. The police surveil the subject, and when they see him in contact with known gang members, they arrest him for a parole violation and send him back to prison.

The POP approach also includes a focus on a specific problem. Rather than focusing on partnerships, shared responsibility, and other traditionally "nonpolice" activity, the police activities are directed toward a tangible crime problem by taking traditional and nontraditional steps to solve it.

Example: Rather than attending community meetings to discuss how to approach a particular problem, the police are staking out a liquor store or saturating a problem area with patrol officers and gang investigators. POP is serious police work.

There has been much focus on solving problems, so it is only fitting to discuss *what the police consider as being a true problem*. Three specific characteristics cause something to become a police problem:

- **Recurring incidents**: This is an *identifiable pattern* to the problem. If there has not been a recurrence of a specific crime at a specific location, it is not going to be viewed as a problem. It only becomes a problem when the same thing keeps happening at the same location.
- **Community concerns**: When evaluating the situation, the police must ask themselves if the situation is important enough, whether it is important enough that citizens are concerned about it. If the community is not concerned about whatever is going on, then the police do not need to concern themselves with it either. (The police have enough to do without fighting battles that no one cares about winning.)
- **Police business**: Before it becomes a true police problem, the police must determine if the situation is within the scope of law enforcement responsibilities.

  Example: If an apartment complex is having problems with tenants using the community pool after hours, that is not a police problem. If the complex is having problems with nontenants sneaking in and using the pool, that is a police problem.

The COP approach to law enforcement asks a lot of police officers: they are expected to continue to fight crime in the traditional sense, as well as take on extraordinary responsibilities that were never expected of them in the past. To help these officers in the pursuit of organizational goals, the creators of COP have created a four-step process to help police officers identify and solve community problems.

SARA MODEL

The creators of COP created a four-step process modeled after a decision-making process to help officers identify and solve problems. *SARA* is an acronym for this process that provides police officers with tangible guidelines for identifying and solving police problems in their communities. SARA stands for scanning, analysis, response, and assessment.

This simplistic process was an effort by the experts to turn the *theory* of problem solving into the *practice* of problem solving.

Scanning

Officers monitor their area for crime problems. For the officers to do this effectively, they must remain in an assigned area for a longer period of time than they have traditionally stayed. Typically, most officers remain in a specific area for about six months, sometimes less, depending on the agency. Experts in community policing recommend that officers remain in a specific area for 18 months or more. This is because it takes a considerable amount of time just to get to know the people in an area—the apartment managers who know everyone, the business owners and their unique problems, the street people who know everything that is going on, the troublemakers and their proclivities, as well as the crime problems and other police-related matters.

Analysis

In this step, *the police define the problem and the underlying causes*. They make sure that they identify the root cause of the problem, *rather than a symptom* of the problem. This is where the expertise of the field officers is important—administrators sitting in an office cannot do this.

During this step, *the officers develop a method to solve the problem and identify the alternatives*. There is no limit to what these alternatives can be and are limited only by the imagination and ingenuity of the officers dealing with the problem.

The following are some examples of alternatives.

- **Zero-tolerance enforcement:** This is a very traditional approach to law enforcement, which can be very effective and is a vital aspect of community policing. If there is a serious crime problem in a certain area, the police will not give warnings to violators; that is, there with be no tolerance—zero—for violations of the law. This means that any violations will result in full prosecution under the law. Once the violators figure out that they will get slammed every time they break the law, they will either stop doing it or will move on to a location where there is less heat.

- **Evictions:** This is a great way to get rid of troublemakers and undesirable individuals. Whether a tenant is a drug dealer or just plays his music too loud all the time, a few telephone calls from the police to the property owner will usually result in the eviction of people and elimination of the problems that the landlords want no part of.
- **Target patrols:** This approach is also a very traditional approach to police work, and one that is also very effective at solving problems. Remember, traditional approaches to police work are often the best way to solve serious crime problems and will always be an important part of the crime-fighting arsenal. With target patrols, the police become aware of a particular problem in a particular area, and focus their patrol time in that area. In other words, when they are not handling calls for service they saturate the particular area with patrols. The sudden presence of many patrol cars can be very effective at reducing certain crimes that rely on defenseless victims and reluctant witnesses.
- **Neighborhood watch:** In conjunction with other police activities, the police may want to involve community members to be additional eyes and ears for them. The police cannot be everywhere all the time. The ratio of police officers to citizens is usually less than 1 police officer for every 1,000 citizens, with only a small portion of them on duty at a time. If the police take the

approach that they must do it alone, there will only be 25 people (the police) watching over a community of 150,000 during the wee hours of the night, which is when a lot of really bad stuff can happen. But by enlisting the assistance of enthusiastic members of the community, the police can increase the number of eyes and ears to detect and report criminal activity. The police have figured out that they cannot fight crime alone; they must rely on the people who live in the community to take on some of the responsibility of protecting and preserving their community.

- **Stakeouts:** Stakeouts are undercover surveillances of certain locations that police have received information about, such that a crime was going to occur there or there has been a pattern of recurring crime in a specific area, that justifies the extensive use of police manpower to covertly observe and monitor activities that, hopefully, will lead to the identification and apprehension of offenders who were observed committing crimes.

- **Other resources:** During the analysis stage, police officers should consider the services available by other agencies and city departments. Rather than continuing with the mentality that the police must do everything on their own, they should seek out the assistance of other private and public agencies that could take on some of the responsibilities that have traditionally been the sole domain of law enforcement.

- **Gang intelligence:** If a particular crime problem involves gangs, it is important for the police to get as much information as possible about its leaders and their activities. Anything less is traditional, reactive policing. The police have specialized units that focus solely on gang activity—their command structure, their goals, their enemies, and anything else that could result in crimes that harm innocent citizens. If gang intelligence can provide the police with information which enlightens them as to the various dynamics going on in a particular area, it can improve their chances of solving the problem, because they will know who is causing the problems, and why they are causing them.

Response

In this third step of the process, officers select one or more of the alternatives that they have developed. The officers, often with the help of other resources, *put their plan into action*. It is at this point that the police work closely with the community and other agencies to solve the problem.

Assessment

In this step, the police evaluate the progress and effectiveness of the alternatives. They may need to make changes or modifications. Actually, it is inevitable that some changes will be necessary. By realizing from the beginning that no plan will ever be perfect, the police build flexibility into their plan, which is a fundamental component of the decision-making process that SARA is modeled after.

During this step, the police also try to determine if the problem was eliminated, reduced, or displaced:

- **Eliminated**: If a problem is eliminated, that obviously means that the problem has stopped occurring, rather than just being moved to another location. This is the optimal result.
- **Reduced**: A problem is reduced if it is not as serious or not as frequent as it was in the past. A reduced problem is better than no change, but not as optimal as being eliminated.
- **Displaced**: A displaced problem only means that it has been moved. When the police put the heat on, often the problem-makers move elsewhere, usually to a more vulnerable area where there is not as much police attention or presence. This is not optimal, because it will probably require the police to follow the problem and work on it at its new location.

THREE-STEP PROBLEM-SOLVING PROCESS

Remember, community-oriented policing is a philosophy, and problem-oriented policing is a strategy—the tactics, methods, and processes that the police use to prevent, reduce, and eliminate crime. Just as the SARA process is a problem-solving approach, there is a three-step problem-solving process that is useful in giving direction to the police when they are trying to develop alternatives and work activities to solve problems.

This three-step process is generally used during the analysis step in the SARA process, which is when the police are evaluating the problem and developing a list of alternatives for consideration in the response stage.

A crime always has three components. Depending upon the crime, one of these three components will be the optimal focus for the police to solve the problem. *The three components are the location, the victim, and the suspect.* Once the police have figured out what their focus should be, they will have a clearer outlook on developing alternatives to solve the problem:

- **Location**: A crime has to occur someplace, so there will always be a specific location where it occurs. If there are many crimes occurring at the same location, the police would focus on that location.

  Example: There is a rash of auto burglaries occurring at a certain location. The focus would be on that location. The alternatives that the police would consider could include surveillances, video cameras, improved lighting, and increased patrols in the area.

- **Victim**: Obviously, every crime involves a victim. If a series of crimes show similarities between the victims, then this could be an appropriate focus for the police as they develop the alternatives.

  Example: There is a date rape trend with the use of drugs, so the focus may be on the victim. The police would make notifications of the problem to potential victims, and provide information and education to prevent further crimes. Also, the police could focus their interviews with the victims to determine any similarities, such as parties they attended, people they know, or activities they are involved in.

- **Suspect:** For there to be a crime, there must be a person who commits it. If the location varies, and there is no pattern regarding the victims, the focus will usually be on the suspect. And if there is a pattern to the crimes, such as a method of operation, the police will develop alternatives which focus on the suspect.

Example: If there is a problem involving a gang that is terrorizing a neighborhood, or there is an active serial killer or rapist, the focus will be on the suspect.

EFFECTIVENESS OF PATROL EFFORTS

So, what is the best use of resources, traditional policing or community-oriented policing? One of the reasons that community policing is being used is because there is some doubt about the effectiveness of traditional patrol activities (driving around and looking for bad guys).

However, critics of community policing say that taking officers away from patrol duties to attend meetings and other community policing activities prevents them from doing real police work. So, we have to look at the true value of patrol versus community policing activity to determine the best use of limited resources.

The effectiveness of patrol activities was examined in the following well-known study, which concluded that *preventive patrol, response time to calls, and follow-up investigations did not reduce crime.*

The 1971 Kansas City Study

In this study, Kansas City was divided into three demographically similar areas. One area had very heavy police patrols, the second area had the same level of patrol that it always had, and the third area had no patrols. If there was a call for service in the third area, the police would respond, handle the call, and then go back to one of the other areas.

After two years, a survey was conducted and crime statistics were analyzed. The results of the study were that the three areas showed no difference in reduction of crime, reduction in the fear of crime, or in the level of satisfaction that the community had with the police. These results were in conflict with the preventive patrol doctrine, which is that the police must have a visible presence to prevent crime and to make people feel safe.

The point of this study as it relates to community policing is this: community policing is manpower intensive, and officers leave their assigned areas to handle nontraditional duties, such as attending community meetings, coordinating work activities with outside agencies, and many other problem-solving duties, but the Kansas City study showed that patrol time was an ineffective use of resources.

It boils down to this: *preventive patrol does not reduce crime, so if officers are busy with problem-solving activities that prevent them from patrolling their area more, it really does not matter, because visible patrol is a waste of time.*

However, one must also consider the activity generated by patrol officers while they are patrolling their areas. On a daily basis, they encounter individuals who are involved in crimes, and are arrested for them. Perhaps just driving around and being visible is a waste of time (according to the study), but *officers on patrol still do a lot to reduce and prevent crime by arresting violators that they encounter during their patrol duties.*

PROBLEM-SOLVING CONSIDERATIONS

Four concepts need to be considered to understand the concept of community policing and problem-oriented policing. These fundamental concepts provide the layperson with a foundation for understanding the complex and changing philosophies and strategies of these modern methods of law enforcement.

Target Hardening

A *target*, in police terminology, is a location that is potentially desirous or inviting to criminals; it is a location or individual that is either easy to get to or that offers a high reward. *Hardening* refers to making the target "harder" for the offenders to get to. Hence, *target hardening* refers to making physical modifications to locations (or individuals) so that those locations are more difficult for offenders to get to.

This is more than just telling citizens to get stronger locks; *officers evaluate crime areas* to determine what can be done to make the area less desirable for criminals. A variety of strategies can be used to harden a target:

- **Lighting:** Oftentimes when lighting is added to a high-crime location, it acts as a deterrent for future criminal activity, because criminals want to conduct their nefarious actions without fear of detection.

But sometimes, adding lighting is not the best solution; if disorderly or marginally criminal activity relies on lighting, such as games in the streets or gambling in an alley, the best solution would be to remove lighting. This concept will be discussed further in chapter 5, "Crime Prevention Through Environmental Design."

- **Modifying areas:** Much of the evaluation of problem areas done by the police requires that they consider modifying areas where troublemakers congregate, so as to make it less attractive for them to stay there.

    Example: Public telephones are used by drug dealers to receive calls for drug sales. By modifying the telephones so that they only allow outgoing calls, or by removing the telephone booths completely, the drug dealers will move on.

    Example: Bus benches are a desirable spot for homeless individuals to bed down for the night, because they get them off the ground and they are the right size for sleeping. By placing a center armrest on the bench, people cannot use the bench for other than its intended purpose, and the transients seek out other sleeping arrangements.

- **Adjust or limit traffic patterns:** If the police can make changes in the physical environment to control pedestrian and vehicle traffic, it can have an effect on crime.

    Example: If walkways in apartment complexes are designed so that pedestrians can more easily get close to doors or windows of apartments without looking out of place, it will make the area more desirable for criminals to commit crime.

Crime prevention through environmental design (CPTED) is an entire field of study devoted to the concept of making physical changes to specific locations to prevent the location from being attractive to criminals. The field of CPTED studies how the design of landscaping, walkways, and walls, among many other things, can have a major impact on crime reduction and resident responsibility. CPTED will be presented in detail in chapter 5.

    Example: A short row of hedges around the perimeter of a front yard is enough to keep people out.

Shared Responsibility

One of the primary objectives of community-oriented policing is for the police to get *community members involved in the law enforcement effort*. This objective of community interaction with the police in solving police related problems is to get the citizens to take responsibility for their homes and neighborhoods through actions such as the following:

- **Improve the appearance of their homes**. If potential criminals get the feeling that the people who live in the area care about their neighborhoods, the criminals are more likely to find a more vulnerable location.
- **Call the police.** Residents should call the police when they see something that the police need to address. The police do not expect nor do they want private citizens to take police action. They only want to turn ambivalent residents into responsible citizens, who want to defend their turf and are willing to be concerned enough about what is going on around them to make a simple telephone call to the police while something is happening, rather than being a reluctant witness long after a crime has occurred.
- **Join groups.** If the police can manage to get residents to join neighborhood groups, such as Neighborhood Watch, whose goals are to be vigilant and watchful, it will go a long way toward developing the objective of shared responsibility.

When this responsibility is established, *the police can let the residents take over much of the policing effort.* It will not be as necessary for the police to maintain a high level of patrol, because the people who live in the area will be doing that for them by being vigilant and watchful.

When true shared responsibility has been achieved, residents will be more willing to report crimes as they occur and confront suspicious persons in the area, because they have become empowered. Too often, residents have come to rely on the police for too much. This reliance can reach a point of dependence on an overburdened, overworked, and understaffed agency that does not have the same personal stake in a particular area that the people who live there have, or should have.

Environmental Change

Another objective of community-oriented policing is to *reduce the atmosphere of crime* by changing the *physical appearance* of an area from looking like a high crime area to a peaceful, orderly area. This is in furtherance of the goal of reducing fear of crime, which also uses a psychological approach to crime prevention, which is a fundamental component of CPTED.

One of the most basic objectives of the environmental change approach is the *redevelopment of rundown areas.* Using this tactic, the police work with and encourage property owners of apartments to improve the appearance of the structures and landscaped areas and to ensure they abide by health and safety regulations.

The police also try to rid neighborhoods of *establishments that generate or attract criminal activity.* Some of these businesses, and sometimes residences, are a constant source of calls for service, and a constant source of crime.

> **Example:** A certain bar, because of its location and clientele, attracts a high level of crime, which results in many calls for service from the police, draining manpower resources, which causes other parts of the community to suffer.

Crimes such as drug transactions, assaults, street robberies, fights, and public drunkenness, as well as many other alcohol-related crimes can quickly turn a quiet, peaceful neighborhood into a skid-row type of environment. The decent people move away, and all that is left is the degenerates who perpetuate the criminal activity and decay of the area.

A very visible sign of urban decay and lack of community control over a neighborhood is graffiti. Gang graffiti is a constant reminder to the people who live in the area that criminals are walking their streets at night, which means the streets belong to them, not to the people who live there.

Police departments that are involved in community policing and are dealing with a gang problem will inevitably have a graffiti removal program. This type of program allows residents to call a "graffiti removal hotline" number to report new graffiti that has shown up overnight. Within 24 hours, a work crew will arrive and paint over the graffiti. (The idea is that if the gang members who put up the graffiti see that it is immediately removed, it will discourage repeat offenses to occur at the same area, because it will be a waste of their time and paint to embark on something that is so temporary.)

Another example of preventing neighborhood deterioration is something as simple as *trash removal*. Many, if not most, of the high crime areas that the police must deal with are high-density, low-income apartment areas. As low-income individuals move into these areas, many more people than are designed to live in the apartments share living quarters to reduce their living expenses.

This results in way too many people living in an area than it was originally meant for. What happens then is that there are too many cars for the area (which causes many parking problems), but, more important, it creates a serious trash problem.

When double or triple the amount of people live in a location than was intended, there is a doubling or tripling of the amount of trash. When the dumpsters in the alleys overflow, which is within a day or two of the trash pickup day, it creates a deteriorating environment, along with health concerns.

What the police must do in this situation, which is far from their traditional responsibilities of fighting crime, is to create ordinances or other requirements that force the property owners to increase trash pickup respective to the volume of trash accumulated. This simple tactic can have a positive visual and health impact on the neighborhood.

This entire concept of the neighborhood deterioration approach is supported by the_*broken windows theory*. A broken window is used as a metaphor for deterioration and disorder. The theory is that *if a window in a building is* *broken and is left unrepaired, the rest of the windows will soon be broken because the broken window is a signal that no one cares.* As the property deteriorates, it becomes fair game for additional damage or loitering. *This lack of caring can spread through the neighborhood, and soon no one cares about the appearance of their houses, and the neighborhood deteriorates, inviting criminal activity.*

A supporting study demonstrated the social and psychological effects of deterioration on the attitudes and actions of residents. A theorist tested this theory by placing an unattended automobile in different neighborhoods and then monitored it with cameras. An intact vehicle remained unmolested, whereas a vehicle with a smashed-out window was quickly vandalized and stripped.

Demographics

The people who live in a particular area play a part in the success or failure of community policing. The police can only get the ball rolling; the residents must eventually take over. If the predominant population of a neighborhood is predisposed to distrust the police or have an inherent apathetic attitude about their surroundings, then the best efforts and intentions of the police will be futile.

Low-income areas are inherently transitory; that is, most of the residences are rental units, and renters are much more transient than property owners. Also, renters do not have as much control over the appearance of the area as homeowners do. (A tenant of an apartment cannot get the building painted nor have the landscaping improved. They can apply pressure to the landlord, but most tenants in low-income area are not likely to make such requests.)

Because the low-income, high-density area is less than desirable for long-term living, *once residents can afford to live someplace nicer they leave the area*. Because of this, these people have little or no personal stake in the community, which results in a *lack of community*.

This means that neighbors are not as close to each other as in the past. In the past, neighbors interacted more, which improved their sense of community. One of the things that caused more interaction in the past was a lack of other modes of entertainment and distraction. But with electronic sophistication in this modern era, conveniences such as television, computer games, and the Internet have replaced neighborliness.

Television has replaced neighborhood social life. People living next door to each other do not know each other near as well as they did decades ago. Hence, the feeling of solidarity and neighborhood responsibility has diminished substantially over time. This makes it much more difficult for the police to get residents to care.

Additionally, in today's real estate market, many people live where they do because it is what they can afford, not because it is what they view as home. When people move to less expensive housing areas, they do not necessarily embrace that area as their community—it is just where they live. Consequently, *they have little or no desire to be a part of that community*.

What this means to the success of community policing is that when the police back off as the community takes over (which is a tactic of shared responsibility), it is only temporary in these areas because most of the residents are gone after a while, and the neighborhood goes back to the way it was as new residents move in. Unless the police come back and maintain a high-visibility presence (which means they start all over again), there will be no shared responsibility, and the area will deteriorate again.

When this is the case, most likely during the assessment stage of the SARA process, the police will view their efforts as a failure. Rather than trying to do the same thing over again (because it did not have any long-term success), they will likely try something different, such as a problem-oriented approach.

Finally, *demographics have changed with respect to an increase in minority populations*. Different minority and immigrant groups may have different social values and attitudes. Getting involved in police problems and issues may not be something they are comfortable with. For example, *many immigrant groups are reluctant to trust the police*, which is understandable given the countries they came from and the corruption and brutality common with the police in those countries. Because the police in their native countries were corrupt, these immigrants may likely assume that the police cannot be trusted.

Also, because these immigrants do not trust the police, they are less likely to call upon the police for help or to report when they are victims of crimes. *This makes these people very attractive victims to offenders*, because if they are assaulted or robbed, and they do not report the crime, the offenders do not have to fear being sought by the police.

Because of these different values and attitudes of minorities and immigrant groups, their reluctance to trust the police, and their vulnerability as victims who do not report crimes, it becomes very difficult for the police to develop a sense of shared responsibility with them.

MANAGEMENT CHANGES

For community-oriented policing to be successful, law enforcement leadership must make many changes in their management approach and expectations. Rather than relying on traditional autocratic management styles and authoritative supervisory roles, police managers and supervisors must reassess and reevaluate their responsibilities in the work environment.

Some leaders can accept this change and adapt to it, whereas others will not or cannot. This ability to change with the changing culture of the police environment will mirror the success in the abilities of these organizations to implement community- or problem-oriented policing.

Police supervisors and managers must consider several different areas, and modify their behavior and expectations accordingly.

Redefine the Role of the Officer

It is the responsibility of police supervisors and managers to ensure that the officers are fully aware of their role in the police department and in the community. They must understand that their normal duties associated with traditional policing have not been eliminated. Rather, they have additional duties of identifying problems and developing innovative methods to solve them.

Redefine Productivity and Quality

Officers must be made to realize that traditional police activity (i.e., arrests, patrolling, and citations) will continue to be recognized, but that the officer's problem-solving efforts will be the greatest measurement of their worth and contribution to the organization. (It will behoove them to make an effort to demonstrate problem-solving skills if they want to be recognized as being good officers, and if they aspire to supervisory and management roles in the future.)

Reassess Officers' Management Expectations

Police managers must realize that noncritical response time, arrest and citation volume, and other traditional measurements of performance must be replaced with individual and team problem-solving efforts. Management and supervision cannot expect that the officers will maintain the same level of traditional productivity when they are given additional responsibilities of community- and problem-oriented policing.

Time Management

As police officers spend more time with nontraditional policing situations, availability of police resources will be limited. This will result in higher response times for calls in nonemergency services. When there are few officers available, calls for service get backed up, and consequently, there is a longer delay in getting an officer to respond to a call.

Both management and the public must be aware of this, and accept that it is a better way of doing business. If they cannot accept this, than the community-policing approach is not an appropriate approach for that community.

Many communities have come to expect a short response time for all types of calls, and the police managers rest their success on short response times. If neither can get past this, there will be conflicts that will result in dissatisfaction—the managers' dissatisfaction with patrol performance, and dissatisfaction of the community with the police response.

New Leadership Style

As quasi-military organizations, it is difficult for police departments to revert from an autocratic to participative or collaborative type of leadership style. But if community- or problem-oriented policing is going to work, officers must be given autonomy and trust to make their own decisions, which is not possible in the traditional autocratic environment.

Revised Reward System

Police managers must make changes in the organizational reward system. Special assignments and commendations must be based on officers' problem-solving efforts rather than just traditional enforcement-generated activity.

Revised Performance Criteria

When police supervisors and managers are completing performance evaluations on their officers, they must not only assess the officers' abilities in their traditional roles, they must also assess each officer in his ability and willingness to become involved in the problem-solving process. The evaluation form itself must be modified to include areas of evaluation that focus on problem-solving.

Training

Police managers and supervisors must understand the importance of training when their personnel are made accountable for additional responsibilities and duties. All officers must be well trained in the problem-solving process. A lack of training will lead to a lack of commitment by the officers, and the process will be in the form of lip service only; that is, they will go through the motions but will not really try, because they will not understand the process.

New Sources of Information and Knowledge

Community- and problem-oriented policing have been around for several decades now, but they are still relatively new concepts. As studies and research results begin to accumulate, police managers must be flexible in their approach. What worked for one agency may not work for them. What worked 10 years ago may not work in a new social environment.

The organization must be flexible and willing to change as new information becomes available. Without this attitude, an organization could easily lock themselves into a community-oriented policing approach that is not suitable for the organization or appropriate for the crime problems of their particular community.

CHAPTER 4

POLICE
ORGANIZATION
AND
MANAGEMENT

Topics

- Transition of Police Management
- Organizational Concepts
- Mission Statements, Policies, and Procedures
- Classical Organizational Principles
- Human Relations Theory
- Systems Theory
- Contingency Theory

INTRODUCTION

Police organizations are unique in that they are designed to be much more controlling and autocratic than other types of public service organizations. Although police organizations are well established and very traditional, they are not stagnant; they evolve and change due to changes in the outside environment and in the dynamics within the organization.

For instance, police departments change the way they function because of changes in society. As explained in chapter 3, changes in U.S. society required many police agencies to examine the concept of community-oriented policing.

Also, dynamics within police agencies cause change. The culture of the emerging workforce is different from that of the previous generation of workers. This should cause police managers to give pause and consider their management style, and how it will be embraced by this new generation.

Although changes occur in these very regimented and established organizations, change is still a slow process, especially when major changes takes place. Over the past 100 years, police management has moved from one extreme to the other, then back again. Change is slow because of the very strong subculture that is entrenched in every police department. So, change is very slow, but it does happen.

TRANSITION OF POLICE MANAGEMENT

Political Era

In the nineteenth century, many high-level appointments into police departments were made by political leaders. These political appointments resulted in a high amount of political control, which resulted in corruption and unethical conduct. (In most cities, the police department is the largest city department, with the largest budget, the most power, and usually a very high profile. For a city politician to have control over this department because of the appointments that he made was important for the politician's professional survival and power.)

The political era of policing was known for corruption and bribery. *Police departments were very open systems, but not in a good way.* They were open to the control of politicians because of political appointments to high-level positions and they were open to bribes by organized crime. There was just too much undue influence from the outside environment.

Reform Era

After the turn of the twentieth century, police managers made efforts to professionalize their departments. They became more organized and tried to isolate themselves from political influence and corruption. To do this, they became a very closed system by necessity. This caused them to become very isolated from the public, but the removal of corruption was a priority at the time.

Police departments adopted rigid, bureaucratic structures and a clear chain of command. They moved away from individual discretion (to reduce corruption) and instituted many rules and regulations, which was important for the control that they needed in order to reform.

Although detaching themselves from the community was not ideal, at the time it was necessary to accomplish the change.

Community Policing Era

The reform approach worked through the 1940s and 1950s, but law enforcement problems changed a lot in the 1960s due to civil unrest and increased responsibilities. Law enforcement managers realized that a closer relationship with the public would reduce fear and improve problem solving. So, by the 1970s, *the police moved back to a more open system*. This move was in the form of community policing, which involved building relationships with the community and getting people to become actively involved in law enforcement efforts.

Comments about This Transition

Over a period of several decades, police organizations moved from an open system to a closed system, and then back to an open system. This type of change takes time, requiring major changes in organizational culture and attitudes. It was the outside environment, and its effect on the organizations, that prompted the police departments to evolve. This history of evolution is an excellent example of how police organizations evolve and change, and why.

ORGANIZATIONAL CONCEPTS

The typical police organizational structure is a pyramid shape, with most of the department members at the bottom (see Appendix A). This type of structure is a typical bureaucratic structure, with two very important characteristics: unity of command and span of control.

Unity of Command

The concept of unity of command is that *officers answer to only one supervisor*; there is a clear-cut chain of command. This hierarchy prevents the issuance of conflicting orders, which can occur if an officer reports to more than one supervisor. Unity of command has both advantages and disadvantages:

- **Provides control (advantage):** When there are multiple supervisors giving input or direction to an officer, it can be confusing, and there is the inevitable potential for conflicting orders. Supervisors have different preferences, and they exhibit these preferences in the direction that they give subordinates. Having to deal with only one supervisor's preferences is much easier on the officer, and it is less likely that there will be problems as a result of these differences in preference.
- **Determines responsibility (advantage):** When there is a discipline or training issue with a particular officer, it is clear who the supervisor is who is responsible for the deficiency or for correcting the problem.
- **Limits input (disadvantage):** An officer who receives direction and guidance from only one

supervisor only learns that supervisor's way of doing things, rather than having an opportunity to see several different styles, which allows him to develop his own style.

• **Reduces flexibility (disadvantage):** If an officer always has the same supervisor, he does not develop an attitude of flexibility, because he has not been exposed to different ways of doing the job. However, if an officer gets moved around to different supervisors, which occurs in many organizations, then the officer can learn to become very flexible.

Span of Control

Span of control refers to *the optimum number of officers that a supervisor can effectively handle.* Several factors have an effect on what the span of control should be. Generally, the span should be reduced as a manager promotes up the organization, because the factors also change.

The following factors can affect the span of control:

• **Complexity of the work:** In a complex job, a supervisor should have fewer officers to supervise. At the supervisory level, a police sergeant should be responsible for fewer officers than a supervisor at the DMV. A police sergeant should not be supervising more than 6 or 7 officers, whereas a construction supervisor could effectively supervise 50 ditch diggers. At the management level, the number of subordinates should be even smaller, because the line-level work that a supervisor deals with is less complex than supervision of supervisors or managers.

- **Experience level:** Experienced officers do not need as much supervision as inexperienced officers. At the supervisory level, older workers with more experience are easier to supervise than newer workers with less experience. At the management level, a manager supervising a supervisor deals with more complex areas of development, such as turning the subordinate into a leader, rather than turning an officer into a productive and competent officer.
- **Stability of the organization:** If the organization is unstable (i.e., the outside environment is constantly changing), then more supervision is needed, which will require a reduced span. Social changes that require the organization to change require retraining or changes in direction of the organization.

MISSION STATEMENTS, POLICIES, AND PROCEDURES

Law enforcement is a very ambiguous job. When dealing with the variety of problems that people bring to the attention of the police, along with discretionary decision making that profoundly affects peoples' lives and applying the complexities of the law uniformly and fairly in ever-changing situations and circumstances, it is clear that this type of work environment needs a great deal of guidance and control so that police officers can complete their duties to the satisfaction of their superiors and to the community.

This guidance and control comes in many forms. A *mission statement* is a very general statement about the organization and is provided so that the officers understand what their true purpose and ultimate goal is.

Procedures and *policies* are provided to assist the officers in conducting their duties proficiently and uniformly, as well as assisting them in critical situations, which often involve life-and-death decisions.

Finally, *rules* and *regulations* provide for continuity and control of all employees, ensuring that each member of the organization is held to the same high standard of conduct and performance.

All of these instruments for guidance and control can be a nuisance to employees. There is so much to remember, and accountability for mistakes or deviations from these guidelines is hard to hide from. Additionally, these instruments can seriously inhibit creative or critical-thinking efforts that many employees desire so that they can achieve a sense of personal fulfillment in their jobs. It can simply be stifling.

This is an unfortunate side-effect of very bureaucratic organizations, of which law enforcement is a prime example. But when an organization is very specialized, which police work is, these instruments become critical for continuity and accuracy. Additionally, without them there would be a great deal more civil liability exposure to police departments than already exists. It is often these guidelines that protect police officers from lawsuits and the subsequent vicarious liability to their agencies.

Mission Statement

A mission statement is a very basic and general explanation regarding the purpose of an organization. Think of it as a "creed," which, simply put, is a formally stated belief. It contains the *overarching goal* of the organization, along with an explanation of how the organization intends to pursue that goal.

Note that an overarching goal is one that will never be reached. If the goal is attainable, this means the organization would be disbanded upon reaching the goal. The goal of the medical community, for instance, is to eliminate pain, suffering, and disease. This will never happen, but it is their constantly pursued, overarching goal. Likewise, the goal of law enforcement is to eliminate crime. In a complex society, this will never happen either. So, besides having job security, the police have a "guiding light" of sorts, a focus.

A mission statement should contain three components to serve the purpose it is meant to serve. (The challenge here is to be brief; many mission statement are way too long.) The following are the three components:

- It is a description of an organization's *general purpose.*

  Example: The general purpose of a police department is to protect lives and property.

- It is a description of the organization's continuing purpose for the existing responsibilities.

Example: In a police department, existing responsibilities will include investigating crimes, apprehending criminals, and responding to calls for service.

- It includes the organization's ideology, values, and operating principles.

Example: A police department may incorporate its community policing and/or problem-solving philosophy into its mission statement.

Example: Many police departments have created mottos that encompasses their mission. The Los Angeles Police Department's well-known motto is "To serve and to protect." That pretty much says it all in a very basic term. Sometimes less is better than more.

The Fullerton, California, Police Department's motto has an acronym, RAP, which stands for response, attitude, and presence. This motto encompasses a great deal of this agency's mission statement.

- *Response*: This word stresses the importance that the agency places on police officers responding quickly to calls for service, and especially to priority calls in which lives and property are in danger. Rapid response to routine calls is also important, as it reflects the high level of service that this agency constantly strives to provide.

- *Attitude*: Sometimes, attitude is everything. Because police officers are human beings themselves, they have good days and bad days just like everyone else. These variances can affect individual attitudes, and may result in a favorable or unfavorable impression about the entire police department. This word stresses the importance that the agency places on all personnel to maintain a courteous and respectful attitude toward members of the public at all times.
- *Presence*: This word stresses the importance that the agency places on patrol officers maintaining a visible presence throughout the community to reduce and prevent crime and to help residents to feel safe.

In essence, a mission statement serves as an *anchor for the community*; residents understand what they should expect from their police, and the police understand what is expected from them by the community. A mission statement clarifies the direction for the agency activities by providing a clear understanding of the purpose, goals, and objectives to both the public and to the employees.

Procedures

Procedures are completely different from the mission statement. Procedures fall just short of being a rule or regulation, which are the carved-in-stone laws of the organization. Although procedures fall short of being these laws, they do become the "operational" rules and regulations of the agency. (If an officer fails to follow proper procedures, it is usually dealt with as a training issue, because the deviation is the result of not knowing or understanding what he was supposed to do. Failing to follow a rule or regulation, however, usually is dealt with as a disciplinary issue, because deviation violates a standard of conduct.)

Procedures are essentially step-by-step descriptions of activities needed to achieve an objective. They are guidelines that are provided to employees to help them in conducting routine work activities.

The more specialized an organization is, the more it must rely on procedural guidelines. And the larger an organization is, the more it needs specialized procedures. For organization, control, and efficiency, very large police departments are extremely specialized. This provides for many areas of expertise, which is great for efficiency, but again, it reduces the opportunities for employees to be creative and to think outside of the box.

These large organizations do not have much choice but to institute procedural guidelines for the many work activities. Without them, too many mistakes would occur, and there would be too many "individualized methods" of completing an activity, which could lead to total chaos from a management perspective.

Procedures help employees who are new to the work unit, or who are unfamiliar with the work activities, to function and carry out their duties without needing close supervision or personal guidance.

These procedural guidelines perpetuate a bureaucratic approach, which always stresses procedural guidelines and job specialization. This becomes important in the long run to maintain the stability and continuity of the organization. (Employees come and go, but procedures last forever. So even if personalities and cultures change and evolve over the years, the activities of the organization remain the same.)

Procedures are specific guidelines that outline the preferred method for handling incidents or work activities. Because it is a "preferred method," this instrument gives a little leeway to employees if they find a need to deviate from the procedure.

Management acknowledges that all situations cannot be foreseen, so the procedures that they provide to employees purposely have "loopholes" for deviation. So, whenever an employee reads a document providing direction, and the word "should" is commonly used, rather than "shall," it should be clear that this document is a guideline, not a steadfast rule.

These guidelines are provided to assist employees in their decision making. A spelled-out procedure will make it clear what the organization's objective is regarding a particular work activity, and the preferred method of reaching it, but provides some leeway for situations in which the employee feels the procedure would be counterproductive to the agency's objective.

As with almost all public bureaucracies, police departments have many different procedures for the many work activities involved. Consider the following types of procedures:

- **Property procedures:** These procedures outline how various types of property should be booked into evidence. This is important to maintain the chain of evidence, prevent contamination or loss of evidence, and to provide continuity of evidence control.

If an officer purposely deviates from a procedure, it would be because an unforeseeable situation had occurred which required deviation, such as having a piece of evidence that was too big to be booked into a standard property locker.

If an officer inadvertently deviates from a procedure, it is dealt with as a training issue. The officer is trained in the proper procedure to ensure continuity by all employees.

- **Jail procedures:** These procedures will outline the many details regarding the handling of inmates, which would include areas such as hours of visitation. The hours of visitation are outlined, along with the number of visits, number of visitors, and location of visits. Occasionally, a jailer many decide to deviate from that policy for an unusual situation.
- **Juvenile procedures:** These procedures outline the situations in which juveniles may be handcuffed, and what type of room or facility they can be detained in. These procedures have to be followed very closely, because federal laws are involved, and agencies are audited to ensure compliance. If an unusual situation occurs, an officer should contact a supervisor before deciding to deviate from the procedure. It would practically have to be an emergency situation. (For instance, a juvenile arrested for a

minor offense cannot be left in a locked room. But if officers suddenly needed to leave to assist with an assault at the front desk, the officer may elect to lock the door.)

Policies

A policy is a clear statement that defines what action is to be taken and why. It provides a statement of purpose, which will include the rationale and action for the purpose.

> **Example**: Every police department has a pursuit policy, which clarifies all aspects regarding a police pursuit. This policy will address several concerns, and the purpose of the policy will reveal itself.

For instance, an *action* within the policy will refer to initiating, continuing, and terminating a pursuit. The *rationale* for each of these three actions will be made clear, which will guide the individual officers in their decision-making when they encounter taking one or all of these actions.

- **Initiating a pursuit:** The policy will explain why this action should be taken. Criminals must know that the police will be relentless in their duties to apprehend criminals. The purpose is to protect the community and apprehend criminals.
- **Continuing a pursuit:** The policy will explain why this action should be taken. The seriousness of the offense and traffic and weather conditions do or do not justify the

actions. The purpose is to have due regard for public safety.

- **Terminating a pursuit:** The policy will explain why this action should be taken. Lack of a serious crime, coupled with dangerous conditions, will justify the action. The purpose is to put public safety ahead of apprehending the violator.

The purpose of the pursuit policy is to clarify to the officers what they are to consider in a pursuit situation, and to provide them with guidance when deciding on the particular action regarding a pursuit.

While procedures explain *how* to do things, policies explain *why* things are done the way they are. A policy is very much like a mission statement, but instead of being general and overarching, it focuses on a specific issue or activity. Think of policies as a bunch of mini-mission statements, just more specific, but not as specific as procedures.

Policies are purposely general in the way they are written and are meant to be a guide to decision making, rather than specific actions, which procedures are for.

> **Example**: A police shooting policy (when to use deadly force) cannot be structured as a procedure. Every incident involving a decision to use deadly force is different, and all possible actions cannot be foreseen or predicted.

A *shooting procedure* would read something like this: "When confronted with a suspect armed with a knife, the officer should fire his weapon when the suspect comes within 21 feet of said officer, as this is within the zone in which the suspect can strike before the officer can react and fire his weapon."

This would be ludicrous, to say the least. Life-and-death decisions cannot be made with a rule book. They must be made based on the unique and individual circumstances presented at the time. It would sure take some heat off the officers, but many more people, both offenders and officers, would die.

A *shooting policy* would read more like this: "Whenever an officer believes that his life or the life of another is immediate danger, he may use any force that is reasonable to protect himself or others, up to and including the use of deadly force."

This guideline makes it clear that the situation must be a life-and-death one, in the mind of the officer, at the time it is happening, without having to follow some procedural blueprint made by someone who could not possibly predict a particular incident.

> **Example:** The shooting policy may state that officers generally should not shoot at moving vehicles. The *rationale* is because of the inherent danger associated with it:
>
> • Low probability of striking the driver
> • Danger of shooting bystanders as the background changes
> • Out-of-control vehicle if the driver is struck

Note that this policy does not absolutely forbid an officer from taking that action. There will be situations in which an action contrary to a policy will be justified. For instance, there is a policy against using a firearm as an impact weapon (pistol-whipping). But during a confrontation with a suspect, the suspect struggles for control over an officer's weapon. A second officer involved in the struggle has his handgun drawn, and strikes the suspect in the head with the handgun to halt the struggle.

This action would be justified, and is certainly better than the second officer shooting the suspect, which also would have been justified.

Rules and Regulations

Unlike procedures and policies, rules and regulations are the unambiguous, clear laws of the organization. And also unlike procedures and policies, rules and regulations are not suggestions or guidelines.

Instead of words like "should," rules and regulations will have the word "shall" throughout them.

Rules and regulations cover a wide variety of topics, including:

- **Uniform standards:** No deviations are allowed whatsoever.
- **Grooming standards:** All employees must conform rigidly regarding hair, jewelry, and other personal issues.
- **Court appearance requirements:** When an officer receives a subpoena, he must respond. If he is called to court, he must appear. There is no gray area.

- **Personal conduct:** A great number of personal conduct items must be followed, from civility toward the public to intoxication while on duty.

Failure to follow a rule or regulation cannot be justified as it sometimes can be with a procedure or policy. Deviations will be handled as a disciplinary issue, not a training issue.

Procedures, policies, rules, and regulations are deeply entrenched principles of the bureaucratic approach to organizations. The following section will describe how these principles evolved.

CLASSICAL ORGANIZATIONAL PRINCIPLES

To truly understand police organizations, we must look at how police organizations have evolved and developed over the years. We will see what has been learned, which has turned into the guiding principles that shape organizational styles and structures of police agencies.

The classical approach to management, which virtually all police departments use, is the foundation for their current structure. The most established and adhered to classical concept is that of the ideal bureaucracy.

Ideal Bureaucracy (Max Weber)

The concept of the ideal bureaucracy was developed by Max Weber, a German sociologist who attempted to find a way to best organize the large organizations that formed and grew quickly after the beginning of the Industrial Revolution. It is important to recognize his name, because so often in academic readings Weber is referred to by name without actual reference to his theory because he is so closely associated with it. So, by knowing the connection of Weber to the concept of the ideal bureaucracy, the reader will understand what is meant when "Weber's approach" is mentioned.

Weber's approach was not developed to be a "how to" guide of running an organization. It was developed as an academic approach; hence, the term *ideal*. In other words, in an ideal world, and an ideal organization, the concepts presented by Weber will work.

After the start of the Industrial Revolution, organizations needed to formalize their structures and procedures. So, this concept of bureaucracy refers to a conscious effort to organize people and activities in order to achieve specific purposes.

This was considered a rational means of addressing the subjective managerial practices that were common in the first part of the Industrial Revolution. Nepotism and favoritism were common practices during this period. It was normal for chief executives to hire and promote friends and relatives into supervisory and management positions, rather than seeking the most qualified candidate for the position.

This concept emphasizes the conscious and formal structural aspects of organizations over their natural, more traditional forms. At the time, an effort to formalize and organize large organizations was very important. Many of the characteristics of the bureaucratic concept may appear to be obvious, but at the time they were somewhat revolutionary.

We will now examine the most important characteristics of an ideal bureaucracy.

Characteristics of a Bureaucracy

1. Positions in the organization are arranged in a hierarchy. Each level of the organization is under the control of a person of authority, who reports to someone of higher authority. There are successively higher levels of authority, which comprise the typical vertical command structure of the organization.

This characteristic is important for control and coordination of employees and activities. In many organizations that require a great deal of control, such as in law enforcement, it is important for the line-level personnel (police officers) to be very clear as to who they report to. Additionally, by using this approach, managers know which supervisor to go to when there is a problem or issue involving a particular employee.

2. Specialization and division of labor. According to this characteristic, individual employees are grouped according to their work, creating *divisions of responsibility*, hence the term *bureaus*, which encompasses the concept of bureaucracy; that is, the *structuring and organizing of employees and their activities for maximum efficiency.* So, with this division of labor into work units called *bureaus*, it creates a clear understanding of where responsibilities of certain work activities lie.

But besides organizing the work to clarify responsibility in the organization, employees are divided into these work units for intensive refinement of the work activities for maximum efficiency, or *specialization*.

The larger an organization is, the more important it becomes for it to specialize positions. When a large organization creates specialized work positions, it helps the organization in four ways:

- **Expertise:** When workers do the same job for a long period of time, they get very good at it, and become experts. For maximum efficiency and effectiveness, it is important for organizations to have a large number of experts.
- **Simplified training:** When there are clear-cut job distinctions, it is easier for management to identify which employees need to be trained when there is new technology or information that must be learned. Rather than having to train the entire workforce, only the employees affected require the training.
- **Placement of responsibility:** When there are clear-cut job responsibilities, it becomes much easier for management to know who to go to when something needs to be done.

- **Administrative control:** And because managers know who to go to for a particular job assignment, and also know who to go to when a particular job is not being done, it provides a great deal of control.

  3. Procedural guidelines. Procedural guidelines are nothing more than a system of abstract rules. The word *abstract* means that the rules are uniformly applied to all the employees. It is supposed to be an impersonal procedure, used throughout the entire organization, requiring all employees to conform to the rules, without regard to their position in the organization.

Over the years, personnel in an organization change. But the rules, regulations, policies, and procedures should remain the same, thus permitting continuity of function. So, even though over several decades the employees have come and gone, the activities and functions of the organization have remained the same, because the rules and procedures have provided the stability and continuity necessary for the organization to continue to reach its goals.

Individual personalities of employees can certainly have an effect on an organization in terms of efficiency and effectiveness. However, because all the employees must conform to the existing rules, regulations, policies, and procedures, their personalities have a very limited impact on the organization itself.

For public-sector jobs, and other service-type jobs, procedural guidelines provide for stability and accountability, ensuring the ongoing continuity of the organization. However, because of the constraints imposed by so many rules, it can limit employee involvement, interest, and creativity. This is because with so many rules employees do not have the opportunity to think for themselves, because all their work activities are predetermined by established policies and procedures.

> **4. Organizational documentation.** By documenting important events and incidents, a history of organizational activities and employee activities can be very helpful to managers, especially new managers who are unfamiliar with the history of the organization.
>
> **Example:** A manager who is deciding which employee should be placed into a specialized assignment can review the employees' personnel files to determine which employee has the most desirable background in terms of training, positive evaluations, and other qualities that would make that employee the most suitable candidate. In a discipline issue, a manager can review the employee's file to find out if there has been a pattern of misconduct, which can help in determining the severity of the discipline.

Way too often, organizations rely too much on their rules and regulations and the importance of documentation. When this happens, which is pretty much all the time, the focus becomes placing the blame on someone (other than themselves), rather than solving the problem.

5. Organizational authority. According to this characteristic, an employee's position in the organization determines the amount of authority that the employee has. This prevents individuals from having authority beyond their position. This is a fairly commonsense approach, but when you consider the subjective managerial practices of the past, a characteristic such as this could be very necessary.

Example: A sergeant in a police department is the brother-in-law of a captain in the same department. Because of this relationship, it is very possible that the sergeant could exercise more power than is granted by his rank in the organization. In the past, this sergeant could possibly have considerably more power than his peers. However, in a modern organization, following this characteristic, the sergeant would have no more formal power than any other sergeant in the organization.

That is not to say that the sergeant would not have some informal power that some of his peers would not have, because, although nepotism is not viewed as a power base in modern times, only an idiot would believe that the sergeant does not routinely discuss work-related issues with his higher-ranking relative.

6. Appointments based on qualifications. This characteristic is one of those commonsense ones, something we all accept as normal practice. But remember, a hundred years ago this was all new stuff. People bought their way into high positions, were placed there by politicians, or were put there because of their family tree. *This characteristic states that selections and promotions should be based on competence and expertise,* not irrelevant considerations, such as nepotism.

Appointing someone to a position is not just based on fairness, which, by the way, is a very important consideration for creating a motivating work environment, but appointing the best candidate for the position is in the best interest of the organization for developing the most competent workforce and management team.

Comments about the Characteristics

The entire concept of bureaucracy is pretty much the theory of choice for most criminal justice organizations, and most certainly law enforcement. Police departments are quasi-military organizations, and with the specific rank structure that closely resembles the military, a bureaucratic orientation fits well with the values and customs of these traditional organizations.

And because police departments of any size have specialized positions, a bureaucratic approach would be an appropriate model for them to subscribe to. The most important characteristic that this bureaucratic approach provides to law enforcement organizations is the high degree of control that is provided. Because police managers are dealing with employees that are carrying guns, driving fast to emergency calls, and detaining and arresting people, it is important that they are in an environment that provides for a great deal of control over their activities. A bureaucratic setting provides this.

Even though some individuals in a highly bureaucratic organization are uncomfortable with the rank and structure of it all, they must learn to live with it, because the organization perpetuates the mentality.

> **Example:** A new police sergeant may be uncomfortable with the fact that everyone calls him "sergeant" or 'sir," but he has to deal with it, because the organizational structure, culture, and attitude demand it.

Problems with the Bureaucratic Approach

No theory has all the answers. They are not all-encompassing answers to all problems. For every theory, there is another theory to counter it. By examining a number of theories, you can determine for yourself which ones are appropriate for the time, situation, or organization.

Keep in mind that theories are not facts; they are beliefs based on studies and other findings. The critics of a particular theory will be able to quickly identify the problems with a theory that they do not agree with, as quickly as they point out the positive attributes of theories that they agree with. So, here are some of the problems with the bureaucratic approach:

- **Human nature is ignored.** The way that these organizations are structured and organized, there is little, if any, consideration given to employees' personal needs. But, in all fairness, the bureaucratic approach was not designed to provide for this. Because most of the decision making is the job of management, it does not allow for line-level employees to make important decisions, which affects their ability to develop and grow professionally within the organization.

  Additionally, this theory assumes that people respond rationally to traditional incentives such as pay and punishment. Because this theory does not address the human needs aspect of organizations, no thought is given to structuring the organization to provide for personal needs of employees.

- **Nonresponsive to change.** Because bureaucratic structures create very distinct divisions (see Appendix A), barriers between work groups can prevent an environment that encourages progressive change.

  Each division in this type of organization has specific duties, which are distinct and different from those of the other divisions. If one division wants another division to make changes to help their own division, cooperation to do so may be difficult if the change does not positively benefit the division being asked to change.

Example: A detective division in a police department wants to streamline its caseload regarding in-custody cases (i.e., cases in which a patrol officer has arrested someone and a detective needs to conduct a follow-up investigation to prepare the case for prosecution). The detective division asks the patrol division to direct patrol officers to conduct interrogations of the in-custody suspects so that the detectives do not have to do it themselves, which will enable them to prepare the case in a more timely manner.

If this request does not positively impact the patrol division, the officers may be reluctant to change. The request will require the officers to spend more time on the case, causing concern that it will make them unavailable for field duty, which is a continual concern for patrol supervisors and managers.

Employees and supervisors alike are comfortable with things the way they are, and are naturally uncomfortable with change, especially if it has the appearance that they are being asked to do the job of another division. Quite frankly, the patrol division will not be overly concerned that the detective division is overworked, because patrol deals with that problem constantly.

- **Poor communications.** Because the organization is divided into specialized groups, this creates natural barriers to effective communication (see Appendix A). As in the previous example regarding patrol and detective divisions, not only do the divisions have very distinctive and different duties and responsibilities, they also differ in other ways that can have a negative impact on communication:

    o The detectives work in an office; the patrolmen work in the field.

    o The detectives work in plain clothes; the patrolmen work in uniform.

    o Even when the patrol officers are in the station, they are usually in a different building or a distinctly separate area from the detectives.

So, not only is there a natural organizational barrier, there is also a physical barrier, as well as a psychological one.

- **Red tape.** When dealing with organizations that have specific task assignments, it seems as though it is always "someone else's job." In other words, it can be very frustrating for a citizen or client who is trying to obtain information or service from a large bureaucratic organization. It is unlikely that this person will be able to walk into a public building and have the first person they contact help them with their problem. It is more likely that this person will be referred to someone else in another office, on another floor, or another building. And, hopefully, the employee that this person has been directed to is not on vacation, because it is likely that there is no one else that can help them.

This situation is not really the fault of the employees, or even the supervisors. The employees are bound by the rules, regulations, policies, and procedures that outline their individual duties and responsibilities. It would be a violation of rules, or at least beyond acceptable protocol of the organization, for an employee to go beyond his job description to help the individual seeking assistance. Obviously, these rules can seriously restrict efficiency.

Comments about the Drawbacks of Bureaucracy

Weber assumed that one type of structure would work for all organizations. The theory of ideal bureaucracy was created to improve efficiency in large organizations, and it is ironic that now the term *bureaucracy* is usually associated with inefficiency in government.

And the larger the organization is, the more likely that it will be even more inefficient. This is because the larger the organization, the more rules and regulations there are so as to properly control and coordinate the many activities. And the more rules and regulations there are, the more it bogs down creativity and innovation by employees, because they are bound by so many rules.

HUMAN RELATIONS THEORY

The bureaucratic approach was used exclusively by large organizations until into the 1930s. During the 1930s, human relations theory, a more modern approach to management, developed once it was discovered that *strong informal groups were developing* within these classically structured organizations. Experts found that *the needs of employees were not being met* by the classical structure. By the 1950s, human relations theory was fairly widely accepted.

Also, researchers finally figured out that workers *did not always act rationally or follow predictable patterns of behavior*, especially when it came to monetary incentives. Managers had always taken the approach that the more they paid someone, the harder the employee would work. When that did not happen, researchers realized that there was more going on in the work environment than just the quest for a paycheck.

Human relations theory is based on two assumptions. We have to make these assumptions because, although there have been attempts through research to quantify the following, they have been unsuccessful because there are too many uncontrolled variables.

The First Assumption

The more satisfying an organizational structure is to a worker, the more efficient the worker will be. This means that if an employee enjoys his job (because the organization has been able to create an environment that provides for this), then the employee will work harder, because he enjoys his work. But this can be difficult for management to provide, because some jobs are just inherently more satisfying than others. An artist would just naturally be more satisfied with his work than a dishwasher would.

What management would have to do to create a satisfying work environment is to alter the organizational structure by removing layers of management (flattening the hierarchy) and make jobs more flexible so that employees could make their own decisions and feel more involved.

The Second Assumption

The work and the organizational structure must relate to the social needs of workers. These needs are things such as the feeling of accomplishment, achievement, belonging, and satisfaction.

All that this means is that the organization has to be set up so that people will feel these things as they do their work. And again, this is easier to do in some jobs than in others. For the assembly line worker putting on right front wheels every day, the organization is really going to have to get creative to provide for those needs. In contrast, police managers can rely on the characteristics of police work to satisfy some of the needs that police officers have. The fact that their jobs put them in the position to arrest dangerous people, solve crimes, and save lives provides a great deal of personal satisfaction in and of itself.

Most managers ignored the human element involved in organizations until there was scientific proof that it was a valid concern. This scientific proof was instrumental in ushering in the human relations approach to management.

The Hawthorne Experiments

In the 1920s and 1930s, Elton Mayo conducted a series of experiments to improve worker efficiency. One of these experiments was at the Hawthorne Works, a large factory in Illinois. It started out as a study to determine how lighting conditions affected productivity. This was very much a scientific management approach.

He started by adding lighting to a work group and monitoring a control group. He then examined the effect the lighting had on worker productivity. He found that productivity increased with the added lighting conditions. More light was added, and productivity continued to improve. But then he reduced the lighting, and productivity still continued to improve, in both the work group and the control group.

So, why did this happen? The conclusion was that *productivity was influenced by special treatment and attention to the workers,* not the actual working conditions. This became known as the *Hawthorne effect,* whereby *human factors (i.e., the social and psychological conditions within an organization) can significantly affect productivity.*

Another study was done to examine how the "piece work" approach of paying employees for the amount of work they did versus paying for the time they put in would affect productivity. The result was that workers adjusted their output so as not to exceed the groups' output.

The conclusion of this study was that *group acceptance was more important than money*. Based on the results of the Hawthorne experiments, they realized that this was the cause of *soldiering*, or intentionally limiting productivity. So based on this information, organizations realized that they had to put social needs of employees ahead of organizational needs or monetary gain.

There was a major flaw, however, with the Hawthorne studies. What the researchers did not realize was the obvious fact that when employees are under close observation (as they were during the lighting experiments), they would most likely increase their productivity. It would be as if their boss had walked into the room; everybody gets back to work. But flawed or not, the studies still were responsible for ushering in the human relations approach.

Theory X and Theory Y

The bureaucratic and human relations approaches are at opposite ends of a continuum. Theory X and Theory Y identify these two approaches. In 1960, Douglas McGregor developed Theory X and Theory Y in an effort to explain and identify two diametrically opposed management approaches.

Usually, a "theory" attempts to explain behavior. In this case, these two theories do not do that. Rather, they identify *two management approaches that are on a continuum.* To prevent confusion, it would probably have been better to name them "Management Approach X and Management Approach Y," but the damage has been done, so let's just work with it.

What this approach does is identify the classical approach to management, pointing out the advantages and disadvantages, and then considers the modern human relations approach, also with its advantages and disadvantages.

Theory X

A Theory X manager uses the traditional approach of dealing with employees, which is through fear and intimidation, and generally has a negative view toward employees. A Theory X manager assumes that the average person has an inherent dislike for work, and will avoid it if possible. And because of the dislike for work, most employees must be coerced, controlled, directed, or threatened with punishment to get them to put forth adequate effort. This typical bureaucratic type of manager believes that the average employee prefers to be directed, avoids responsibility, has little ambition, and wants security.

There certainly could be some truth to this evaluation of employees, and experience as a manager probably reinforces his beliefs. But a Theory X approach to managing employees can be a self-fulfilling prophecy in which people act as they are expected to act.

Example: If a supervisor treats his employees as mature, responsible adults doing a very important job, they will respond accordingly. If a supervisor treats his employees as misguided children that need to be punished, then he will constantly be punishing them for their misbehavior.

Theory Y

A Theory Y manager is at the other end of the continuum and manages based on having an understanding of people's needs. This is the humanistic approach to management. *The belief is that when employees obtain these needs, they become more productive and content,* as is obvious when they reach a level known as *self-actualization.* This is a level of motivation at which employees reach a high state of satisfaction, to the point that they work for the sheer joy of achievement and accomplishment from doing a worthwhile job.

A Theory Y manager assumes that expenditure of effort in work is a natural part of life and that control and punishment are not the only effective ways to control people. So, if there are other ways to control people, managers should choose those other ways so people will stay happy.

Note that many managers strive to keep employees "happy" because happy employees are productive employees. It is not because managers are really great people and want their employees to love their work and be happy, but rather because happy employees make money for them. Let's face it, if a study came out today that frightened employees did the best work; by tomorrow, supervisors would be chasing employees down the hallways with baseball bats.

A Theory Y manager has a much more positive impression of employees. He believes that people will exercise self-control and direction when committed to objectives and that under the right conditions will seek responsibility and be capable of imagination, creativity, and ingenuity.

Theory Y is based on the assumption that management has the responsibility to assist each employee to reach his potential. To effectively use this theory in the public sector, it would mean fewer layers of management; broad guidelines, rather than a plethora of rules and regulations; and minimal front-line supervision.

For employees to reach their full potential and have a high degree of job satisfaction, they would have to become involved in the decision-making process that is usually reserved for high-level management positions. And completely revamping public organizational structures solely for an increase in employee satisfaction levels for the purpose of increasing productivity based on two "assumptions" related to human relations is probably a fairy tale. So, in reality, a serious change from Theory X to Theory Y in public sector management is probably not realistic in the near future.

Besides the fact that inverting the hierarchy, flattening the hierarchy, or revamping the hierarchy are unlikely given the fact that those in charge (i.e., at the top of the hierarchy) like things the way they are, Theory Y was initially deemed a failure. *The problem was that it was overdone.*

To counter the top-down approach of Weber, this theory went too far with a bottom-up approach, with the result that not much got work done. Modern management uses a balance of the two theories; hence, the concept of the continuum, in which virtually no organization is on the extreme end, but rather, finds itself to the left or right of either end of it.

The human relations approach evolved into what was known in the 1990s as *participative management*, and which is now called *collaborative management*. This approach is designed so that officers can meet their personal needs.

Many theories have been developed to describe what these needs are, and how managers can help officers to reach them so that the officers are satisfied, which will cause them to work harder. The best-known theory about personal needs is Maslow's hierarchy of needs.

Maslow's Hierarchy of Needs

According to Maslow, *every person has certain types of needs that follow a progression* (i.e., a hierarchy). The most important concept in this theory, as far as managers are concerned, is that *when the primary needs are reached, motivation ceases, so the next level must be available* (see Appendix B).

Five Levels of Needs

The following are the five levels of needs as identified in Maslow's hierarchy:

- **Survival:** Basic physiological needs such as food, air, shelter, and clothing. In an organizational setting, it is having and keeping a job.
- **Security:** People need to feel safe and to have stability in their lives. In an organizational setting, this refers to job security and pension plans, as well as an environment they feel comfortable in.
- **Social:** People need a sense of belonging. This results in personal interactions and friendships. In organizations, this creates social and work groups. Management must understand that informal work groups are important to fulfill needs.
- **Ego:** People seek to be recognized and appreciated. They seek self-esteem through status. In organizations, this is obtained through job titles and responsibilities.
- **Self-actualization:** This is the need for personal growth and development, to reach one's maximum potential. In an organizational setting, challenging jobs and involvement can lead to self-actualization, in which employee performance is maximized.

Only about 10 percent of employees reach self-actualization, and most of these workers are at the high end of the organizational structure. Let's face it; the most satisfying jobs in terms of achievement and acknowledgment are in the upper management positions. Many top managers in organizations are past retirement age. They are literally working for free, but choose to do so because of the great level of personal satisfaction they receive from working.

> **Example:** A police captain could have retired two years prior. With the excellent safety employees' retirement system, he is actually losing money by staying on the job. So, why does he do it? Well, he worked so hard for so many years to be the head of a police division, he just was not ready to give it up yet. Additionally, the chief of police was many years past retirement age, but when you run an entire police department, that is not something someone gives away easily. High levels of job satisfaction are hard to give up.

Remember the old army slogan: "Be all you can be?" This is the essence of self-actualization. This slogan was probably not coincidence, but rather a reflection of how the challenges of army life provides for self-actualization needs to be fulfilled. It is doubtful that "Join the army and fulfill your self-actualization needs" would have been as catchy.

Problems with This Theory

As mentioned earlier, *people want different things.* Maslow's theory does not address this issue and basically generalizes about the needs of people. Some employees after a long career are simply interested in retiring without problems and new challenges to face. Other employees, perhaps those new in their careers, are looking to get ahead in the organization and are seeking out additional responsibility for advancement. Others in the organization just want to be left alone to do their job without fear of additional responsibilities being placed on them. To them, work is just a paycheck, and they are not looking to advance in the organization or to fulfill some inner need.

To be fair to Maslow, his theory was not designed for use in the workplace. But the theory is immensely helpful for managers to understand the personal needs that people have.

> **Personal observation:** Look at the pyramid structure of the hierarchy of needs, and then look at the typical organizational structure of an organization. Besides the obvious observation that they have the same pyramid shape, note that they also mirror each other in another way. *The structure of the hierarchy of needs reflects the organizational structure in that the higher an employee ascends in the organization, the more attainable those higher level needs are.* So, one's position in the hierarchy mirrors the hierarchy of needs in ones' ability to fulfill needs.

> **Example:** Those at the bottom of the organizational structure are really only able to achieve the lower level needs in the hierarchy of needs structure in the average organization. Those as the top of the organizational structure can much more easily achieve higher-order needs, because they have the fun and fulfilling jobs of running a team, work group, or entire organization. So the higher up an

employee goes in the organization, the easier it is to reach those higher-level needs. *The challenge for managers, then, is to make higher-level needs attainable at the lower levels of the organization. This is the biggest challenge that managers and leaders face when it comes to creating an organizational climate that fosters motivation.*

About the only way officers get self-actualization is through participative management; using the human relations approach, management attempts to satisfy employee needs by improving the work structure. This is done by including officers in decisions, allowing them to participate. In some organizations this can work, but in others that require a lot of control and structure, such as police departments, it can be difficult to do. A consultative approach, where management asks for input, is probably the best that they can do.

Police try to do this with vertical staff meetings, in which members at all levels of the organization attend management meetings; problem-solving groups, such as community policing activities; and quality circles, which are group problem-solving committees that examine organizational problems and make recommendations for change.

A good way to look at how police management gets things done is by examining the systems approach to organization. The classical approach focuses on the formal structure of organizations, and the human relations approach emphasized interpersonal relations. The systems approach emphasizes relationships between and among groups and subgroups within an organization.

SYSTEMS THEORY

A system is an interrelated set of elements functioning as a whole. From an organizational perspective, systems theory emphasizes organizational structure and operational methods. This concept is borrowed from the scientific community, which focuses on how one thing has an effect on other things (see Appendix C).

By using this scientific approach in an organizational setting, *systems theory allows managers to view organizations as a unitary whole and to understand that the activities of one part affect the activities of other parts.* It forces management to view the organization from a "big picture" perspective, recognizing that a change in one subsystem will have an effect on the other subsystems.

With this theory, managers within an organization would keep in close contact with each other to ensure that *their activities are congruent with one another,* and with their objectives. The term *congruent* means that the activities may not be the same, but they are in harmony with each other; that is, there is no conflict.

Besides managers keeping in close contact with other managers within an organization, the systems approach also is meant to get managers to keep in contact with managers of other organizations to ensure that activities and changes would not negatively affect the other subsystems outside the organization. By following this approach, *managers would monitor the environment outside their organization or division within the organization and respond to change.*

General Framework

A system receives something from the environment, transforms it, and returns it to the environment. Again, from a scientific perspective, consider the following example: a plant takes carbon dioxide from the environment, transforms it through a process called photosynthesis, and returns it to the environment as oxygen.

In general, a system has inputs, throughputs, and outputs:

- **Inputs:** This is what the organization *takes from the outside environment*, such as materials, people, money, and information.
- **Throughputs:** This is the *transformation process*, in which the inputs are turned into outputs. The throughputs consist of work activities, rules and regulations, goals and objectives, and other organizational processes that bring it all together.
- **Outputs:** These are the products, services, profits, losses, and information that are produced by organizations in order for them to reach their goals and objectives.

With the systems approach, management must consider the effects of decisions on all the subsystems.

> **Example:** A police narcotics unit plans a sting operation in which a hundred drug

dealers are identified and warrants issued. If the police department did not use the systems approach in its activities, thereby failing to involve and consult with the other subsystems (i.e., courts and corrections), the District Attorney's Office, the trial calendar, and the county jail would be severely impacted by the police operation.

By involving the other subsystems, and considering the impact of the subsystems from the operation, the level of success, and that of future success, would be enhanced, not to mention the importance of maintaining a positive relationship with the other subsystems.

Open versus Closed Systems

The difference between a closed system and an open system has to do with the relationships that they have with their environments. No organization is completely closed, and no system is completely open; rather, they are on a continuum, with few at either extreme.

It is important to realize that it is not the organization itself that is either open or closed, *it is their view of the organization and their relationship with their environment*. For instance, Weber had a closed system view of organizations. His concept focused on the internal environment of organizations. From his viewpoint, the environment outside of the organization was not a factor in his theory.

Closed System

Managers in an organization that take the approach (in their activities and decision making) that they are affected only by the internal environment of the organization are operating as a closed system. In the past, most organizations were viewed as being closed; that is, that decisions were made in a vacuum. Issues and incidents that occurred outside the organization were not variables that factored into management activities and decisions.

> **Example:** During the Reform Era of policing, police departments detached themselves from the community in their effort to professionalize and organize. And at the time, it was necessary to do this to prevent corruption and unethical influence from those outside the organization. The problem was that when they did this the police lost a lot of public support and information from the public.
>
> So, until the internal changes in police departments took place, police managers focused their activities and decisions based on the dynamics and issues that occurred within the organization, not those that were occurring outside the organization.

The closed system approach to organizations is a simplistic view of organizations that views activities and situations occurring in the organization as being unrelated to anything outside the organization.

> **Example:** For an organization to be
> completely closed it would have to be self-
> contained, such is being in a biosphere.
> This is because the employees watch
> television, see the news, and interact with
> other people. And because of this, they
> bring their beliefs, opinions, and attitudes
> with them into the work environment.
>
> And as long as employees do this, it will
> have an impact on the activities of the
> organization, resulting in the organization
> being affected by the outside
> environment, thereby making them an
> open system to some extent.

There is an irony regarding the incentive for private
organizations to be open, versus the incentive for public
organizations to be open. Private organizations must
interact with the public so that they can make a profit.
The more clients and customers they have, the more
money they make. Public organizations, in contrast, are
on a fixed budget, and no matter how much more work
they do, the personnel and organization will not make
more money, because profit is not part of the
organization's goals.

So, not only is there no incentive for public organizations
to be open (by advertising their services or seeking out
clients), there is an incentive for them to be closed
(because extra work will not result in a larger budget).

Open System

Managers in an organization that take the approach (in their activities and decision making) that they are affected by both the internal and external environment of the organization are operating as an open system. When taking the human factor into consideration, most organizations are open. This is due to the attitudes, values, and problems that employees bring into the organization with them. Of course, the activities and functions of an organization will determine how open or how closed it is.

> **Example:** After law enforcement professionalized and moved away from corruption and political control, it found that it had to become much more open again, so that officers could regain the trust and support of the community.

> **Example:** The CIA is a fairly closed system because of the confidential nature of its work activities. A police department would be more of an open system, based on officers' constant interaction with the public and their high-profile status within the community.

On the systems continuum, public organizations are on the open end of the continuum because of the major influence that the external environment has on them. Because of the reliance of public organizations on the budget process, which is controlled from outside such organizations, as well as public scrutiny of public organizations, these types of organizations are going to be more open than closed.

Obviously, most public organizations, including police departments, are on the open end of the continuum. When managers operate and make decisions with an open-systems mindset, it aids them in adapting to the ever-changing outside environment, which allows them to plan ahead and to anticipate change.

There are advantages and drawbacks of both the classical and human relations approaches, and there are special problems implementing these in law enforcement. Police departments must rely on some of the positive characteristics of the classical approach; they are organized, there is a high degree of control, and there is an emphasis on specialization.

Elements of both approaches can work in some situations and some organizations, and not work in others, with special needs for police agencies, making implementation even more difficult. With the need for flexibility in police management, a much more situational approach was needed.

CONTINGENCY THEORY

The classical approach to organizations has provided a great deal of value to the evolution of modern organizational structure, as has the human relations approach. The systems approach also provided modern managers with important tools on which to base their activities and decisions. But none of these approaches provided modern public managers with the insight and guidance to properly lead their organizations effectively.

A situational approach was developed when it was found that certain methods and practices worked in some situations but not in others.

In 1967, Fred Fiedler developed *contingency theory* to resolve the problem that a manager felt he had to subscribe to only one type of management style. The other theories were not considered realistic. *Earlier theorists had looked for a universal answer for all situations.* For instance, Theory X did not apply in all situations, because it did not provide for meeting the personal needs of employees, and Theory Y did not apply in all situations, because it did not provide for sufficient control and direction when it was needed.

Contingency theory states that no single organizational style fits all situations; it is a blend of different management styles. Fielder contended that management approaches must be contingent on three variables: the organization, the task and goals, and individual situations.

The Organization

Organizations are stable or unstable. A stable organization is one in which there is very little change required to keep up with its goals and objectives. An unstable organization is one in which there is constant change in the environment, requiring ongoing training and closer supervision.

> **Example:** The DMV is a very stable organization, there is not much change that would require an autocratic or directive style of management. A police

department, however, is in a constant state of change because of changes in case law and societal attitudes caused by high-profile police incidents.

So, in a police department, managers must maintain a higher level of supervision and control than would be seen at the DMV. If managers in the DMV used the same type of management style that the police used, it would not be effective.

Organizations can have bureaucratic or loose structures. If an organization requires a bureaucratic structure, it will very likely need a management style that provides for control and direction. So, the structure or the organization, based on the type of activities involved, dictates the type of management style that should be used.

Example: In a loosely structured organization, such an in an artistic endeavor, an autocratic style would not be appropriate or effective.

The Task and Goals

Tasks and goals may be ambiguous or clear. If the organization's tasks and goals are ambiguous (i.e., they are not clear cut or straightforward), then more direction and control is needed by management. If the task and goals are clear, not as much direction and control is needed.

Example: The task of police officers is ambiguous (discretion offers officers a wide range of options for solving problems) as are the goals (it is not clear if visible patrol prevents crime). In this type of work environment, police officers need more guidance and supervision than in a work environment where the task and goals are more clear cut.

The task and goals at the DMV are much clearer. Supervision does not need to be as controlling and directive as it is with police officers. If DMV. managers were to use the same style as police managers, it would likely be detrimental to morale, and ultimately have a negative effect on the organization.

Organizations also differ with regard to the types of responsibility. Managers have an obligation to their organization and the public they serve to provide a leadership style that is in the best interests of the organization and the public.

Example: Police officers have dangerous and dynamic jobs that sometimes result in life-and-death decisions. In a work environment in which employees carry guns and have a high degree of authority and responsibility, it is incumbent upon management to monitor and control the activities of the employees.

The work activities of DMV employees do not compare to those of police officers. To use the same controlling management style in both organizations would not be appropriate or effective.

Individual Situations

Situations may be crisis or routine. In a crisis situation, a manager should be very autocratic; making important decisions quickly, without participation by line-level employees. But in routine situations, the same manager can allow employees to be involved in important decisions.

Motivation also plays a role. With a motivated employee, a manager does not, nor should he be, overly directive and controlling. However, with a nonmotivated employee, the manager should be more directive and controlling, for the benefit of the employee and the organization. Using the same style on both types of employees would be ineffective.

Comments about the Situational Approach

The bottom line about choosing a management style is that there is no one best way to run an organization, an incident, or a situation. The style of management (autocratic through participative) should be contingent on the above variables to have an effective and efficient organization.

Sometimes participative management will be appropriate, and other times it will not, and an autocratic approach (by the same manager) will be the best and most appropriate style.

The behavior of individuals and groups within the organization will also determine the appropriate style. What is effective and successful with one individual or group will be ineffective and unsuccessful with another.

CHAPTER 5

CRIME PREVENTION THROUGH ENVIRONMENTAL DESIGN

Topics

- Crime Generators
- Territoriality
- Surveillance Opportunity
- Traffic Patterns
- Displacement Concept

INTRODUCTION

The community policing approach to law enforcement requires police officers to take on many complex responsibilities that they have not had to deal with in the past. Those involved in this approach are expected to develop long-term solutions to crime-related problems. They are expected to devise original, creative, and ingenious ways to do this.

But without understanding some of the dynamics that actually cause these crimes to occur, officers do not have the tools to help them make these decisions. The police officers burdened with the responsibility of devising plans that can have such a tremendous impact on the lives of everyone in the community *need tangible direction and knowledge of specific processes to guide them in this quest.*

Crime prevention through environmental design (CPTED) is a field of study that provides for this. CPTED is a complex field of study that uses human psychology to analyze how crime can be reduced at different types of locations through the proper design and effective use of the environment to reduce crime and the fear of crime. *CPTED is an attempt to reduce crime and the fear of crime in a particular setting by reducing criminal opportunity while simultaneously fostering positive social interaction.*

With CPTED, the police examine *specific locations* to figure out ways to make them *less desirable to criminals*, while also making the location *more desirable for the people who legitimately use them.*

This complex goal can be accomplished by analyzing two factors: the pattern of criminal behavior in an area and the behavior and perceptions of legitimate users.

Pattern of Criminal Behavior in the Area

A key consideration with regard to this factor is the presence of a pattern. Unless there is a pattern of criminal activity, it is not a recurring problem that would require the focused attention of the police to develop CPTED tactics to resolve it.

If there is a pattern, the police have to look at what it is about a location that appeals to the criminal element, and then take steps to remove the appeal. As a *tangible element* that police officers are desperately seeking to identify a real problem, this activity of figuring out what the appeal is provides the officers with something of substance that they can realistically focus on and construct real-life solutions to in extremely ambiguous and vague social anomalies. (In cop talk, this means that finally, by understanding CPTED, they have something they can sink their teeth into and actually do something that works, rather than the same old song and dance of rhetoric and politically correct go-nowhere, do-nothing dialogue.)

> **Example:** Criminals are attracted to deteriorated areas (*the appeal*) because the legitimate users are signaling an apathetic attitude, telling criminals that they are not inclined to challenge disruptive or illegal activity and that they are not inclined to report it to the police.

This is not necessarily a conscious thought process; it's not like criminals drive around and think to themselves, "It doesn't look like anybody cares here, let's set up shop." Rather, the criminal element gets a feeling about an area just as we all do—we feel comfortable or we do not. If we do not, we find someplace else to go. What the police try to do is to make the criminals feel uncomfortable, so they will go someplace else.

This attempt at identifying a criminal appeal and then removing it takes place in the scanning step of the SARA process. The police have been told for decades now that they are supposed to scan for problems in their area, and then take steps to remove them. But the police officers are never told what exactly they are supposed to be looking for. *Finally, with CPTED, they have tangible information to help them to do this.*

> **Example:** If a location is well concealed (*the appeal*) from public view, it makes it easier to break in or do other illegal things without fear of detection.

Behavior and Perceptions of the Legitimate Users

This factor means that the police evaluate how a particular location or area is being used by the legitimate users, and if it is not being used properly, then *they make modifications so that the area is used properly*, which, in turn, prevents the area from being open to unwanted intrusion.

Basically, CPTED looks at how design *involves the good guys* and *appeals to the bad guys*. If the police just take away the appeal, that would only be a temporary fix. By making legitimate use of the location, it keeps criminals away.

Example: If a park is designed so that there are activities for legitimate use throughout the day and night, it will keep illegal activity away. For instance, if there are facilities for daytime activities and facilities for evening activities, then there is less dead time at the location that nonlegitimate users can take advantage of.

Example: If locations are designed so that the users have better opportunities to monitor the activity in the area, it increases their control over the area, which prevents disorder and crime. For instance, if a park is well lit and is surrounded by houses with windows overlooking the park, it will appear less inviting to potential offenders.

So, based on these two factors of CPTED, the police take a *dual approach* to identifying and solving problems:

- **Modify the physical environment**. Modifying the physical environment involves such things as improving lighting for better observation by residents and discouraging potential violators, adding windows to structures to again improve observation opportunities by occupants and lessen the appeal to offenders, and providing activity areas to increase use by legitimate users and remove opportunities for nonlegitimate users.
- **Use social tactics.** Social tactics can be used to provide opportunities for residents or users to interact, which increases the commitment they

have to protect their area. This involves more than just a target-hardening approach of building fortresses. The successful use of these social tactics increases the sense of propriety felt by residents, which is something commonly felt by homeowners as opposed to renters. This sense of propriety increases their commitment to protect their area.

CPTED addresses four specific areas: crime generators, territoriality, surveillance opportunity, and traffic patterns. In some of these areas, police officers can make or suggest changes that can easily be accomplished, but in other areas any changes are beyond the scope or authority of law enforcement.

In those cases in which the police cannot make changes, at least they will have a frame of reference to help them to understand why crime is occurring in a particular area, which can help them in their problem-solving efforts.

CRIME GENERATORS

Crime generators are any structures or locations that, because of their purpose or characteristics, attract or generate criminal activity. Crime generators can be bars, liquor stores, convenience markets, vacant lots, and vacant houses. These places often invite theft, drinking, loitering, robbery, assault, and general disorder.

Unfortunately, this is one of the areas that the police do not have much control over, and, as such, is beyond their scope and responsibility. However, as stated earlier, it is good for law enforcement to understand that these types of locations exist so that they can use traditional police strategies to control the crime problems that are generated from these locations.

Addressing crime problems that are due to crime generators may mean removing the structure or condemning it. Demolishing a liquor store may not be a realistic alternative to solve a problem, but at least if they know why the crime is occurring at a location police can take other enforcement steps, such as:

- **Increased patrols:** As a traditional policing strategy, the *presence of the police* at a problem location can be very effective in preventing crimes. Regardless of what the studies say, if a couple of blacks and whites are sitting in the parking lot of a bar at closing time, there will be fewer fights and other crimes occurring if the police are present.
- **ABC operations:** The police often solicit the assistance of the state's Bureau of Alcoholic Beverage Control to ensure that bars and liquor stores follow the law. The police also conduct sting operations in which they send in underage agents (usually police cadets) to purchase alcohol.

When these operations reveal violations, the liquor licenses of these establishments can be suspended or revoked. When this happens, the lack of alcohol sales causes these problem locations to shut down, which can have a dramatic impact on the area's dynamics.

- **Aggressive follow-up investigations**: Generally, a criminal investigation that is characterized as a bar fight (two drunk losers beating the daylights out of each other, no loss) has no jury appeal, which means the prosecutor's office is not interested in filing criminal charges and pursuing these types of cases. However, if the police department develops a cooperative effort with the prosecutor's office with a *zero-tolerance policy* to solve a specific problem by prosecuting these cases, it can be instrumental in reducing the cycle of disorderly behavior at the location.

In some jurisdictions, such as in Canada, police departments have officers who are specially trained in CPTED, and these officers are consulted by city planners before any new structures are approved. They bring their specialized combination of knowledge of CPTED and law enforcement to the planning process. By doing this, they are preventing crime generators from ever being built.

The best that the police can do about crime generators is to *acknowledge that they are there*, and accept that these types of locations generate crime. Armed with this commonsense approach, the police can use *traditional law enforcement tactics* to reduce crime.

Some of crime generators, however, can be corrected through recommendations from law enforcement. Locations such as vacant lots and abandoned structures can be changed to prevent crime:

- Abandoned structures can be *demolished or refurbished* and occupied by legitimate users.
- Vacant lots can be eliminated by *building structures or placing activity areas* at the location. Even if this is not possible, lots can be changed

in their appearance so that hidden areas are removed or fences installed.

- *Adding lights* to a problem area can make the location less desirable for criminal activity. However, the addition of street lighting may not be the answer; the lighting will depend on how the location is being used.

Example: A park being used for drinking and sex could have *lights added* to the location, which would deter the activity.

A park being used for sports activities after closing time could have *lights removed* to make playing more difficult.

Subtle lighting could be added, just enough to observe illegal activity, but not enough for activity that requires a lot of lighting.

TERRITORIALITY

This concept of territoriality uses tactics to foster a stronger sense of ownership over space. This "defensible space" idea suggests modifying areas so that it is apparent to outsiders that the occupants are vigilant and have control of the area. This is done through modifying exterior areas so that a signal is sent to anyone who might happen by that the occupants of the area have *control over their space;* the residents are vigilant about what happens on the street, and they have a high *sense of responsibility* for the area, to the extent that they may intervene or confront those who do not belong. (Not that they *will* actually confront people, but the location *gives the appearance* that they will.)

This concept ties in directly with the concept of neighborhood deterioration, which is a community policing concept. *Neighborhood deterioration* is the idea that if an area is run down, it sends a message that the people who live in the area do not care, because they obviously do not care about the appearance of their homes or apartments. When it is apparent that the residents do not care, it is an invitation for others with nonlegitimate purposes to move into the area and take over.

The following tactics can be used to announce control over a space:

- **Improve the appearance of the space.** Residents can announce their control over their space by improving the appearance of an area. This concept is usually presented as a fundamental component of the broken windows theory, which suggest that a single broken window, left unrepaired, can ultimately lead to the deterioration of an entire neighborhood.
- **Extend semi-private areas:** Improving the appearance of an area is very important, but residents can do other things to announce their control over their space. A common way to do this is to place fences or shrubs around the front yard, which extends the home's semi-private area.

  When an area is fenced in, it gives *the allusion that this is a private area.* This is often enough to keep criminal activity away from the location; a criminal simply does not feel comfortable on the other side of the fence, which is obviously a private area, because he knows it look like he does not belong there.

Fences or shrubs can be tall and oppressive to the point that it actually does prevent nonlegitimate users for entering the semi-private area, but the placement of short fences or shrubs, which appears to be cosmetic only, can actually be as effective in announcing that an area is semi-private. This makes people who have no business in this area from being comfortable enough to enter these areas.

• **Focal point entrances:** By its very nature, a single family home is its own statement of territorial claim. It becomes more of a design problem when dealing with apartments, because, from an architectural standpoint, it is difficult to make a large apartment complex look like a single family home.

However, *limiting the number of entrances* to an apartment complex and *making the entrance a focal point* of the structure can increase the sense of territoriality. Of course, the design portion of this concept is beyond the purview of law enforcement, but by understanding the importance of focal points, at least they can explain to tenants and apartment managers that these characteristics inherent to apartments could contribute to these areas being more prone to crime and disorder.

SURVEILLANCE OPPORTUNITY

Surveillance opportunity is simply the ability of the occupants of homes and businesses to be able to see activity outside of the structure. When homes and businesses are designed so that the occupants can see out, outsiders can also see this.

If someone is planning something illegal outside the structure, they are less likely to do it where they can be seen. The effect of surveillance is to put the offender under *threat of being observed*, which could lead to identification and apprehension of the offender.

The following techniques can be used to improve surveillance opportunity:

- **Simple modifications:** Police officers can do a lot in the area of improving the natural surveillance of a location, usually by making suggestions to the property owners to make simple modifications, such as the following:
  - **Keep store windows free of clutter.** This will allow the police and passersby to see into the location, which potential offenders will also realize.
  - **Arrange aisles perpendicular to the front windows.** If the aisles are parallel to the front windows, this gives potential offenders many opportunities for concealment from outside the location. If the aisles are perpendicular, then police officers driving by can see down

each aisle as they cruise through the parking lot.

○ **Keep trees and shrubs trimmed.** All too often, residents of single family homes let their landscaping get out of control, to the point that it conceals portions of the structures. When this concealment includes doors or windows, it allows offenders with the concealment necessary to break in without fear of detection. (Ironically, this is not as much of a problem with apartment complexes, because they all have gardeners who maintain the landscaping.)

• **Design:** In the design stage, activity areas, such as the kitchen, can be placed at the front of home, which is generally the most active area in the average home. Most kitchens in modern homes are in the back of the house, as are family rooms. This design is to provide the residents with a greater amount of privacy, but it does not provide for much surveillance opportunity.

When homes are backed up to parks, the placement of many windows overlooking the park can improve the surveillance opportunities of the residents, with the added benefit of providing the residents with a desirable view.

• **Surveillance cameras.** Businesses can install surveillance cameras to monitor activities inside their businesses as well as parking lots and parking structures. The conspicuous placement of these cameras can send a not-so-subtle message to everyone around that they are under constant observation. Some businesses believe so much in this concept that they install facsimile (phony) cameras to give the appearance that people are being observed and recorded.

TRAFFIC PATTERNS

Designs of walkways and layouts of streets can have an effect on crime. Offenders want to appear that they are legitimately at the location. If traffic pattern designs do not allow this to happen, the offender will not feel comfortable.

When people who do not belong in the area are provided with opportunities to be in the area legitimately, by way of streets and walkways, it improves their opportunities to go about unchallenged. Minor changes in traffic patterns can often reduce or remove an ongoing nuisance or crime problem.

> **Example:** A resident living at a corner house keeps calling the police about people trespassing by cutting across his lawn to get to a bus bench at the side of his yard. By moving the bus bench to the corner, the traffic pattern is changed, and is no longer a problem.

Traffic Studies

Studies have shown that there are *more burglaries to houses on major streets*. This is because there is more opportunity to appear to be legitimately at the location than on quieter streets. Major streets have a lot of street signs, and when a street has many street signs, it is an indication that it is a more public area than streets with few signs.

Studies have also shown that *more burglaries occur at corner houses*, again because of the more public appearance of homes at corners. The risk of burglaries is lowest for homes at the end of cul de sacs. Because of the inherent increase in surveillance opportunity in cul de sacs, offenders do not feel comfortable at these types of locations due to the increased potential of being detected.

The more private an area looks, the less comfortable a criminal will feel being there.

DISPLACEMENT CONCEPT

If the police are successful in their CPTED efforts, it does not mean that they have eliminated a crime problem. At best, they have moved it to another location, and hopefully, for the police department, to another city, making it someone else's problem. This is called the *displacement concept*, in which the problem simply moves from an area in which changes have been made to a more vulnerable area. This is considered *negative displacement*. The second half of this concept is *positive displacement*, in which the criminal activity is *moved toward legitimate activity*, such as disorderly behavior being moved to a recreation center or other legitimate activity area.

> **Example:** If there is a problem with individuals playing sports games in a closed park after hours, which creates a nuisance for the surrounding neighborhood, turning the lights off will stop the activity. If, concurrently, the

police arrange to allow the sports games at another location, perhaps in an area not surrounded by homes, along with adding the lights, the activity remains the same, but has been converted from illegal activity to legal activity.

Community policing concepts require officers to evaluate problem areas that are not just frequent crime locations, but also disorder locations, which is a breeding ground for future criminal activity and deterioration.

The four components of CPTED are not the entire answer to these problems; they are just one part of a variety of social, economic, political, cultural, and environmental tools. Suggestions for modifications based on CPTED concepts may not solve the problem, but they may reduce the problem, and in any case, will not likely make the problem worse.

CONCLUSION

The goals of CPTED are to:

- **Increase the effort required to commit crime**. This is accomplished through target hardening techniques, such as installing fences and adding lighting.
- **Increase the risks for committing crime**. By modifying the physical environment so that there is an increase in offenders being seen, or not looking like they belong at the location, the risk increases, which will likely cause an offender to go elsewhere.

- **Reduce the rewards of crime**. With sufficient target hardening and modifications to the physical environment, which makes a target undesirable to potential offenders, it just is not worth the risk, no matter what the reward would be.

CHAPTER 6

CIVIL LIABILITY

Topics

- Three Areas of Liability
- Reducing and Preventing Liability
- Supervisory Responsibilities
- Three Components of Managing Liability

INTRODUCTION

Civil liability exposure is a major concern for managers when they make decisions. In criminal justice organizations, it is a huge concern. Probation and parole agencies have exposure, but law enforcement is more prone to liability exposure than any other segment in the criminal justice system. In fact, the medical profession is the only profession with a higher level of liability exposure than law enforcement.

When it comes to management decisions, the question of liability is often a major consideration. Personnel decisions, training issues, and especially discipline decisions are as much about liability protection as they are about changing behavior.

THREE AREAS OF LIABILITY

A criminal justice employee or agency (especially law enforcement because of the nature of the work) will become involved in civil litigation due to three areas of liability: intentional acts, negligence, or violation of a person's Constitutional rights.

Intentional Acts

Intentional acts are actions that are intentionally done. These acts are often defended as being a mistake, consent, self-defense, denial, or privilege. These include acts such as battery, assault, false arrest, infliction of mental distress, and conversion of property (theft).

Negligence

Negligence is a violation of a standard of conduct, which is the most intense area of litigation. Negligence is different from an intentional act because there is no intent for the consequences of the act. In law enforcement, there is constant liability exposure in the form of negligent driving, negligent discharge of a firearm (known as an *accidental discharge*), and negligence in the use of lawful force to effect an arrest (such as breaking a suspect's arm while making an arrest).

The three levels of negligence are:

- **Simple negligence:** This is simply a lack of due care, such as when someone is involved in a traffic accident because he was not paying attention to his driving.
- **Gross negligence**: This is more than just not paying attention; this is committing an unsafe act, such as reckless driving that causes a traffic accident.
- **Willful/criminal negligence:** At this level, there is intentional misconduct, such as being pursued by the police and getting into an accident.

Negligence is a major concern for management. For example, an agency may be liable for the negligent retention of an employee if they do not fire them when they should have. This is a major reason for the concept of progressive discipline, in which employees receive progressively more severe levels of discipline as violations continue.

> **Example:** A police officer who gets in a traffic accident is reprimanded the first

time. After the second accident, he gets
suspended and is sent to a driver training
course. After the third accident, he is
suspended for a longer period. After the
fourth or fifth accident, management must
start to consider the liability exposure that
they have if they continue to employ this
officer. If the accidents continue, the
officer will certainly be terminated.

In addition, negligent hiring, negligent supervision, and
negligent training can also expose a public organization
to liability. This potential liability exposure explains why
the testing process for law enforcement candidates is so
exhaustive. Police officer candidates undergo polygraph
examinations, psychological examinations, and
background examinations to screen out potential
problems; these are attempts to reduce liability exposure
right from the beginning.

To prove negligence, the plaintiff must establish:

- **There was a duty or obligation for the person to
  conform to a standard of conduct**. For instance,
  in a traffic accident, the driver had a duty to
  stop for a red signal.
- **There was a failure of the person to conform to
  the standard of conduct.** For instance, in the
  traffic accident, the person failed to stop for the
  red signal.
- **There was a reasonable relationship (proximate
  cause) between the failure of the person to
  conform to the standard of conduct and the
  resulting injury.** For instance, because the

person failed to stop for the red signal, the collision occurred.

- **There was actual damage occurring to the plaintiff.** For instance, collision damage and/or physical injury occurred because of the accident.
- **Personal observation:** Sometimes in news stories, alleged victims or their attorneys will go into great detail about the emotional trauma that they were subjected to, which resulted in a loss of sleep, loss of consortion with a spouse, use of sick time at work, seeing a psychologist, wetting their bed, whatever. This is because there must be some economic loss or personal injury to sue for damages. So, absent of physical injury, the victim must have some sort of injury which resulted in an economic loss or physical pain.

Violation of Constitutional Rights

Most civil actions based on a violation of Constitutional rights are filed pursuant to Title 42 of the United States Code, section 1983. Criminal actions that are a violation of Constitutional rights are filed based on Title 18 of the United States Code, section 242. These sections cover those under color of authority who deprive a person of any of their Constitutional rights, which are acts that go beyond their authority granted by law.

One area of liability exposure that law enforcement often faces regarding Constitutional rights is *false arrest and false imprisonment*. With all the detentions and arrests that police officers make on a daily basis, this area of liability is eventually going to catch up with every police agency.

Officers must have probable cause to detain someone; that is, they must believe that criminal activity is occurring, and that the person they are detaining is connected to the criminal activity. Officers must also have probable cause to make an arrest.

If officers are not properly trained, and retrained because of continual changes in the law, an agency's exposure will be much more significant than that of an agency that provides quality and timely training. And of course, close supervision is vital to prevent false arrests and detentions.

Police departments have a number of legal protections that prevent civil suits from crippling law enforcement efforts:

- **Officers are not civilly liable for accepting a private person's arrest**. Officers must meet a number of requirements in accepting an arrest, which limits their liability. However, recent changes in the law state that an officer is no longer required to accept what is an obvious unlawful arrest, which could bring more liability exposure to him than in the past.
- **Officers are not liable if arrests are made in good faith, based on the information they had at the time**. For instance, an agency mistakenly tells an officer that an arrest warrant is valid, when in fact it is not. If the officer arrests an individual on this invalid warrant, the officer will not be liable because he made the arrest in good faith, believing that the warrant was valid.

A less common occurrence related to a violation of rights is in the area of false imprisonment. The police must release an individual once all charges have been dismissed or it has been determined that charges are not going to be filed. For instance, say that a detective investigates a suspect who is in custody for an alleged crime. He investigates the case, and then presents the case to the district attorney. The DA refuses to file charges. The detective must have the suspect released from custody in a timely manner. If he fails to do so, such as going home for the weekend and having the suspect released at a later date, this is false imprisonment.

Another area of liability regarding a violation of rights other than false arrest and imprisonment is excessive use of physical force. The law provides that a peace officer making a lawful arrest may use reasonable force to affect an arrest, to prevent escape, or to overcome resistance. Any force that is used beyond what is reasonable is considered to be excessive.

Peace officers do not have to retreat or desist from their efforts because they are met by resistance; they will not be deemed the aggressor, and they will not lose their right to self-defense.

> **Example:** As an officer is making an arrest, the suspect's friends try to interfere. Even if it would be prudent for the officer to back off and wait for assistance, which could lead to a peaceful resolution with a show of force, the officer is not required to do so. So, if he chooses to do so, the officer could use any force necessary to maintain custody of his

suspect, which would likely mean using physical force on the friends.

Example: As an officer is making an arrest, the suspect fights and struggles with the officer. The officer is not required or expected to back off because of the resistance. The officer may use any force necessary to overcome the resistance, even if it means serious injury to the suspect.

Personal observation: People rely on the police to protect them from harm by others. If the police had to retreat when met with resistance, what good would they be regarding their obligation to protect the public from physical harm?

REDUCING AND PREVENTING LIABILITY

Elimination of civil liability is a two-pronged approach:

- Officers and management must *do* their job right.
- They must be able to *prove* they did their job right.

Doing the Job Right

Officers do not intend to do something wrong. Usually, someone gets involved in a complex situation and makes a mistake. These mistakes are highly predictable and can be eliminated.

One of the responsibilities of management is to predict what will happen, and then take steps to prevent it. The two best ways to prevent officers from doing something wrong are:

- Proper selection of personnel
- Effective training of personnel

Selection of Personnel

The organization must take care to select personnel who are *even-tempered*. In a dynamic, stressful and violent job, such as law enforcement, there is too much potential for excessive use of force if officers are prone to anger.

This is one of the reasons that police salaries are comparatively high for the actual amount of work that they do. It is not because of the danger (per capita, more construction workers, taxi drivers, and convenience store clerks are killed each year than police officers). It is because there is a very high expectation of the officers; they are expected to be very controlled in extremely stressful and hostile conditions.

> **Example:** After fighting for his life with a suspect, several other officers arrive to assist. The suspect surrenders with the show of force and is taken into custody. The officer, bloody and injured, punches the handcuffed suspect. If the officer was just an average citizen, this reaction would be typical, and not unexpected. But the officer is held to a much higher standard, and this conduct would be unacceptable. The officer would face

severe discipline and potential civil liability.

Besides selecting officers who are even-tempered, *the organization must select personnel who have a strong learning aptitude.* Not only do police officers need to have the intelligence to learn the complexities of the law, they must also have the ability to apply their knowledge in a variety of situations under stressful conditions. If an officer does not have the cognitive skills to understand the law and apply it appropriately, he will make many mistakes in the form of unlawful detentions and arrests, which will expose the agency to potential civil liability.

Training of Personnel

If police supervisors fail to adequately train their officers, it may bring about liability exposure. *A proper training program can protect an agency from negligent training liability.* An effective training program can also *keep skill levels high,* which will decrease the incidents that produce liability cases.

> **Example:** A police officer gets in a shootout with a suspect, and during the gunfire a bystander is shot by the officer. The bystander sues the police department for failing to properly train the officer in the use of a firearm.
>
> The police department shows the court that the officer received training with his firearm on a monthly basis, supported by documentation by the department range master. Records also show that the officer

received a qualifying score for every training period. This well-documented program will significantly reduce the liability exposure for the department. There will always be vicarious liability, which means the department will still be responsible for the actions of the officer, accident or not, but punitive damages would be minimal, if at all.

A good training program is sort of like an insurance policy for the department; it is a protection again punitive damages for failure to properly train. But other than that, if officers do receive quality and timely training, incidents, such as the shooting of a bystander, will occur much less often because the officers' skill levels are high; they hit what they are aiming at, and nothing else.

> **Example:** In a highly publicized incident, a suspect was struck numerous times with a police baton. If the officer had been more skilled in the use of the baton, a few well-placed, powerful blows would have ended the suspect's resistance sooner, and the officer would not have had to strike him so many times.

So, to prevent civil liability exposure, and to reduce the amount of liability by the agency, proper selection of personnel and effective training of officers is the best way to ensure that the job is done right.

Proving They Did the Job Right

As previously stated, police managers must recognize that some mistakes made by officers are highly predicable, and it is their job to prevent these mistakes from happening. One expert in police liability, Gordon Graham, has identified three potential liability incidents. *When one of these types of incidents occurs, the incidents themselves must be carefully documented.* This documentation is how the police prove that they did their job right.

When it comes to documentation, the information needed in a police report for successful criminal prosecution is different from the elements and information that may be needed in a future civil case, which allows the police to be able to prove that they did their job right.

> **Example:** In a criminal case in which a suspect resisted arrest and the officer had to use physical force to affect the arrest, resulting in an injury to the suspect, the officer needs to describe the event in enough detail to incorporate the elements of the crime for successful prosecution.
>
> But this incident, as we will soon see, is a potential liability incident, and further documentation is required. Besides providing information to satisfy the criminal elements for prosecution, the officer's report must go into great detail so that the reader gets a clear picture of the incident, which would typically include

minor details that the criminal case would not require.

Consider the following potential liability incidents:

- **Any injury to a person or damage to property caused by the police.** The element of injury or damage must be present, because there must be some loss incurred by the plaintiff. When the police are involved, it can be inviting for attorneys because the police are easy targets, in that they are often looked upon unfavorably by judges and juries, depending on the social climate. (After the Rodney King incident, the police had a very negative image, after 9/11, they were heroes.)

  Besides the police being an easy target for lawsuits, attorneys seek defendants who have "deep pockets." That is, there is no value in suing someone who has no money. Even suing a police officer is not worth the effort, because he does not have the millions that are being sought. So the big money is with the officer's employer. Vicarious liability is the avenue that attorneys take to go after those who can pay a large judgment, which would be the city that employs the officer.

- **Any major injury requiring hospitalization and the police are on scene or there is public property involved.** Only a major injury is worthy of an attorney's attention. Minor injuries do not net much in monetary damages.

The element of hospitalization is twofold: (1) it ensures that there is a significant injury that can yield significant monetary damages and (2) many attorneys have contacts at hospitals who notify them when a patient meets the above criteria.

And again, deep pockets are involved. The police (who are not sympathetic victims in civil court) are connected through vicarious liability to their employer, as is the case when public property is involved.

- **Anytime someone says that they will sue.** We live in a very litigious society, and if someone says that they are going to sue, it is likely that they will. Forewarned is forearmed.

So, to prove that they did their job right, the police must show proof through documentation:

- *The police reports need to include the precipitous acts by the police,* such as, "In uniform, driving a marked police unit, dispatch to . . ." This shows that *the officer was duty bound to respond* to the incident. It was not as if he was looking for trouble with the plaintiff, he was simply doing his job.
- The wording of the report is very important. *It needs to show that the officer was simply reacting to the actions of the suspect.* The officer needs to carefully choose his words, such as "the suspect fled" rather than, "I chased the suspect." The reports generally tell too much about what the

police officer did, and not enough about what the suspect did.

- The report needs to include all the precipitous acts committed by the suspect that escalated the incident. The officer needs to describe the objective behavior of the suspect. If he fails to do this, and he later describes this behavior in a civil trial years later, the plaintiff's attorney will likely try to show that the testimony is fabricated to aid in the officer's defense. The argument will be that if the information was important enough to testify to now, it would have been important enough to put in the arrest report.

- Generally, officers do not include any verbal abuse by the suspect in the crime report, because it has no bearing on the elements of the crime. However, in an incident which could lead to civil liability exposure, verbal abuse by a suspect can show a noncompliant attitude, as well as the mindset of the suspect just prior to the incident leading to the lawsuit.

The goal of police management in the area of civil liability is to maximize effectiveness of the officers while avoiding lawsuits. And if they are sued, they want to be in a position to win the suit or at least reduce the damages.

SUPERVISORY RESPONSIBILITIES

Management approaches the goal of maximizing effectiveness while avoiding lawsuits by taking two approaches: (1) providing policies that give guidance in complex situations and (2) providing training to ensure that the officers know the policies and laws.

- **Policy:** A policy manual is supposed to serve as guidance for officers in difficult situations, such as when entering someone's home. Too many policies focus on grooming standards and other issues irrelevant to civil liability.
- **Training:** Proper training ensures that the officers are aware of the policies and the law concerning these difficult situations, thereby preventing many of them from happening in the first place.

The key to success is effective supervision. Without training by the supervisors and reinforcement through discipline, management's efforts will be futile. But discipline can only be fairly dispensed when officers intentionally violate policy. So the *policies must be clear* and *supported by training and supervision* so officers know what is expected of them. Also, the *policies must provide guidance*, which means they are merely guidelines rather than steadfast rules.

To maximize effectiveness and reduce lawsuits, the police must approach their job differently. It is the job of supervision to make sure that this happens. They can do this by continually reinforcing three concepts that can prevent or reduce liability exposure: consent, confession, and cooperation.

Consent

Supervisors must make sure that officers *constantly consider the role of consent* in the course of their criminal investigations. Many of the contacts and activities that the police are involved in are because people are consenting to it. *Consensual contacts, searches, and entries can protect officers and their departments from lawsuits based on civil rights violations that would otherwise stem from unlawful detentions and searches.*

> **Example:** If a police officer sees someone walking down the street, and the officer wants to talk to him, perhaps because he looks suspicious, but there is no probable cause, the officer is entitled to ask the person if he may talk to him. If the person consents to this, it is a consensual contact, not a detention. Likewise, people can consent to have their person, vehicle, or home searched just because an officer is asking. Officers recover vast amounts of contraband simply because people allow the police to conduct a search.

So, let's say that an officer thinks that he has probable cause to detain or search someone. But to be on the safe side, he asks for consent for the detention or search, and the person gives it to him. If the courts later decide the officer did not have probable cause, the evidence is not excluded, because the officer had consent anyway.

The point is that an officer is not going to get consent unless he asks for it. As a safety measure against liability based on a violation of civil rights, *officers should get into the habit of always asking for consent even when they have probable cause.* It is the responsibility of supervisors to make sure that officers develop this habit. Additionally, officers are not going to get consent if they are overly officious or otherwise display a poor attitude toward the individual.

Confession

Officers should try to get admitting statements from suspects that could refute later allegations that they may make against the officers. For instance, if an officer makes an arrest and the suspect has struggled with the officer, the officer should question the suspect to obtain a confession that he resisted arrest.

When a suspect is injured by an officer, or an officer uses a weapon on a suspect, a sergeant usually conducts an administrative investigation to determine if the officer's actions were within department policy. As a normal course of action, the sergeant will interview the suspect, and during the course of the interview will attempt to illicit statements from the suspect admitting that his actions precipitated the injury or use of force.

These statements made to the officer during the criminal investigation, or to the sergeant during the administrative investigation, are carefully documented in the event the suspect later files a civil action against the officer and department. *The confession will likely protect the agency from an unfavorable judgment.*

Cooperation

Supervisors must show officers that tact and diplomacy with suspects is much more effective than using verbal and physical force. Officers should be made to understand that it is in their best interest to behave in way that prevents use-of-force incidents, which can lead to liability exposure.

Studies have shown that female officers have better verbal skills than male officers. Perhaps this is because they generally do not have the physical strength of their male counterparts, and thus must rely more on tact and diplomacy. This results in fewer use of force incidents involving female officers. Part of this may also be that a male suspect will never feel good about fighting a female officer, whether he wins the fight or not.

The most important aspect of cooperation deals with the ability of officers to take advantage of the concepts of consent and confession by properly utilizing the concept of cooperation. If an officer does not display an amicable attitude that would illicit cooperation, he will not be successful in obtaining consent or confessions.

Officers must demonstrate tact and diplomacy in their contacts with suspects so that they are willing to be searched and will confess to their misdeeds. This will only occur if there is a spirit of cooperation between the officer and suspect, which will only happen if the officer *treats the suspect with respect and dignity*, whether or not he deserves it.

So, the way that officers conduct themselves impacts whether consent, cooperation, and confession occur. *Anger—either the suspect's or the officer's—will cause a blockage of all three of these valuable liability protection tools.* Officers need to treat people as well as possible, especially when they do not deserve it. If they are in a situation where the suspect does not deserve good treatment, it is because there is a great amount of hostility occurring, which prompts many people to file civil actions.

Some people will get angry with a situation involving the police no matter what the officers do or say. But what supervisors need to do is to make sure that officers do not make the suspect unnecessarily angry.

> **Personal observation:** Police officers are used to people being angry at them, and they can take it in stride. Officers do not get personally involved in the situation and can control any anger they may be feeling. However, sometimes an angry suspect or citizen is actually amusing to the officer, because the person is making a fool out of himself.
>
> To continue or heighten the amusement, some officers may be tempted (and sometimes do) to add fuel to the fire by saying and doing things to make the person even angrier. These activities are usually very subtle, and would not rise to the level of inappropriate conduct. But still, it is conduct that could come back to hurt the officer and the organization if a civil suit is filed because the suspect wanted to get even.
>
> Instead, officers should control their urges to egg people on, and use tones and inflections to diffuse someone's anger.
>
> **Example:** Often, someone being arrested will get angry with the arresting officer.

This is especially true in drunken driving cases, in which the alcohol exacerbates the anger, and the offenders often involve citizens who are not typical 'criminal types" that are used to being detained or arrested. They transfer their anger for making a stupid error in judgment to the officer.

If the officer maintains a neutral attitude, and even tells the suspect that "This is nothing personal, I'm just doing my job, trying to keep the streets safe for you and everyone else," this often causes the suspect to transfer the anger back to himself, rather than the officer. This may prevent a violent confrontation, which can lead to injury and liability exposure.

The three things that cause most lawsuits are greed, injury, and anger. Anger is the root cause. Knowing this, officers should try to prevent people from getting angry. Supervisors need to show them that treating people as well as possible is good for them, because it maximizes effectiveness and prevents lawsuits.

When police officers maintain a professional and civil attitude when contacting people, it allows consent, cooperation, and confessions to occur and reduces anger. This prevents lawsuits. The key to this goal is the use of effective human relations training so that officers learn techniques to diffuse hostile situations and reduce people's anger.

Whether or not the person deserves good treatment or not is irrelevant. Those who create the most negative contacts with the police are the ones most likely to complain or sue.

One way that supervision can modify the behavior of the officers so as to minimize liability exposure is to *get the officers to view themselves as good and clever investigators.* A big part of successful investigations and confessions is by playing "mind games" with the suspects. That is, an effective strategy in the criminal investigation process is treating people well as a way to reach their goals.

> **Example:** A detective who works child sexual assault cases certainly does not have sympathy or concern for child molesters. But to an outsider watching the interaction during the interrogation, one would think the detective cared about and understood the offender, and almost seemed to side with the offender at times. What the detective was doing is common practice for investigators; he was subtly breaking down the defenses of the offender by pretending to understand and sympathize with him, which enables the detective to obtain a confession. A detective will never get a confession from a child molester by yelling at him and calling him a pervert.

Another challenge that police supervisors have is that the subculture that police officers are immersed in is contrary to the concept of treating offenders well. Treating offenders well is viewed as "not cool." Supervisors must retrain officers to believe that this new strategy is cool. A personality change by the officers is not required, only a change in behavior by way of a different attitude to reach the goal of successful prosecution and reduction of liability exposure.

Supervisors must also make sure that officers understand that they do not have absolute authority over others. Routine consensual encounters can turn into detentions without the officer realizing it, which can then result in a civil rights violation, resulting in liability exposure.

> **Example:** Officers commonly make contacts with individuals by asking for their consent to do so. Usually, the officer says something to the effect of "Hey, can I talk to you for a minute?" Almost always the individual consents. The process becomes so routine that officers, if they are not careful, can get lulled into a false sense that they can talk to anyone they want any time they want.
>
> After years of making these consensual contacts, when "asking" for consent, the requests sound more like "Hey, come here." And suddenly, a consensual contact becomes a detention. Without probable cause to detain the individual, the detention becomes a federal civil rights violation. This could subject the officer and agency to civil liability and expose the officer to federal prosecution.

The police have no authority without a combination of facts. When certain facts are present, the police have authority to detain or arrest. So, without this authority or power (because the facts necessary to establish probable cause are not present), police officers must rely on human relation skills to be effective.

> **Example:** A Supreme Court decision regarding a case involving detentions makes it clear how important it is for officers to use consent whenever possible, such as when they lack sufficient facts to detain an individual.
>
> Officers received a radio call that a man sitting at a bus bench at a certain location was armed with a handgun. The caller did not give his identity, and it was not known how the caller knew this information. Officers arrived at the location and observed a man fitting the description given by the anonymous caller. The subject was detained, and a gun was located on his person.
>
> The Court stated that the information that the officers had was not sufficient for a detention. (If there had been additional information, such an identified caller, and how the caller knew the subject was armed, this could have helped the facts problem.) So, in situations like this, officers must rely on consent. The officers could have contacted the subject and asked him for permission to conduct a

search. Efforts such as this can lead to more successful prosecutions, and can prevent Supreme Court decisions that can negatively affect law enforcement efforts.

So, officers should try to make voluntary contact with subjects when the officer has nothing more than investigative curiosity, with no reasonable suspicion or probable cause.

To make matters even more challenging for police supervisors, the contempt of cop theme is the most likely cause in a majority of civil liability cases. Contempt of cop is when an individual shows contempt for an officer or his authority through his insolence. The way officers who do not properly manage their anger "get even" is to arrest the subject with questionable probable cause or to use too much force when the hostile suspect resists arrest.

The officer's anger creates liability exposure for himself and for his department. Officers must learn to accept that there are situations where they will have no authority, and there will be situations where their judgment will be impaired if they allow themselves to get angry or personally involved in an incident.

Additionally, they must accept that ordering people to talk, sit down, shut up, whatever, does not illicit a cooperative attitude that can lead to admissions and confessions.

THREE COMPONENTS OF MANAGING LIABILITY

Human Relations Training

Human relations training should encompass the following:

- *Officers* must be skilled in the art of anger management.
- *Supervisors* have to help officers manage their own anger and manage the anger of the suspect.
- *Management* must consider the anger management issue during the selection of personnel.

Knowledge of Authority

It is the responsibility of police supervisors to make sure that their officers are properly trained in the law and in the policies of the organization to prevent liability exposure, such as probable cause and search and seizure.

Skills and Equipment

A situation that the police are involved in can evolve from using no force to using deadly force for several reasons. In some situations use of force could have been prevented, but in some situations the officer lacks the skills and equipment needed to de-escalate a situation.

- **Lack of tools or equipment.** If an officer is not properly equipped to deal with a violent confrontation, he may be forced to use more force than would have been necessary if he had the proper tools. For example, some detectives only carry a firearm, and maybe handcuffs. They usually do not carry chemical agents or batons. So, if they get in a fight with a larger and stronger suspect, they must resort to their firearm to win the fight.

• **Lack of skill or training.** Officers need continual and ongoing training in specific weapon skills, including firearms, baton, and other less-lethal weapons. If they lack the proper skill in the use of a weapon, such as a baton, they will have to use more force than would be necessary if they had the skill to use the weapon properly.

• **Lack of physical conditioning.** If a police officer is in a fight, and the officer is in poor physical condition, he will likely not be able to hold his own. An officer who maintains a high level of fitness is much more likely to be able to control a combative suspect. A lesser-conditioned officer may have to resort to weapons to get him out of trouble.

• **Fear.** Fear is a powerful force. When someone, even a police officer, is in fear for his life, he will resort to any means necessary to protect himself, which would include using weapons that he has at his disposal. Fear is removed when an officer is confident, which occurs when the officer is properly equipped, trained, and conditioned. Self-confidence can even prevent physical confrontations. Officers have more confidence in facing these situations when they are prepared.

Personal observation: The cops who are the most prepared, (in good physical condition, mentally ready, and skilled with their weapons) seem to be involved in fewer use-of-force incidents. Perhaps it is because the suspects can sense the self-confidence that the officer has, and because it looks like he spends more time in a gym than a donut shop.

CHAPTER 7

USE OF FORCE

Topics

- Reactionary Forces
- Levels of Force
- Justification Factor

INTRODUCTION

A very unique characteristic of police work is that it is inevitable that *every police officer will be involved in a violent confrontation with a citizen* requiring him to use physical force in the course of his duties. And, these use-of-force incidents are not rare occurrences. On the contrary, they occur much more often than people think.

There is no time to prepare for these confrontations; they happen instantaneously and without warning. Police officers must always be prepared—both mentally and physically—for violence at any moment. What most people do not realize is that *every fight that a police offer is involved in involves a gun—the officer's gun.* A police officer cannot afford to lose a fight; if he does lose, the suspect will have access to the officer's sidearm and can use it against him. Many officers have been killed in just this fashion.

This unique characteristic of physical violence as a job descriptor does more than just make police work an unusual and dynamic occupation; it is a catalyst to the most powerful subculture in society—the brotherhood of law enforcement.

No other civilian occupation calls upon the courage of fellow employees to protect each other and place themselves in harm's way for one another than police work. And, because of this demanding job requirement, there is a bond between all police officers that only another police officer can understand. This dynamic topic of police culture will be discussed in chapter 10.

Police officers must tread a fine line in this area of use of force. The law describes what actions an officer can take but is intentionally vague in its language, because all possible situations cannot be forecast. This leaves it up to individual police officers to make split-second, life-making or -taking decisions, which police administrators and courts scrutinize and analyze in tedious detail for years.

State statutes give the police certain authority to use physical force, and *case laws* provide them with additional guidelines resulting from what are perceived as mistakes by officers that these after-the-fact decision makers impose (okay, generously provide) police officers with.

The law provides that a peace officer making a lawful arrest may use *reasonable force to affect an arrest, to prevent escape, or to overcome resistance.* The officer does not have to retreat or desist from his efforts because he is met by resistance. He shall not be deemed the aggressor or lose his right to self-defense.

> **Example:** As explained in chapter 6, sometimes it would be safer for the officer and result in less injury to an offender if the officer were to back away from a potentially violent confrontation. But, if the police had to consider this as an option, their effectiveness in protecting the public would be significantly diminished.
>
> **Personal observation:** Society wants the police to do the things that they are unable or unwilling to do, but they still do not like it. *The actions of the police, especially in use of force incidents, are the lesser of two evils* — the greater being anarchy and the demise of civilized society, and the lesser being the reliance on human beings (police officers) to do the dirty work that a civilized society does not want to acknowledge that they rely on to perpetuate their very existence and future.
>
> These provisions in the law clearly tell us that the police are expected to use

physical force in the course of their duties. Case law decisions second-guess the police when they do, which makes that fine line a very fine one indeed.

REACTIONARY FORCES

The police are reactionary forces; that is, they react to the acts of others. The acts of others that lead to another incident, such as a use of force, are called precipitous acts.

Precipitous acts bring trained responses by officers, which can lead to a use of force. If a subject runs from the police, the police will chase. Electing to run from the police is a precipitous act that increases the risk to both the officer and suspect.

> **Example:** The police do not initiate use-of-force incidents. In all lawful use-of-force situations, the police simply respond to an aggressive, hostile, or violent act by the offender. When the police observe this type of behavior, they respond to this precipitous act with a level of force that is considered reasonable for the level of resistance that they are encountering.

When an officer recognizes noncompliant behavior, he must respond in a *reasonable manner* to gain control. The officer must instantly decide how much force to use; what weapons (control devices) to use, and exactly to what degree; and then decide exactly when he should reduce or increase his level of force, based on the offender's actions.

This notion of a reasonably measured response is known as the *escalation* and *de-escalation of force*. The police increase or decrease the amount of force as the level of resistance increases or decreases.

> **Example:** A suspect attacks an officer with his fists, attempting to strike him. The officer uses his baton to strike the suspect. After being struck several times, the suspect stops his attack and drops to the ground to avoid further baton strikes. With this de-escalation of resistance, the officer should de-escalate his force. He would stop using baton strikes and use a lesser degree of force to control the suspect.

> **Example:** A suspect takes a fighting stance and makes comments to the effect that he will not comply with police commands. The officer administers a burst of a chemical agent at the suspect, who immediately drops to the ground and holds his face. If the officer then uses his police baton to strike the suspect, this would be an escalation of force when the suspect's resistance is clearly de-escalating. The appropriate response by the officer would be to reduce his level of force to a hands-on level of controlling and handcuffing.

The officer must evaluate the level of resistance he is encountering and meet it with enough force to overcome the resistance. In previous years, the old standard was that an officer met resistance with the next highest level of force. The problem with this standard was that every situation is different; to simply require that the police use a baton when a suspect is using his fists is to presume that violent confrontations occur in controlled settings in which a step-by-step procedure will always be the best option.

One of the criticisms of the Rodney King case in Los Angeles was not with the amount of force that was initially used, *but rather the lack of de-escalation once the suspect appeared to be submitting.* When King first charged an officer (which was footage the public did not see), King was struck with a baton. But when King was on his hands and knees, baton blows were no longer needed, and a lesser degree of force (such as a swarm tactic in which several officers pile up on him) would have been more reasonable for the level of resistance being encountered.

Additionally, one of the defense arguments by attorneys representing the officers was that the officers were not properly trained in the use of their batons. This was demonstrated in the video in which there were several ineffective baton blows as well as several glancing blows. A fewer number of properly placed baton strikes could have caused compliance and incapacitation of the suspect, resulting in proper de-escalation.

What most people do not realize is that *a baton is not a pain-compliance tool*; that is, a baton is not used for the sole purpose of inflicting pain to gain compliance of a violent suspect. A police baton is a very serious weapon. When used properly by a police officer, it is meant to cause injury to the point that it immediately incapacitates the suspect. If an officer strikes a suspect on the back or upper leg, these baton strikes will cause pain, but will not cause the suspect to cease his violent behavior, unless the pain he is experiencing is enough for him to stop.

As the level of resistance decreases, so must the level of force. The key is to use a level of force that overcomes resistance, and nothing more. Where resistance ends, and de-escalation does not occur, excessive force begins. For instance, a suspect fights with an officer, and when backup arrives, the suspect surrenders and is handcuffed. The officer involved in the fight, who wants to get his pound of flesh, strikes the handcuffed suspect. This is clearly excessive force.

LEVELS OF FORCE

The levels of force available to police can be placed on a continuum. The level of force used will be based the level of resistance the officer is encountering and many other factors, such as the size and strength of the suspect, the number of suspects, information about possible weapons, and the seriousness of the offense, just to name a few.

Note that the *seriousness of the offense* can in itself cause an escalation of force. For instance, if a suspect commits a violent crime such as a murder, rape, or armed robbery and is running from the police, the police may use deadly force to stop the suspect from escaping. With lesser offenses, this level of force would be excessive.

The following levels of force start at the lowest level and end at the highest level, but the exact sequence of levels varies from one agency to another. But, with *reasonable force* being the operative word, the sequence holds less importance than in the past.

Uniform Presence

A police officer in uniform is usually enough to make most people submit to their authority. As an example, police officers make consensual contacts with people every day. Even though these people do not have to submit to the contact, most people do, because the sight of a police officer in uniform can be pretty intimidating.

Anecdotal evidence suggests that police officers who are not in uniform, such as detectives or other plain-clothed assignments, have more difficulty getting people to comply with orders than officers who are in uniform.

Additionally, when a police officer puts on his uniform, his transition into "cop mode," in which the officer takes on his expected occupational role, is probably much more intense than for an officer who is not wearing a uniform. In other words, a cop in uniform acts more like a cop than one out of uniform, and this cop-mode attitude results in a higher level of command presence than an officer who is wearing a T-shirt and jeans.

Verbal Force

Command presence and a commanding voice can prevent the use of physical force. A physically imposing officer with a deep, strong voice will rarely have to use physical force. When an officer lacks a powerful voice, it will impede the officer's ability to control volatile situations without resulting to physical force. Right from the police academy, instructors force those who are vocally challenged to improve their voice projection and power.

Firm Grip or Gesture

If a police officer grabs onto someone's arm to prevent them from leaving, it can often be enough for the person to comply. Obviously, they know that if they pull away things could go badly for them.

If someone is trying to leave, and a police officer stands in front of them, blocking their path, it is also usually enough to make most sober individuals to rethink their plans, knowing that if they push past the officer they will be making a regretful error in judgment.

Chemical Agents

Improvements in the effectiveness of chemical agents have had a tremendous impact on use-of-force incidents. In the past, the chemical agent known commonly as mace was marginally effective, and was ineffective with many people. Because of this, police officers did not have much faith in it, and as a result were reluctant to use it.

However, with the advent of pepper spray (oleoresin capsicum) the use of chemical agents has become much more widespread now that officers realize how much more effective it is than mace. The use of pepper spray can be very effective in preventing a volatile situation from turning into a violent one.

> **Example:** In the past, a police officer facing a drunken idiot looking for a fight would get just that, a fight. But with pepper spray, when the idiot takes his fighting stance, the officer hoses him down with a chemical agent, and the fight

is over. This results in the suspect not being injured, the officer not being injured, and a reduced likelihood that there will be civil liability exposure because of any resultant injury.

Physical Force

This is where the police use all their fancy control holds and pain compliance techniques (these rarely work, because the suspect is too drunk, too crazy, or too wired, which is usually the case). When this happens, then it is a good old wrestling match, with a bunch of "distraction strikes" (punches), kicks, and other street-fighting techniques. In reality, when an officer must resort to physical force, it is usually nothing more than a street fight.

Impact Weapons

An impact weapon is a politically correct term for a police baton, which used to be called a nightstick. Whatever it is called, it is long, straight implement made of wood, plastic, or metal that is designed to strike the human body and inflict serious injury so as to immediately incapacitate an attacker.

This is serious stuff; it is not pepper spray or wimpy control holds. This is a weapon that is meant to inflict serious injury. Officers target their batons on elbows, knees, and the solar plexus. When a knee is properly struck with an impact weapon, it will likely result in bone fractures. These types of debilitating injuries notoriously result in civil recourse, making the use of this tactic a very serious decision indeed.

Carotid Restraint

When a police officer applies a carotid restraint on a suspect, he is temporarily cutting off the flow of blood to the suspect's brain, which renders him unconscious without any ill effects. To do this, the officer places his arm around the suspect's neck, flexes his bicep and forearm against both sides of the suspect's neck, places his free hand behind the suspect's neck, then pushes down. After a few moments, depending on how well the restraint is applied, the physical characteristics of the suspect, and other factors, the suspect will pass out. He can then be taken into custody with further force.

The problem is that there have been several times in which suspects have died after this technique has been used. If used improperly, such as placing a forearm against the throat, the suspect's larynx is crushed, resulting in suffocation and ultimately death.

Because of the potential for death with this technique, many police departments have placed this method as a very high level of force, equivalent with deadly force.

Electronic Weapons

The most effective and popular electronic weapon that the police use is the Taser. This is a handgun type of weapon that fires darts attached to spools of wire that imbed themselves into the skin of the suspect. An electrical charge then is transmitted into the suspect, which causes a loss of muscle control, rendering the suspect incapacitated.

The only injury to the suspect is the superficial wounds created by the darts. Some of these Taser weapons are designed for use in close quarters, which involve the use of extended probes, such as the old-fashioned television antennas, to administer the electrical shock, which leave no marks or injury.

Less Lethal Weapons

The weapons in this category are called less lethal rather than nonlethal, because, depending upon how the weapon is used, it can actually result in death. These weapons are generally projectiles fired from firearms are other firearm-type devices that are intended to strike the suspect without the projectile actually penetrating the body. The result is to create pain and incapacitation, without causing traumatic injury.

This type of weapon is a good tactical choice when dealing with a suspect with a knife or a suicidal subject armed with a weapon other than a firearm. (If a suspect is armed with a firearm, less lethal weapons are not even considered.)

One of the advantages to the use of this weapon is the psychological effect that it has on the suspect. When a police officer is pointing a shotgun at a violent suspect, and the officer suddenly shoots the suspect, the suspect instinctively believes that he has been shot with a firearm and falls to the ground, not realizing for a moment that he has not been mortally wounded. This gives the officers enough time to swarm the suspect and take him into custody.

Deadly Force

Obviously, this highest level of force involves the use of firearms. But no matter what weapon is used, if the use of deadly force is justified, any weapon can be used. Police officers have used their vehicles to run down a suspect, and less lethal weapons have been used when lethal force was justified.

JUSTIFICATION FACTOR

If a police officer can justify a use of force, even if it is unusual or not with normal policy, it can be deemed appropriate if it was reasonable for the situation. Often, when officers cannot get control of a combative suspect they will punch him. These are called *distraction strikes*, with the desired result of the suspect becoming distracted from his resistance due to the sudden pain he is experiencing. This often results in the officers being able to overcome the suspect's resistance and take him into custody without escalating the force to a much higher level.

> **Example:** When officers are fighting with a suspect in close quarters, the use of chemical weapons or impact weapons is not an option. Often, an officer cannot get to these weapons to use them, but he can get to his flashlight. If an officer uses his flashlight as an impact weapon, and the level of force can be justified for the level of resistance being encountered, the use of a flashlight can be justified.

Use of force policies are guidelines, that is, they provide guidance to officers for most of the encounters they will experience, but not every incident can be forecast.

> **Example:** Three police officers are trying to take a combative suspect into custody. One officer has the suspect in a bear hug; the other officer grabs onto the suspect with one hand and has his gun in the other. The third officer attempts to strike the suspect with a shotgun, but the suspect grabs the shotgun and struggles with the officer over possession.
>
> The officer with the handgun does not like how things are going, and quickly ends the struggle by striking the suspect in the head with his handgun. Although this is not generally an acceptable use of a firearm, in this actual incident it was deemed as a justified use of force.

CHAPTER 8

ORGANIZATIONAL ETHICS

Topics

- Values
- Ethics
- Ethical Relativism
- Integrity
- Principle versus Preference
- Ethical Problems in Law Enforcement

INTRODUCTION

Police organizations and their employees are held to a higher ethical standard than are private organizations and their employees. But most police departments have not undertaken active programs to promote an ethical work environment. Management expects employees to behave in an ethical manner, but they do not take steps to develop this.

By their very nature and structure, many large bureaucracies tend to promote unethical and dishonest behavior. Many workers find themselves feeling they must compromise their ethical standards to fit in or to be successful:

- **Fitting in:** In a police subculture, some officers are verbally abusive to suspects, so a new officer does the same.
- **Being successful:** In a police department, if there is pressure by a supervisor to make drug arrests, an officer may invent probable cause to make vehicle stops that can lead to these arrests.

Many dynamics are involved: wanting to fit in, but also wanting to do the right thing. So, ethics can be very personal, but in this chapter we will also look at ethics from an organizational perspective. Personal and organizational ethics can sometimes conflict, but they must be congruent. For instance, if an officer has to be unethical to get ahead in the department, the ethics of the officer and the ethics of the department are not congruent.

> **Example:** Everyone is getting along fairly well in an organization. Then comes an announcement that there is going to be a testing process for promotion. Suddenly, a false rumor surfaces about a candidate who is a frontrunner for promotion. Rather than the organization ignoring or

quashing the rumor, they perpetuate the process by conducting an investigation on the candidate. The candidate, to save himself, creates rumors about the other candidates, to take the heat off of him and spread it around a little.

Many terms and concepts are associated with organizational ethics. Understanding them will provide a good introduction into the subject.

VALUES

Values are the things that are important to the individual, the things that motivate them. Values are a person's *enduring preferences*, and they are the beliefs that guide the person's behavior. Values include such things as relationships, money, success, honesty, appearance, and health, just to name a few.

Values vary between social classes. Criminal justice personnel generally have middle-class values, which are conservative. *Conflicts can develop when these values are pushed onto those who have different values.* Research has even shown that there is a link between hostile, even prejudiced activity, and conflicts in value systems.

> **Example:** A police officer may be so disgusted by a homeless person's lifestyle or by someone on welfare that it may lead to an insensitive or hostile confrontation.

So, personnel must make a conscious effort to maintain a neutral stance on imposing their values onto others, which could lead to a negative encounter. The goal of this effort is providing unbiased and fair treatment of all people.

Values are developed during a person's formative years, but they can change as time goes by. People choose their values and prioritize them.

> **Example:** A teenager smokes pot, hangs out with his friends, and takes advantage of his parents. But as he gets older, his values change; he gets a job, cleans up his habits, and helps out his family.

> **Example:** A young man enjoys the company of different women. He always has something going, and gains a reputation as a player. As he gets older, he no longer values the next conquest, but rather wants to settle down with one woman and have a family.

Many work-related problems are the result of value conflicts. Managers must be aware of their values and the values of others. A good manager will realize that his values may not be the same as those he manages and will take steps to prevent conflict.

> **Example:** A supervisor does not get promoted into that position by accident; it is because he values success and achievement and has worked hard to get that position. The supervisor has an employee who has no aspirations of supervision or management; he is one of those people who just wants to do the job they were hired for and go home at the

end of the day. (And there is nothing wrong with that; there are not enough positions at the top of the hierarchy for everyone anyway. Organizations need people like this.)

But this supervisor, who values success and achievement highly, views this employee as being lazy and lacking motivation, rather than having different values. If this supervisor fails to recognize the distinction, the relationship between him and this employee will suffer, and undoubtedly lead to poor performance by the employee who is now encountering a hostile work environment.

Example: As will be discussed in chapter 9, the emerging workforce culture values recreation time, which makes alternative scheduling so desirable to them. The older workers, many of them supervisors to the younger ones, did not have it as well in their day; they worked five days a week and were not allowed to use vacation time except once a year.

These new employees are constantly asking for vacation time off, even when they have three or four days off every week. An old school supervisor, who is not aware of changing values from generation to generation, may take a very negative approach to these requests, resulting in hostility between supervision and employees.

So, it is very important for managers and supervisors to recognize that these differences can lead to conflict in the organization. If there is a conflict, it will likely result in a negative outcome for the organization. (In the above example, if the employee is not allowed to take a vacation day because the supervisor does not think he needs it, the employee will most likely just call in sick.)

ETHICS

Ethics are the rules that ought to govern human behavior. There are not a lot of them: honesty, truth, the Golden Rule, hard work, equality, justice. These are the things that we know are right. Ethics involves a process of clarifying what is right and wrong, and acting on what is right.

The real concern about ethics is not in what one does value, but what one should value. Our ethics do not change. We have a choice about following them, which is a choice about who we are.

Remember, *it is our values that guide us, not our ethics.* Ethics are the "rules" that we are supposed to follow, but that does not mean that we follow them.

> **Example:** A thief knows that it is wrong to steal (ethic), but he has a stronger personal value which creates this choice to be a thief (easy money).

So, knowing the right course of action does not necessarily mean that an individual will follow it. But true leadership instills a desire in others to be ethical. A true leader does this through leading by example.

An ethical person has values that are congruent with ethical standards; they know what the right thing is, and they do it.

Police organizations are very concerned that the employees they hire have high ethical standards. One way to assess for ethical standards is by conducting a background investigation on candidates. The purpose of this investigation is to determine if the candidate has led an ethical life. This is done by examining the candidate's *pattern of behavior*.

> **Example:** A candidate was arrested for shoplifting when he was 14, but there have been no other similar incidents. Therefore, this would not be a pattern of behavior that the investigator would be concerned about.
>
> However, if the candidate was also terminated from a job when he was 16 for stealing the petty cash and a neighbor tells the investigator that at age 18 the candidate went joyriding in his car, this would be a pattern of unethical conduct that would be of concern.

Another step that police departments take to determine the ethical standards of potential employees occurs during the oral interview process. Generally, a scenario-type question is posed to the candidate, geared toward determining what the candidate values as higher, honesty or loyalty (maintaining membership in the informal group versus telling the truth).

The question will be along the lines of a fellow employee (with seniority and in good standing with the organization) doing something obviously wrong or illegal. The candidate is asked to explain what he will do about it.

Many times, the value of loyalty is so strong that the candidate actually does not know the right answer to the question. He values loyalty so highly that he assumes the organization does, too. Often, the candidate with this conflict will dance around the issue, and usually stop short of actually reporting it to a supervisor. Unfortunately for this candidate, he has shown the interview panel that to him there is a gray area when it comes to honesty.

ETHICAL RELATIVISM

Ethical relativism is the belief that some actions are moral in some circumstances and immoral in others; that is, that they are *relative to the situation*. According to this approach to ethics, there is no absolute right or wrong and no universal rules of conduct.

An example of ethical relativism is *utilitarianism*. According to this concept, an action is right, compared to other actions, if the result is the greater good for the greatest number of people.

> **Example:** Here is a scenario commonly used to stimulate discussion in ethics

> workshops: five people are on a life raft,
> and there is only enough food and water
> for four. If the group kills one person, the
> rest will live; otherwise, everyone will die.
> The question is: Would it be ethical to kill
> someone in this situation?

You can take this even further. What if it is a family of
five? Most people would rather face death than live the
rest of their lives knowing they had killed a family
member so that they could live. But what if none of the
people on the boat knew each other? What if one of them
was as escaped child molester, who was already injured,
and would probably die in a few days anyway?

Many public-sector decisions are based on this approach,
such as fund allocations. Other decisions that can have a
negative effect on some people are also based on
utilitarianism, such as a decision to put a freeway through
a neighborhood, causing many families to be displaced.

Another area of management, the disciplinary process, is
based on the concept of utilitarianism. When a supervisor
or manager is considering discipline for an employee, a
guideline that is followed is, "The good of the
organization must supersede the good of the individual."
What this means is that although the discipline hurts the
employee, maintaining discipline benefits the
organization.

INTEGRITY

An ethical person has *integrity*. A person with integrity
consistently follows an ethical standard that does not
compromise his values, because his values are ethical

ones. If someone does the right thing only because they are afraid of being caught, that is not integrity.

PRINCIPLE VERSUS PREFERENCE

Organizations lose effectiveness when preference is chosen over principle when making decisions. Preference is the imposition of personal values over doing what is right. Often, this occurs because it is easier, safer, or because of personal benefit or satisfaction.

This conflict between principle (doing the right thing) and preference (doing what you want to do) happens a lot when employees have to follow orders. Line-level employees have often been faced with dilemmas involving individual morality versus obedience and loyalty. It is common for employees to succumb to this pressure because it is easier to just follow orders than to be personally accountable for actions.

> **Example:** During the Vietnam War, the My Lai incident involved soldiers killing innocent civilians because they were ordered to. During World War II, Nazi soldiers facing war crime charges said they were just following orders. In both instances, soldiers had to commit crimes disguised as orders or face a potential firing squad for insubordination during wartime.

So, we can either *excuse* the individual from personal moral decisions when they are following orders or we can *condemn* the behavior in support of *disobedience* of laws or orders that conflict with ethical principles.

These are difficult positions for employees. They raise difficult questions: Where does personal accountability begin? Is this accountability absolute, or is someone absolved if they are following orders?

> **Example:** A police sergeant is dealing with a belligerent subject outside of a bar. The sergeant orders an officer to arrest the subject for being intoxicated even though he is not.
>
> If the officer makes the arrest, he is committing an act completely contrary to the standards he has sworn to uphold. If he refuses, the sergeant will make his work life miserable, because if this sergeant is unethical enough to order an unlawful arrest, he is likely unethical enough to retaliate against this officer for his lack of loyalty.

These are the most difficult choices people must make in their careers, choosing personal values that conflict with colleagues or supervisors, which could lead to complete alienation from the work subculture. To add to this difficulty, organizations do not create an atmosphere that helps people to make the right choice.

ETHICAL PROBLEMS IN LAW ENFORCEMENT

No other occupation possesses greater control over personal destiny than law enforcement officers, because of the elements of *authority*, use of *physical force*, and *discretion* inherent in the job. Unethical behavior in the field of law enforcement is usually an abuse of one of those three elements:

- **Authority:** This refers to the authority that police officers have to detain and arrest people. Officers have the ability to control others due to their position. Even when officers obtain consent from people to talk to them (consensual encounters), most people are too intimidated by the uniform to refuse. An abuse of authority amounts to a violation of individual rights.
- **Physical force:** This refers to the use of physical control granted by law to affect arrests, prevent escape, and overcome resistance. Abuse of physical force takes the form of excessive use of force. This occurs when an officer uses more force than is reasonable for the level of resistance that he is encountering.
- **Discretionary power:** This refers to the ability to choose between two or more courses of action, with none of the alternatives potentially being wrong. This is the power that officers have when they decide when and how to enforce laws, how to handle disputes, and how much and what kind of force to use.

Discretion differs from standard decision making, because decision making generally is making a choice between almost right and probably wrong, whereas discretion is choosing between a right course of action and another right course of action. *Abuse of discretion occurs when an officer bases his behavior or actions on personal feelings or prejudice rather than doing what is right.*

There is a potential for abuse in such a volatile and dynamic occupation that requires critical and immediate decision making. Officers must remain calm in hostile and dangerous situations without succumbing to the temptation to abuse these elements of authority, force, and discretion. Because of this, the selection process for police officers is exhaustive because it is so important to hire people who will not abuse their position.

During the testing process, the oral interview will generally contain an "ethical dilemma" question, which will give the interview panel clues as to whether this candidate will uphold the ethics of the organization, or whether he will weaken under pressure or frustration.

CONCLUSION

None of us are perfect. Sometimes we will choose what we know is not right, because of immediate rewards, convenience, or lack of courage. That just makes us human. But, when we choose that course of action consistently, where it becomes a "pattern of behavior," we choose to be unethical.

CHAPTER 9

POLICE DISCRETION

Topics

- Discretion Defined
- How Discretion Varies
- Variables That Affect Discretion
- Reducing Discretion

INTRODUCTION

As explained in chapter 8, it is extremely important that police departments hire individuals as police officers who have a high ethical standard. The biggest reason for this quality is because of the *high degree of discretion* that police officers have in enforcing the law and exerting their authority.

If unethical people were hired to be police officers, the opportunities for corruption, illegal activity, and abuse of authority would be out of control. This is because police officers are out on their own, without much direct supervision because of the solitary nature of the work. This makes them true professionals—workers who subscribe to a written code of conduct, and are held accountable to it.

There is much controversy in the area of police discretion, which will be discussed in this chapter. Most professional occupations have discretionary characteristics, but very few have such enormous arbitrary control of the personal destiny of other people. It is this distinctive difference which separates law enforcement from other occupations.

DISCRETION DEFINED

Discretion is the ability to choose two or more courses of behavior. Note that this is not the ability to choose *between* two or more courses of action, which is simply decision making. Rather, discretion is when the effective limits of a police officer's power leaves him free to make a choice among a number of possible courses of action.

> **Example:** At virtually all incidents that the police respond to, officers can take a number of different courses of action, any of which would be acceptable. For instance, the police go to a loud party. They can warn the people to be quiet, they could disperse the party, or they could

> arrest the people for disturbing the peace. Any of these courses of action would be appropriate; and it is up to the individual judgment of the officer to decide what he is going to do.

When involved in a job that deals with human behavior (such as law enforcement), new and unique situations always come up that require the use of discretion. Although many situations that the police encounter are similar, no two situations are ever exactly the same. Each situation involves different people, at different times, at different locations, with different problems—well, you get the picture.

So, although discretion is inherent in all professions, it is absolutely essential in law enforcement, and it is the foundation of the entire criminal justice system. No one would advocate full enforcement of all laws. First of all, it could never be done—half the population would have to be police officers—one for each citizen. Second, do we really want the police to issue tickets to people for driving two miles over the speed limit?

We expect the police to use good judgment when they enforce the law, because it is not possible to make rules for every possible situation that might arise. The point here is that jobs that require discretion also require more dependence on the individual's ethics.

Patrol officers encounter more situations that result in ethical dilemmas than any other police assignment. Probably the most significant dilemma that officers face in exerting their discretion has to do with the decision to involve the criminal justice system in an incident.

Example: When a police officer makes a vehicle stop for a traffic violation, it is entirely up to the discretion of the officer whether he issues a citation or gives a warning. It is the same situation when he elects to arrest or not arrest a violator of the law. If an officer stops a drunk driver, there is no requirement that he arrest him. He can, of course, but the officer can also call a taxi for the driver, call a friend to pick him up, make him walk home, or even let him drive home.

Besides deciding what course of action to take in a variety of incidents, the police have another area of significant discretionary decision making. This is determining *what laws they will enforce and what laws they will ignore*, which extends to even which areas they will patrol in their assigned beats.

Example: An officer may not feel that speeding is a big deal, so he chooses not to enforce speeding laws. Or because he was a frat boy in college, he does not think that drunk driving is a serious violation, so he does not enforce those laws either.

Example: In a daily briefing session, the sergeant reads a patrol check request from an irate citizen demanding that officers patrol his street more often. The officers all laugh, because this citizen, without realizing what he has done, has effectively stopped all patrols on his street for years. No, it is not the right thing to do, but because police officers are still human beings, there is just so much they will take in the way of demands from people who have no clue about what their jobs really entail. And, because they have discretionary powers, human nature can sometimes supersede ethical responsibility, often resulting in juvenile responses to obnoxious and impertinent demands.

We hope that officers are fair and equitable (which they generally are, because the police take great pains in assuring this through the exhaustive testing process), but human nature is human nature (prolific, huh?). So, society must accept that as long as they hire human beings to do their dirty work for them, they have to buy into the whole deal; this means that from time to time these human beings are going to make their decisions and base their actions on the same imperfect and flawed reasoning as the rest of us do.

And, because society still uses human beings as police officers, these people bring into their jobs their unique personalities as well as their biases, experiences, and preferences. Only 1 percent of all police applicants ever become police officers, because only a small segment of the general population have the ethics, courage, intelligence, and disposition to do the job.

This 1 percent staves off their personal preferences in their discretionary decisions most of the time. But given the fact that they are still human, once in a while, when they have had a bad day and some idiot has pushed their buttons, the idiot will likely not get the same level of service or understanding as someone who has the intelligence to understand that you do not call a police officer an asshole when you want them to help you.

What most people do not realize is that the legal authority that officers have is not much more than that of a private citizen. About the only difference is that the police can arrest for suspicion of a felony, they can issue citations, and they can carry guns.

Other than that, much of what the police are empowered to do has more to do with accountability and responsibility rather than true power over others. They do not really have that much power over others; they just have a job that makes them exercise the power that everyone has.

> **Example:** Because of their jobs, the police are sent to locations in which they detain and arrest people. You are not going to get a call from the police station to go handle these things. If you did, you would be detaining and arresting as many people as police officers do.

Where the real power comes in is in their day-to-day discretionary decisions to enforce or not enforce a law. It is this indiscriminate discretion that is the true power that the police have over people's lives.

> **Example:** Would you rather be arrested by an officer who is predisposed against drunk drivers or one who is predisposed against college students? The end result is the same, but in the long run it is more

equitable if the officer's decisions are made for the right reasons.

HOW DISCRETION VARIES

The discretionary decisions that police officers make are affected by factors other than their personal ethics and beliefs. *The environment that these officers work in plays a large part in how they decide on a particular course of action.* Whether they realize it or not, their discretionary choices are partially controlled by their surroundings.

Discretion varies from officer to officer, from locale to locale, and from situation to situation.

Officer Variations

Police officers develop preferences through their experiences and their own lives. One officer may be strongly predisposed against drunk drivers, causing him to take a zero-tolerance approach, whereas another officer may think that drunk driving is no big deal, so he is not inclined to arrest drunk drivers.

Experiences in each of these officers' personal lives likely have caused these differences in the discretionary decisions that they make. The officer predisposed against drunk drivers may have had a friend or family member killed by a drunk driver. The officer who is more tolerant of drunk drivers may have had a history of drunk driving himself when he was younger, such as when he was a frat boy in college.

Besides their discretionary decisions being based on their personal experiences and beliefs, a police officer may target certain types of offenders because it is within his comfort zone or because it will help him to reach a goal.

> **Example:** A police officer may target drug users because he has developed a high level of expertise that makes it easy for him to spot them. This makes his job easier; because he makes a lot of drug-related arrests, his reputation improves and his experience base expands.

> **Example**: Another reason an officer may target drug users is that by arresting a large number of them he will get a reputation of being knowledgeable in drug enforcement, which will help him in getting assigned to the drug interdiction unit, which was a personal goal of his.

Locale Variation

Different cities have different problems, and the police officers in these different cities must deal with them differently, which affects how they make their discretionary decisions. A gang-infested city may need a more legalistic, authoritative, and strict style of policing than a quiet bedroom community that has very few serious crime problems.

> **Example:** A city with a serious gang problem will need their police officers to be less discretionary; that is, officers will need to take much more of a zero-tolerance approach to law enforcement to solve the crime problems. This means that

the officers will not give as many warnings in this type of working environment.

Example: A city that is primarily composed of upper-middle-class suburbs can afford to have its officers be more discretionary; that is, officers can be more oriented to a community policing approach, as well as be more forgiving for minor violations, as long as the serenity and harmony of the community remains intact.

The bottom line is that a doctor stopped for drunk driving in a bedroom community is more likely to be dealt with informally than a gang banger in a gang-infested neighborhood, not because of value systems or prejudice, but because some locations need more strict control and others do not.

Situational Variation

The situations that police officers find themselves in vary in the level of danger or threat that they perceive, and this affects their discretionary decisions. Some situations call for more moderation than others, depending on the ultimate goal of an incident or event.

Obviously, if a police officer is in a situation or area where he perceives a *high level of danger,* he will take on a much more law-and-order approach than if he were in a safe area. And, depending on the *goal of an incident or event,* the police may decide to be more tolerant of minor offenses, making their decisions much more discretionary.

> **Example:** If police officers at a Metallica concert were to take a zero-tolerance approach to all violations of the law, the entire audience would be in custody by the end of the night, which would bog down the courts and overfill the jails. The goal of the police presence at an event such as this would be to keep the peace and to be available for major incidents.

The enormous power that police officers have when making arrests can lead to unethical decisions. An unethical patrol officer may base his decisions on bribes or other personal interests, such as his biases and prejudices.

VARIABLES THAT AFFECT DISCRETION

A variety of factors have an effect on police officers' discretionary decisions. Some of these factors simply affect the course of action that an officer takes, whereas others actually affect the officer's decision of whether or not to make an arrest, which is the most significant discretionary decision that officers make, because it has such an enormous impact on the lives of the people involved.

Variables That Determine a Course of Action

The following variables determine the officer's course of action. In essence, these are the variables that affect an officer's discretionary process:

- **Officer's attitude:** This is where the human factor comes into the equation: police officers have personal problems just like everyone else. We hope they do not take them to work with them, but that is a little too hopeful. Besides that factor, we must consider other influential factors, such as the time an officer has on the job and how seriously he takes his job, which usually go hand in hand. For example, a newer officer is pretty "gung ho" and is out to save the world and make a name for himself. And, according to police culture, he does have to prove himself. He is less likely to warn a violator or let an offender go. With time, perhaps decades, he will loosen up a little and realize that he will never save the world and that individual situations require individual judgments, which will change the way he makes discretionary decisions.
- **Citizen's attitude:** If a traffic violator denies wrongdoing, how can an officer give the driver a warning? If a driver runs a red light, then refuses to accept responsibility for it, the officer will have little choice but to issue the driver a citation, because a warning would have absolutely no value if the driver is not accepting of the fact that he made a mistake.

Additionally, if the traffic violator or criminal offender is *nonreceptive* to any warning or admonishment that the officer may give, how can a police officer just walk away? If a traffic violator is rolling his eyes as an officer tells him that his driving was dangerous, the violator may as well get on his knees and beg for a ticket, because that is what he is going to get. An officer is not going to warn a violator who is not receptive to the warning.

- **Seriousness of the offense:** Minor offenses are easily overlooked, but a serious offense begs for attention—by both the police and the criminal justice system.

Variables That Affect a Choice to Arrest

Making arrests is one of the major ways that the police solve problems. It is also discretion at its highest level, because these decisions, which involve thrusting an individual into the criminal justice system, are among the most life-changing events in a person's life.

Offender Variables

Several offender-related variables factor into a police officer's decision-making process when he is deciding whether to arrest someone. These categories of variables, developed through scientific studies, provide insight into the thought process involved when making these difficult and life-altering decisions.

- **Race:** Studies show that blacks are treated more harshly than other races, but that the area that the incident is occurring in determines the amount of force that is used. If the officer is in a dangerous area, he is more likely to use more force to maintain control of a situation. This sends a message to the gangs and other offenders that the streets belong to the police; they have to talk tough and be tough, they are not trying to make friends in dangerous areas.

But, if the area that the police are in is not dangerous, the police are more likely to show more discretion by letting minor violations slide. This is because in some low-income or minority areas, a minor offense (such as drinking in public or playing loud music) is a lifestyle characteristic. To be hardcore about such offenses that the residents view as normal activity could result in an even more negative relationship between the police and the community, which could create a more dangerous environment for the officers.

- **Age:** Adults who complain to the police about a problem are usually taken more seriously than juveniles making the same complaints. Also, if a victim of a crime is older than the suspect, the officer is more likely to arrest the suspect. This is possibly because, in the eyes of the police, adults are more credible than juveniles. Additionally, the police probably think that an adult is more likely to expect that the police should take action than a juvenile is.
- **Demeanor:** When an offender defers to an officer, it usually results in the offender being treated more fairly. For instance, when an offender is

detained by a police officer, and the officer asks the offender to step out of his vehicle, the best thing for the offender to do is to comply (defer) and do what the officer asks. To argue or to accuse the officer of violating his rights will very likely result in the officer using his discretionary power, which will result in the harshest of the available options toward the offender.

Note that antagonistic complaints are not taken as seriously by the police. If the police respond to a call, and the informant is ranting and raving at the officer as though all this is his fault, the officer is not likely to be sympathetic with this person. Demanding, overbearing people think that this sort of behavior will get them what they want, but most of the time, especially when dealing with the police, who have discretionary power, it will backfire on them.

When the police respond to a call, they view themselves as being in charge of the situation. If the informant tries to take that position, it will create a conflict that will likely not result in what the informant thought was going to happen. When the police are on scene, they are in charge; offenders and informants alike should defer to the officer. This will prevent conflict and a less than suitable outcome for the others involved.

Additionally, when irate citizens call the police for service, the officer or dispatcher on the telephone is not going to be sympathetic or eager to help. And, when a citizen comes in to complain to a supervisor about an officer, if the citizen is antagonistic and angry, the supervisor is going to write it off as just another angry person who wants to get his pound of flesh as revenge against getting a ticket or being arrested.

Lastly, and this should go without saying, *antagonistic suspects are more likely to be arrested than suspects who defer and are cooperative.* Let's face it, human nature is always going to be human nature, and while human beings are still being hired as cops, they will subtly respond as such. If a suspect acts like an asshole, he will be treated like one, each and every time, guaranteed. Police officers have as much compassion and empathy for people as anyone else, probably much, much more than others realize. But they are not going to take crap from some drunken idiot who is screaming at them and making demands.

- **Socio-economic status:** According to studies, middle- and upper-class individuals get more attention from the police and are less likely to be arrested. This information probably does not come as a shock to most people; on the contrary, a statement this obvious is rather humorous. But we can only guess as to the reasons.

One reason is possibly the *lack of value conflict.* As explained in the previous chapter, the police generally have conservative, middle-class values. When dealing with people with similar values, there is less of a chance that there will be conflict. The result of which could be a discretionary decision that would be favorable to the offender.

Another possible reason that this class of people gets more attention is that *they have contacts and political pull.* And because upper-class people are used to getting their way, when they do not, they are more likely to call and complain—directly to the chief of police, who is their golf buddy. Cops do not like problems with supervision, and if it means letting some snobby doctor slide on a ticket, it is well worth it to avoid a major headache.

Situational Variables

- **Seriousness of the offense:** The seriousness of the offense is the single most important factor that helps an officer decide if he is going to arrest someone. A police officer can more easily justify ignoring a minor offense and will be more compelled to take action when a major offense has occurred.

- **Prior record:** If the offender has a prior arrest record, and especially if he is on probation or parole, the officer is more likely to make an arrest. The mindset behind this is that if the suspect did it before, he probably did it this time also. (For every time that a person is arrested, it is estimated that he committed the same or similar offense 100 times.) So, if a suspect has a lengthy arrest record, then, in the mind of the officer, the suspect has committed hundreds of crimes, and very likely, committed this one.

Even if he did not, it will make up for one of the crimes that he committed and did not get caught for. If civil rights-oriented folks read this, it will likely make their heads explode. I'm not saying this is right; I'm just giving some insight into how people think and rationalize their decisions, and remember, cops are still human beings.

- **Weapon involved:** When a weapon is involved in a crime, the officer is much more likely to make an arrest. This goes along with the seriousness of the offense. If a weapon is involved, it is generally a serious offense, and begs police action.
- **Officer-initiated activity:** When a police officer initiates a contact with someone, often he has already decided to take action, or at the very least he has seen something worthy of his attention. What the officer has seen is a probable violation of law. And, because he has

witnessed something or has uncovered a crime, he will feel more compelled to make an arrest if one is appropriate.

Also, *many of the calls for service that the police respond to are not crimes,* they are marginally criminal activity at best, public service requests, or disturbing or suspicious activity that just needs to be quickly resolved. So, most of the time, the police are not going to scenes that an arrest would ever be considered. However, when they see criminal activity in front of them, this is the stuff they have been looking for all day, and they are not likely to just let it slide.

System Variables

- **Department size:** Large police departments generally have a higher ratio of officers to supervisors, so there is more autonomy, and officers therefore have more latitude to make their own decisions. Conversely, in a small department, which many have just three officers and a supervisor in the field, the supervisor will likely show up at many calls and contacts that the officers are involved in. Some supervisors tend to take over the calls and make the decisions. Others tend to exert their opinions as to what they think the outcome should be, causing the officer to defer to the supervisor's authority.
- **Alternative resources:** If nonpolice resources are available and sufficient, such as detox centers

and mental health facilities, officers are more likely to intervene without making an arrest.

Example: If an officer encounters a drunk who is passed out on a sidewalk, he usually has no choice but to arrest him and take him to jail to sleep it off. But if a detox center is available, the officer can take the drunk to that location and drop him off without making an arrest.

Example: If an officer gets a call of a crazy person in the middle of the street, he cannot just warn the person to stop. The activity will likely continue, and the officer is going have to take some action to stop the activity. He could arrest the person for disturbing the peace, but if there is a mental health center available the officer can drop the individual off, and avoid making an arrest.

- **Peer pressure:** The pressure that fellow officers place on each other regarding the level of activity that they produce can have quite an effect on the actions that an officer chooses to take. For instance, if an officer is making a lot of arrests, it may make his peers look bad, so the other officers pressure him to slow it down. Or, an officer is not carrying his fair share of the workload, and officers pressure him to step it up a little.

Many offenders have been arrested only because the officer felt pressure to make more arrests. Conversely, many offenders have been released because the officer felt pressure to reduce his activity. This concept is called *soldiering*, which was identified in the early years of motivational theories. This concept addresses the fact that *employees will maintain a certain level of activity so as to blend in with the activity of their peers*. Their concern for acceptance into the group is more important than recognition or monetary incentives.

REDUCING DISCRETION

Some critics of law enforcement are not in favor of the level of discretion that police officers have. Critics have made efforts to reduce police discretion by requiring that the police provide guidelines to improve consistency. The problem is, no matter how many guidelines are provided, discretion will always be present in law enforcement.

Police officers work alone, and most instances of discretion cannot be controlled by rules or supervision. Unless there is a supervisor riding with each officer on every shift, it will still be up to the individual officer to make discretionary decisions.

Those arguing for control of discretion say that arbitrary enforcement leads to discrimination. This could certainly be true, and over the years, this has undoubtedly happened, even with the rigorous controls that police agencies use to hire only ethical individuals who make the right decisions for the right reasons.

Those against discretionary control argue that decision making is an important function of the police and it is not practical to eliminate discretion. This is certainly true; no situation that a police officer deals with is identical to the last, so having rules or policies to cover every possible situation is unreasonable and unrealistic.

So, the question becomes, *how much structure and control should be placed on police discretion?* The police are subject to *internal controls*, such as the many policies, procedures, rules, and regulations that they must follow in everything they do. They are also subject to *external controls*, such as police review boards, legal mandates, community policing programs, and case law, such as the exclusionary rule, injunctions, and lawsuits.

But, even with all of these controls, *it all still rests on the individual police officer's willingness to comply*. These officers in the field will always be the ultimate policy makers. The best that the criminal justice system can hope for is that police agencies continue to hire highly ethical individuals, and also take great pains in creating a work environment that perpetuates ethical decisions.

A good example of an external control that has been put in place to reduce police officer discretion is in the area of domestic violence laws. Over many years, the laws related to domestic violence have changed in such a way that places additional responsibilities on and requirements for police officers investigating these cases.

Historically, police officers were reluctant to take action in these types of cases; they felt it was a private family matter, they were dealing with reluctant victims, and there was potential harm to the family if the breadwinner was in jail. The problem with this, however, was that a cycle of abuse would continue without the involvement of the criminal justice system.

To reduce this cycle of violence, laws were changed so that the police were required to make an arrest if there was sufficient evidence (often just the victim's statement) that a crime had occurred. In the past, the police could not make a domestic violence arrest because the crime was a misdemeanor not committed in their presence, and they had to rely on the victim to make a private person's arrest. But with the changes in the law, the police are now allowed to make the arrest, and in fact, are required to.

Pros and Cons of Police Discretion

- **Pro:** All violations of law cannot be enforced. Therefore, police officers must choose to enforce some violations and ignore others. They are expected to do this. Fairness, common sense, and an unbiased mind are important traits for all police officers to possess to ensure that discretion is being exercised properly.
- **Con:** Arbitrary discretion between individual police officers reduces consistency.

  Example: Two individuals are drinking at a bar. Both have the same level of alcohol in their systems when they leave. Subject A is stopped by a police officer who observes driving consistent with being under the influence. Subject B is stopped by a different officer at a different location for the identical driving. The facts of each case are identical, the only difference is the officer making the stop. Subject A is arrested for drunk driving, and Subject B is sent home in a taxi.

Is it fair that one person gets away with what another is arrested for? No, it is not. But, because of the individual discretion that officers have in conducting their duties, there is nothing to control this from happening. What critics of police discretion wants is some *meaningful distinction* when there are differences in these decisions, rather than arbitrary enforcement that leads to inconsistency and a lack of fairness.

Discretionary authority is a breeding ground for corruption, where police officers potentially could be paid to exercise their discretion. This was a serious problem in the early years of law enforcement, but society can be assured that the vast majority of today's police officers would never even consider such behavior.

Thirty or forty years ago, in some areas of the country, it was not uncommon for a traffic violator to attach a twenty-dollar bill to his license, in hopes of paying his way out of a citation. If someone were to attempt this today, the violator, at the very least would be severely chastised by the officer, and could possibly face arrest for attempted bribery.

It all comes down to the quality of officers that police departments hire and the ability of the organization to maintain an ethical work environment.

CHAPTER 10

RECRUITMENT, SELECTION, AND PROMOTION

Topics

- Social Environment
- Problems with Public-Sector Recruiting
- Legal Considerations
- Promotional Testing
- Traditional Test Methods
- Modern Test Methods
- Recruitment Issues

SOCIAL ENVIRONMENT

The biggest budget expense of any public organization is employee salaries, which are 80 to 90 percent of an organization's budget. So, if for no other reason than the cost, the methods used to find qualified personnel should be scrutinized.

The most important factor that must be realized about recruiting police officers in this decade is that *the target population comes from a different social environment*. The target population is young men and women of good moral and ethical character, free of mental handicaps. In some occupations, such as law enforcement, the target population must also be free of physical handicaps. The term *target population* refers to the highly desirable candidates; it should not be assumed that it is easy to get a good job in the current economy.

Several characteristics of the target population separate them from the previous workforce generation:

- The target population is generally *better educated* than those recruited in the preceding generation. Many police officers went straight from high school to work. Vietnam War veterans went straight from military service to law enforcement. Consequently, these police officers had to proactively pursue higher education, which can be easy to defer as one is focusing on a new career.

  The complexity of modern public-sector jobs, such as those in law enforcement, demand higher education levels than the jobs of the previous workforce generation.

Those workers entering the workforce now, who believe they can excel without higher education, will be left behind by their counterparts who are entering their careers with college degrees.

- The target population *grew up in a peaceful era* and, consequently, few have military experience. *This creates a whole new attitude toward discipline and autocratic management styles.* The emerging new workforce is more likely to question authority, not out of disrespect, but because of their modern culture.
- The affluence of the 1980s led the target population to place more *emphasis on salary and benefits* than on career satisfaction.
- The *demographics* are also different; fewer people are entering the workforce due to a decline in the birth rate. The previous generation of workers, the "baby boomers," had to face stiff competition because there were so many other people applying for the same job. As a result, the target population can afford to be picky about where they work, rather than feeling lucky that they got an offer at all.

What This Means for the Recruiting Process

Management must do its best to ensure that the salary and benefits offered by the organization to its employees are competitive with those offered by other organizations. This must be a priority for those agencies wishing to seek the most qualified candidates. Failure to do so can very well result in the organization turning into what is called a training ground for a particular career field, in which only mediocre personnel stay with the organization.

> **Example:** The lowest-paid police department in the county is looking for officers. Thirty years ago when there were too many candidates for too few jobs, the department could still have its pick of many quality candidates, but in today's candidate-friendly job market the best that this agency will do is to pick over a handful of mediocre candidates who were not viable candidates for more desirable departments.

What ends up happening is that this department has an agency full of marginal and mediocre new officers, whom they send to the police academy, struggle with afterwards with a variety of training difficulties, and eventually manage to hang on to a few of them, and then firing the rest because they just could not do the job, no matter how hard the department tried to train them.

Over a period of time, as these remaining officers learn the job and gain experience, they get better at their job, and are actually considered competent, thanks to the effort and expense exerted by supervision and management. Now that these officers are more marketable, they start looking around for a better-paying job at other departments. And now that they are trained and experienced, other agencies are interested in them, and these officers leave for the higher-paying departments.

So where does this leave the low-paying department? It leaves them looking for more marginal and mediocre candidates that they can hire and train, just to give them experience so that they can also leave for a higher-paying department. It becomes a vicious cycle in which this agency, which is "saving money" by offering lower salaries, is spending even more on training costs, only to get the "bottom of the barrel" candidates and then lose them to other departments once the agency has trained them and given them experience.

Besides offering competitive salaries and benefits, organizations must also offer *alternative scheduling programs* because the target population has a priority interest in free time and recreation.

> **Example:** Condensed work schedules that allow for more days off have become very popular. Employees would rather work ten hours days for four days a week than eight hours days for five days. And when shift work is involved, such as in law enforcement, employees can work three days a week, twelve hours a day, giving them four days off every week. This is extremely desirable to the emerging workforce.

Good retirement packages also are important considerations for recruitment. Retirement packages have been highly publicized lately, and public employee retirement options are considered to be the envy of the private sector. Safety retirements (police and fire) are even better, because they provide for early retirement (age 50) at up to 90 percent of their salaries, not including specialty and incentive allowances. Most quality candidates will not consider applying at an agency that does not offer these premium retirement packages.

Management must also accept the fact that the *autocratic management style* that worked well with the baby boomer generation of workers *will not work well with the emerging workforce* that questions authority and consequently will not adapt well to an authoritative leadership style.

PROBLEMS WITH PUBLIC-SECTOR RECRUITING

Public Perception of Government Jobs

The media portray a negative image regarding government jobs. They are stereotyped in movies and television as not being challenging or intellectually stimulating. (The exception of course, is the glamour and excitement of law enforcement.)

A survey showed that 90 percent of college students did not seriously consider working for the government. But apparently, this survey did not break down the percentages by college major. Obviously, business majors are not considering government work, whereas public administration majors are.

The Salary Factor

The three primary inducements for potential employees, no matter what kind of job they want or what type of organization they want to work for, are:

• Job security
• Opportunities for promotion
• Salary and benefits

The private sector offers better salaries than the public sector, but the public sector is catching up, especially in line-level positions. Candidates looking at public-sector jobs certainly are not looking to get rich; if someone aspires to be wealthy, they must go into the private sector. But when you compare salaries, a police sergeant makes more than a retail store manager or a new lawyer working 70 hours a week at a law firm.

The most that public-sector jobs have to offer is job security, which is not quite as secure as it used to be, based on diminishing economic conditions. It was once unheard of to lay off public employees, whereas now it is just uncommon. This is still leaps and bounds ahead of the private sector.

According civil service guidelines, *public employees have a "substantial property right" to their jobs,* which creates more security than in the private sector, where employees can be arbitrarily terminated.

> **Example:** A public employee cannot be fired because he is doing a mediocre job. If he is incompetent, supervision must build a case, carefully documenting performance problems, attempts at retraining, and disciplinary issues. After years, the agency would then have sufficient cause to terminate the employee, who would then have the option of arbitration to get his job back. In

the private sector, if an employee "just isn't working out" the employee is terminated, with no recourse.

LEGAL CONSIDERATIONS

Four specific legal actions have dramatically impacted recruitment, selection, and promotional procedures in the public sector.

Title VII of the Civil Rights Act of 1964

Title VII prohibits employment discrimination of people based on race, color, religion, sex, or national origin. The Civil Rights Act evolved to encourage minorities to apply for jobs and to ensure that selection methods are free of bias.

Equal Employment Opportunities Act of 1972

The Civil Rights Act applied only to the private sector (apparently the government did not need fixing). When the 1972 act was passed, it *extended the provisions of the Civil Rights Act to cover public employees.*

Griggs vs. Duke Power Plant

This Supreme Court decision stemmed from a case that dramatically affected selection and promotion procedures. In 1964, Duke Power Plant had 14 black employees, all of whom worked in the labor department, which was the lowest paid of the five departments. In 1965, *the company required a high school education for all departments except labor, which prevented any of the black employees from transferring out of the labor department.*

The company then added a requirement of two aptitude tests for positions outside of the labor department. These tests measured intelligence and comprehension; they were not designed to test for any work-related skills, and were actually more restrictive than the high school education requirement, because only half of high school graduates could pass the aptitude tests.

In 1966, 13 of the black employees filed suit after failing the aptitude tests and being denied promotions. (The remaining black employee had been promoted in 1965.) The 13 employees alleged that *the tests were intended to discriminate against them*, in violation of Title VII of the Civil Rights Act of 1964. (The Civil Rights Act did not prohibit aptitude tests, provided there was no intent to discriminate.)

The case went to the Supreme Court, which ruled that *testing procedures for selection and promotion had to be related to job performance*. Although the aptitude tests and a high school education were considered useful, they were not shown to be a measure of the person for the job.

Uniform Guidelines on Employee Selection Procedures of 1978

The following are the central set of rules for selection procedures that apply to the following public and private sectors:

- All federal agencies and public agencies that have 15 or more employees or receive federal assistance.
- All private-sector employers with 15 or more employees working 20 weeks a year or work with any government contract.
- All "employee decisions" are covered, such as applications, hiring, performance tests, written and oral tests, and evaluations. This is for promotions, separations, performance review and training, as well as the recruitment and selection process.

These legal guidelines require that testing procedures for selection and promotion be valid and reliable:

- **Reliable:** A test is reliable when the test results are consistent. For instance, a written test is reliable because the process of determining the scores does not vary. Scores may vary in tests such as interviews because of their subjective nature or because they are not properly structured.

  Example: A multiple choice test will have more consistent results than an essay test. This is because anyone can grade a multiple choice tests and have the same outcome. But when an essay test is graded, the opinion of the grader comes into play, and his opinion will vary from that of another grader. Consequently, the outcome of an essay test will not be as *reliably consistent* as with a multiple choice test.

- **Valid:** Validity is a measure of the job-related character of a test (as required by *Griggs vs. Duke Power*). For instance, taking a typing test for a job that requires typing would be a valid test.

After these guidelines were established, many agencies had legal problems because they were not conforming to the new testing requirements required by law. For instance, many police departments had physical agility tests that measured strength and stamina, but were not directly related to the job requirements. (Pushups and sit ups had to be replaced with obstacle courses and body drags.)

PROMOTIONAL TESTING

The goal of *promotional testing* is to predict future performance of the candidates so that the most-qualified candidate is selected to maintain the efficiency and effectiveness of the organization. The test methods that are being used consist of both *subjective* and *objective* methods:

- **Subjective:** A test method that is subjective in nature is based on personal judgments and personal opinions. Some test instruments traditionally have reputations for being subjective because of the difficulty in analyzing their performance objectively. Among these are performance evaluations, essay examinations, and oral interviews. The problem with a subjective testing process is that the test results are not very reliable.

Example: Many test instruments are designed to measure intangible qualities that cannot be measured in a more objective fashion. The instruments call upon the grader to give his personal opinion, based on his knowledge, expertise, and experience. But because individuals have different backgrounds, obviously the results will vary from one grader to another.

• **Objective:** A test method that is objective is free from the individual judgments that are very much a part of subjective test instruments. An objective test method is not distorted by personal experience or perceptions. Written tests (question/answer examinations) are usually considered the most objective test instrument because the test results are not affected by individual judgments. So this test method is considered to be extremely reliable in terms of consistency of results.

TRADITIONAL TEST METHODS

Three basic traditional test instruments are used, alone or in combination.

Written Examinations

This is the traditional *question/answer examination* described above. This type of examination usually consists of multiple choice, true/false, or fill-in-the-blank questions. This type of examination is almost always used in promotional procedures, especially at the supervisory level, in which it is important to measure the candidates' technical knowledge.

The following are the advantages of this test instrument:

- **The examinations are easy to administer and easy to grade.** Anyone can hand out the examinations, and anyone can grade them, with identical results. It is not time-consuming to grade such exams, and often the tests can be graded electronically.
- **The results of the examinations are obtained objectively.** And because personal opinions and perceptions are not involved, the results are consistent, making the process reliable.
- **The process is easily defended in court if a candidate sues on the basis that it was not a valid or reliable test instrument.** The process is easily defended as reliable, and can be easily defended as valid, as long as the test measures knowledge that is needed to perform well in the position being sought.

The following are the disadvantages of this test instrument:

- **The process is effective in measuring job knowledge, but not the application of knowledge to situations.** For this reason, a written examination should only be part of a comprehensive examination process that would examine for job knowledge in the written test and the application of knowledge through a different test instrument.

- **It is difficult for a written examination to predict future performance.** Note that this is the fundamental goal of promotional testing. A high score on a written test can certainly be an indicator of future success, because job knowledge is valuable, but other test instruments would also be needed to accurately measure the potential for successful future performance. The use of written examinations is useful for determining job knowledge for entry-level positions, but promotional examinations also need to have what is called *criterion-based validity*, which means the test instrument is designed to predict future performance.

Oral Interviews

The *oral interview* consists of a panel of evaluators who question the candidate regarding his qualifications and job knowledge. The panel also evaluates the candidate's *interpersonal skills and other intangible personal qualities*. This is a popular test instrument used for promotional processes, because, in combination with a written test, it can measure the application of job knowledge.

This testing process often is *criticized for its subjective nature*. The scores are based on the perceptions and opinions of the evaluators, which can be influenced by uncontrollable factors such as stereotyping, prejudice, and early bias.

> **Example:** Scores of books are available to prepare candidates for the subjective variables in the interview process, which include proper clothing and grooming and other factors that could affect the evaluators' opinions. Experts say that the most important time period in an oral interview is the *first seven seconds*, in which the evaluators size up a candidate before the first question is even asked.

A promising way to reduce the degree of subjectivity is to use an *outside oral board*, in which the panel members are from an agency other than that of the candidate. This prevents personal judgments toward individual candidates based on prior contacts or knowledge.

> **Example:** If a candidate for police sergeant in a medium-sized agency were to face a panel of lieutenants from his own agency, they would all know each other fairly well. The panel would come into the process with preconceived opinions about each candidate, and it would be doubtful that the process would fairly evaluate each candidate on the performance demonstrated in the interview. Rather, it would be based on past performance within the organization, thus turning the process into a performance evaluation rather than an oral interview.

The interviews must also be structured so that each candidate is asked the same series of questions to ensure that all the candidates are evaluated on the same material.

Otherwise it would be like a written examination that asked each candidate different questions. All candidates need to be taking the same test to ensure a level playing field.

> **Example:** After a candidate answers an interview question, an evaluator asks for more details, which takes the interview off on a tangent. This is fine, as long as the course makes its way back to the original list of questions that is asked of all the other candidates. Without this structure, the reliability of the process is in jeopardy because everyone is being tested on different material.

Performance Appraisals

A *performance appraisal* is a process in which the organization evaluates the abilities of a candidate based on past performance. Performance appraisals are designed to evaluate the intangible personal qualities necessary for supervisory and management positions.

In this regard, the process is valid. The problem is with the reliability factor. Remember, any test instrument must be valid *and* reliable. A test is reliable if the test results are consistent. But in this testing process, because of individual perceptions, it cannot be expected that one set of evaluators would produce a score on a candidate that would be the same as produced by a different group of evaluators. Without this necessary consistency, there is a lack of reliability. Thus, strict guidelines must be in place regarding the use of performance appraisals for it to be a valid and reliable process:

- **Ratings must be based on observed behavior and performance, not on general opinions or impressions.** Supervisors and managers may think they know an employee, but unless they actually observe the employee at work, they are only guessing, which is not a fair method of evaluating an individual for promotional consideration.
- **Only those managers and supervisors who have worked closely with the candidate recently should be evaluators.** This time period ranges from two to five years, depending on the agency's preferences. The continuum of the range depends much on the type of work environment involved, which determines how much experience affects performance.

Example: A police sergeant has a rookie officer working for him. Five years later, this "rookie" has worked patrol, traffic, and is currently a detective working robbery and homicide cases. If this sergeant is permitted (or required) to complete a performance appraisal on this officer who is testing for promotion, this sergeant's perception will be based on the candidate's performance as a rookie police officer, not as an experienced homicide detective. In an occupation such as law enforcement, where work experience greatly improves job performance, a shorter time period requirement would make the process much more accurate, and certainly more reliable.

MODERN TEST METHODS

The more a process attempts to evaluate intangible yet essential traits needed for management, the more difficult it becomes to maintain objectivity, due to the personal judgments required of the evaluators. The major effort in modern promotional processes is to evaluate these important traits even more effectively than is possible with traditional methods and to *maintain a more objective process*. Two modern promotional processes that have been designed to evaluate important intangible qualities, while maintaining a valid and reliable process, include assessment centers and essays.

Assessment Centers

An *assessment center* is not a location, as the name implies, but rather a variety of testing techniques designed to allow candidates to demonstrate, under standardized conditions, the skills and abilities needed for the job. The assessment center (assessment process would be a better title) is designed to predict future performance through simulation exercises in a controlled setting.

The performance-related exercises resemble actual work activity. Two such exercises are the leaderless group exercise and the in-basket exercise:

- **Leaderless group exercise:** A group of candidates work together to resolve mock personnel and organizational problems and issues. As the group interacts, the assessors examine the dynamics to identify the informal leader, the candidate who tries to take over, and the candidate who does not contribute, and so on.

- **In-basket exercise:** Candidates are given a scenario in which they are promoted into the position but must leave in two hours for a two-week training course. They first must handle all of the correspondence on their desk. This exercise examines the candidate's time management, prioritization, and delegation skills, among others.

Many other exercises are also possible, such as a mock press conference, a traditional oral interview, a mock city council presentation, and a biographical presentation.

As with any process, there are advantages and disadvantages to the assessment center process:

Advantages

- **Studies show that the process is valid and reliable.** It is valid because the process measures actual performance; it is reliable because the assessors who evaluate the performance of the candidates are trained so as to base their evaluations on specific criteria. (Evaluators on oral interviews have no training or instruction on how to rate the candidates, making it extremely subjective.)
- **Most candidates involved in the assessment center process view it as being fair.** Unlike an oral interview, in which a candidate must sell himself to three strangers in 20 minutes, the assessment center process runs the candidate through a series of simulated work activities in a period of one to three days.

• **The assessment center process is a good training tool, even for those who are not promoted.** It gives the candidates vast amounts of information as to their strengths and weaknesses, giving them valuable insight on how to improve for next time.

Disadvantages

• **The assessment center process is expensive to operate.** The process requires the salaries of the candidates, the assessors, and the facilitator. There is also the cost of the facility that is used, as well as the costs of meals and lodging if the process is more than one day.
• **Candidates prefer to be judged on actual performance rather than simulations.** Simulations (or mock exercises) are no more than acting. Some people are better actors than others, and some people just do not act in a simulation as they would in reality.
• **Candidates who fail an assessment center risk a negative stigma at work.**

Example: A candidate who has taken promotional examinations in the past has always failed. He has a good reputation for the job he does, and his peers and supervisors say, "he just isn't a good test taker, but he would be a great supervisor." But if this candidate participates in an assessment center in which he is tested on his performance of simulated work activities, and fails here also, the perception of his peers and supervisors may change, and they may accept the fact that perhaps this candidate just does not have the skills for the position he is seeking.

Essay Examinations

This test instrument is a replacement for the standard written examination. This technique is used for evaluating analytical and writing skills rather than technical skills. The standard written test is fine for measuring technical skills, but for management positions the essay examination is a much more valid process.

This test is valid if it effectively analyzes the skills needed for the position. Virtually all management positions in public-sector organizations require analytical and writing skills. An essay examination designed to measure for this skill will be valid.

This test is reliable if the scoring procedure is designed to ensure consistent results. The essay examination requires that the grader use his personal opinions and perceptions in the grading process. Because of this, the process is inherently subjective, which can lead to unreliability if the process is improperly structured.

To ensure reliability and consistency, each essay must be graded by more than one evaluator. Any inconsistency in score would require evaluation by an additional evaluator. Or, in some processes, the scores of three evaluators are averaged.

RECRUITMENT ISSUES

The selection of candidates for such an important occupation is much more involved and complex than most people realize. The physical, mental, and emotional personal challenges that these individuals must be able to endure is far beyond what the average person can appreciate or understand. Police administrators have the daunting task of selecting personnel who will be an asset to the organization, a champion to the community, and a steadfast comrade to his fellow police officers. Administrators cannot take this task lightly—the very lives of these candidates, their fellow officers, and the citizens they will protect rely on their ability to recruit, select, and train only the very best.

This section will address two specific current issues regarding the recruitment process, an area of great contemporary concern for police administrators. These areas have to do with the importance of diversity within the ranks of the police and the focus on modern skills necessary for police officers to be successful in the twenty-first century.

Diversity in Law Enforcement

Until recent times, law enforcement was a career predominantly filled by white males. Up through the 1960s, racial discrimination prevented most minority groups from joining the police ranks. And to many minority members, the police were the enemy, which they did not want to be associated with, much less work with.

By the 1970s, many returning Vietnam veterans went to work for police and sheriff departments. It was a natural transition from military service, and the two types of organizations were similar in many respects. Primarily, both have very rigid command structures and autocratic leadership styles.

Also, both have specialized positions, and many policies, procedures, rules, and regulations that many people, who are not conditioned to so much control in a work environment, would find undesirable. Former military personnel are accustomed to this type of environment. And actually, law enforcement is lax in comparison to the discipline of military life.

So, by the 1970s, as these veterans returned home, and racial discrimination and segregation was becoming a thing of the past in most parts of the country, minorities began to slowly make their way into law enforcement.

At about the same time, more women were being hired as police officers. Prior to then, women in law enforcement were primarily restricted to clerical and matron duties and investigation of juveniles and sex crimes.

The first women who broke the barrier into the patrol ranks had to deal with a lack of acceptance from some of their male counterparts and from some segments of society. Today, however, most police departments actively recruit women. Studies show that female officers are involved in fewer use-of-force incidents per capita than male officers, which may be a result of better verbal skills and less of a macho attitude regarding problem resolution.

> **Personal observation:** Because most female officers are not as large in stature or as physically strong as male officers, they have found it to their advantage to use tact and diplomacy to accomplish their jobs, rather than relying on force and intimidation. Concomitantly, this approach by female officers can also serve to improve relationships between the police department and its citizens.

The recommended standard for diversity within the ranks of law enforcement is that the composition of the police department should reflect the composition of the community it serves.

> **Example:** If a police department has a 5 percent minority population, but the city has a 20 percent minority population, then the department is considered to be underrepresenting the minority population. The department would be expected to actively recruit minority applicants to balance the composition of the department to match the composition of the community.

Diversity in law enforcement, when it comes to gender, involves other issues. Forty percent of the U.S. workforce is female. A police department with a high number of female officers may reach 20 percent, but such representation is rare. Part of the problem is that law enforcement is just not an appealing occupation to many women. It is male dominated, and the work environment is aggressive and authoritarian. Additionally, the physical agility tests usually require significant upper-body strength, which many (otherwise qualified) women do not have. (It is generally assumed that this strength is important to be an effective police officer, but there is no evidence that supports this notion.)

The U.S. Supreme Court has held that diversity in the workforce is a "compelling state interest," which basically means that organizations should take the diverse composition of the employee populations seriously and take overt steps to reach an ethnic composition that reflects that of the community.

Law enforcement agencies must ensure that discrimination, which is a violation of federal law, is not occurring. But diversity is not just an issue of legality. Some experts maintain that minority officers can better serve minority areas. In addition, community relations can be improved when the workforce reflects the community makeup.

Desirable Qualities of Candidates in a New Era

Law enforcement is not the same job that it was in decades past. With complex social problems, the complexity of law enforcement has increased also. As "agencies of last resort," the role of the police in modern society has developed into a wide range of responsibilities far beyond what they have faced in the past. Because of this, ideal police candidates will possess more skills and knowledge than their predecessors. Failure of police departments to seek out these ideal candidates will place their agencies in jeopardy of mediocrity. The following are just a few areas that modern police candidates will be evaluated on.

Computer Literacy

Because of constantly evolving technology, police officers must be proficient in computer use. Information is critical for solving crimes, and the computer is the optimal way to obtain this information. Also, with the use of computers in police cars and on detectives' desks, those who lack the knowledge to use this technology to its limits will not be as effective as those who do.

Higher Education

Many police administration experts have been proponents of higher education in law enforcement for decades. Those in favor of higher education requirements for employment argue that because of the complexity of the job, officers need a great deal of knowledge that cannot be obtained in the police academy or through experience.

Additionally, a college education provides more than just knowledge. Graduates tend to be more mature, well-rounded, and more accepting of opposing viewpoints. They become critical and analytical thinkers, which is very valuable for community policing and problem-solving activities.

There are administrators, however, who are not entirely supportive of higher education requirements for entry-level positions. It is not that they fail to see its value, but rather they see this requirement as a barrier to recruitment efforts.

Much of the candidate pool comes from the standard working-class workforce, which does not have an immensely high percentage of college graduates. Consequently, a requirement such as this will limit the pool of viable police candidates.

Additionally, many police administrators fear that such a requirement would not withstand the scrutiny of the courts in regards to the validity requirement (i.e., requirements for the position must be directly related to job performance).

Bilingual Skills

It is estimated that by the year 2050 minorities will outnumber whites in California. With the continuing influx of immigrants from other countries, there will be a greater demand for police officers who are able to effectively communicate with this emerging segment of the community.

Police departments often have to rely on translation services to communicate with non-English-speaking residents. But in critical situations, when time is paramount, such a delay could result in disastrous consequences. Therefore, until there are residency requirements calling for English-language proficiency, the police must take proactive steps to recruit or train police officers who have bilingual skills.

CHAPTER 11

POLICE CULTURE

Topics

- It's a Cop Thing ...
- Use of Forces
- Ugly Side of Life
- Occupational Socialization
- A Dangerous Job
- Three Core Elements of Police Culture

INTRODUCTION

Work subculture can be very dynamic and interesting, or it can be very subtle and less than stimulating. It all depends on the *type of work* involved, the *types of individuals* the work activities attract into the occupation, and a combination of *social and psychological factors* that make the culture a unique and interesting one or one that barely acknowledges its own existence.

When experts want to examine the dynamics of workplace culture, they usually find themselves examining police culture. This is because, according to social scientists, police subculture is probably the most dynamic subculture in the country. The only other workplace subculture that even comes close is the military. But even with the military, the culture may be strong in the beginning, during basic training, and of course during war, but then these soldiers go on to lead normal lives. Few military personnel make a career out of this service. On the other hand, most police officers are career officers: they work with the same people, in the same city, for their entire work lives.

So, although the bond between soldiers is strong, the actual working relationship only lasts a few years. Police officers, working side by side, protecting each other and putting themselves in harm's way for each other for decades, become like family. Actually, family is not an accurate analogy, because most cops' families have no idea what officers deal with at work and how much they are relied on and rely upon their fellow officers for their very lives.

Most people cannot realize the bond that is created between police officers, and if they could they probably could not comprehend it lasting an entire lifetime. The police subculture is reinforced even more by the many other dynamics that are unique to police work.

IT'S A COP THING, YOU WOULDN'T UNDERSTAND

The above heading is actually the title of a chapter on police culture written by a social scientist. To begin an examination of police culture, this phrase pretty much says it all: *only cops will ever understand what it is like to be a cop.* It is nothing like what people see on television or in the movies; it is the danger, loyalty, cynicism, excitement, solidarity, anticipation, bullshit, respect, isolation, fear, fun, camaraderie, frustration, anger, and a hundred other things that make up the life of a cop, as well as the culture of a very intense occupation.

Getting back to the heading, the "thing" is police culture. Those who are not part of it cannot really understand it, just as people who have not experienced combat cannot understand it either.

This culture—this dynamic and unique connection that police officers have—is what *gives meaning to police work.* Being a cop is a state of mind; the subculture is so strong that the job shapes a police officer's personality. So, if you were to ask a police officer what it is like to be a cop, he would probably ask you what it is like not to be.

Police officers have very distinct personalities; other people often peg them as being cops. They do not even realize that they give off this vibe that others pick up on. It would be interesting to find out how different police officers' personalities would be if they had not become cops. Maybe it would be significant, but maybe not; maybe the personalities of police officers are one of the factors that drew them toward police work in the first place.

Police officers have many personality traits in common. Some of these are acquired through the police culture, but some of the traits drew them to police work. Most cops will tell you that they like the fact that their job entails outdoor work and excitement and that it is challenging and unpredictable.

The *unpredictability* is the magic of police work—the danger, and the *seduction of street life*, which is the constant potential for action, as well as an ongoing challenge to *discover the truth*, wading through the lies and bullshit, and taking pride in getting to the bottom of something.

Police officers develop a sixth sense that they cannot describe. This is the sense of knowing when someone is lying or when something does not feel right, such as a dangerous situation. This sense cannot be articulated in a police report; the officer cannot specifically identify certain behaviors or statements that led him to believe that someone was lying or was dangerous, he just knew. Perhaps, because of his experience, something at a subconscious level told him that what he perceived was not good.

> **Example:** An inexperienced police officer cannot discern suspicious activity and statements from other activity. Consequently, he spends as much time investigating innocent activity and individuals as he does with suspicious ones. An experienced officer, on the other hand, knows within a minute if he is dealing with an incident or person that requires further investigation or if this is

nothing he needs to spend any time on. But if you were to ask this officer how he is able to determine this, most likely, he would not be able to explain it, he just knows.

But, by far, the most intense area of police culture and solidarity is the *inevitable prospect of violence*. Other than the military during war, no other occupation deals with the constant threat of violence as an inevitable part of the job.

In no other job does an employee rely so much on fellow employees in life-and-death situations. Officers are forced to rely on each other's' courage and their willingness to take personal risks for one another—and officers do this willingly. The culture of police work forms an attitude that there are things more important than their own personal safety. With the daily risks that police officers take, this is obvious. A person is not born this way, but because of their strong subculture, this is the kind of person they are now.

Another thing that reinforces police culture is the way that police officers view their jobs in comparison to other jobs. The work life of a cop can be so dynamic that *they constantly have to readjust to "real life," which is flat in comparison to theirs.* To them, other people's jobs are boring and mundane, and cops cannot understand how they can live such boring and uneventful lives.

> **Example:** At 6:00 a.m., as an officer is on his way home from an incredible night of emergency calls, chasing bad guys, fighting with suspects, and all the other

exciting events of a given night, he sits at a red light thinking about his shift. He looks over to the car next to him—a guy in a suit, drinking his coffee on his way to the office. The officer is grateful that his life is not so incredibly uneventful and void of challenge. He pities this pathetic individual and his mundane life.

USE OF FORCE

As has been mentioned, *the use of physical force, as an inevitable part of the job, is a characteristic that is unique to law enforcement.* This has a tremendous effect on police culture. The constant threat of violence is met with an expectation that any encounter could be a violent one. A lifetime of this mindset will obviously have an effect on police officers' personalities and solidarity.

> **Example:** When a police officer makes a vehicle stop, he always unsnaps his holster. Usually, and especially at night, he will have his hand on his sidearm as he approaches the vehicle and makes contact with the occupants. Why is he doing this? Because he is anticipating that the occupants of the vehicle will try to kill him, and he wants to be as prepared as possible for a gun battle.
>
> Many times, especially at night with suspicious-looking occupants, the officer will have his gun out if its holster, down to his side where no one can see it, until

he is assured that the situation is safe for him.

Hence, all public contacts, at least initially, start with the anticipation in the officer's mind that things could go south. This dynamic is instrumental in creating the "us versus them" attitude that is so pervasive in police culture.

Officers are trained for the inevitable—using physical force in the performance of their job. Consequently, cops view themselves as crime fighters, and gun fighters, literally because they are fighters, hundreds of times throughout their careers.

This attitude develops to the point that not only do cops not try to avoid physical confrontations, they look forward to the challenge, if they are mentally and physically prepared, otherwise they try to avoid it. Unfortunately, some officers go over the brink and seek out violent confrontations.

When this happens, it is an *obvious sign that the police subculture has taken over the positive values of the job*; these are the cops that are an embarrassment to the profession. These are the bullies who became cops because they can assault people with immunity. Fortunately, there are not very many of them these days, and those who are bullies usually end up making so many mistakes that they lose their jobs.

But, all these physical and dangerous confrontations— foot pursuits, fights, car chases, and shootings—all *add to an officer's experience base.* One does not learn to be a police officer from reading books, or even from the police academy, it only comes from experience. Cops rely on experience to get better at their jobs. This is the type of occupation in which workers learn a great deal in a short period of time. Therefore, these high-profile, experience-rich incidents are extremely important to round out an officer's experience.

And, more important, *these types of incidents raise their worthiness and credibility in the eyes of their peers*, because they have proven themselves under fire. Newer officers know that when things go bad, they will be able to handle it—fight the bad guy, chase him, shoot him, whatever it takes. But his fellow officers do not know that yet, because he has not proved himself. And until that happens, the other officers will not be entirely confident with him as their backup officer. But once he does prove himself, the other officers accept him into their very exclusive club.

THE UGLY SIDE OF LIFE

Police officers see the "ugly side of life," which is another characteristic of the job that affects police culture. *Police officers see people at their very worst*; they see family fights every night, they deal with decent people who lash out of the officer when they get a ticket, and they see human bodies in various states of mutilation, some accidentally, and some at the hands of another.

Because of all of these negative experiences, police officers develop what the social scientists call *gallows humor*, which is finding humor and making jokes about human tragedy. The reason they do this is because it provides them with an *emotional defense mechanism*, which allows them to deal with these scenes and situations without it taking a personal toll on them.

The police respond to dead body calls, fatal accidents, suicides, homicides, and many other death scenes on a routine basis. They see the frailty of the human body and realize the reality of mortality, how quickly and unexpectedly a life can be taken away.

And, they see so much of it, that after a while their senses are deadened, which is a good thing, because otherwise police officers would be ineffective in handling these death investigations. With no personal involvement, humor finds its way into otherwise tragic situations.

Most of the time police officers can keep up this front, this emotional detachment, for their own sanity, but not 100 percent of the time. Every once in a while, an officer is affected by an incident that he handles. Those who deny it are either psychopathic, in denial, or lying to protect their image.

About the only time gallows humor does not rear its ugly head is when a death involves a child. Even the most seasoned, cynical, and hardened street cop does not find humor in dead children. These are the cases in which it seems that officers are more personally affected. For instance, a detective handling a child homicide all night goes home and appreciates his own child much more than before.

Obviously, this desensitizing of emotions can take its own toll. Personal relationships that police officers are in can suffer if this lack of sensitivity carries on into their personal lives.

So, when someone is entering such a dynamic job with an incredibly strong subculture, it is important that they be prepared for it. It requires a certain amount of socialization even before entering this career field, which is explained in the concept of occupational socialization.

OCCUPATIONAL SOCIALIZATION

Occupational socialization is the process of indoctrinating new members of a group into their unique culture. During this period, these new members' behavior is molded to match that of the organization. (The socialization of police officers is often referred to as the most dynamic and intense example of this process.) This process of occupational socialization occurs in three stages: anticipatory, formal, and informal.

Anticipatory Stage

During the anticipatory stage, individuals considering a certain career field begin to anticipate the demands and expectations of their future job. They usually start by reading about the occupation, watch television shows about it, and talk to people who are in that career field. And while they are doing that, they develop attitudes and beliefs that are consistent with those in that particular career field. Before they know it, they begin to feel like part of that culture.

In most criminal justice occupations, individuals anticipate entry into the career field early enough to make a smooth transition. But in the area of corrections, the attraction to the job is usually the pay, benefits, and job security. It usually is not the job "they always wanted." So, because of this, individuals who become correctional officers usually have not anticipated the demands and expectations of the job. With this lack of an anticipatory stage, they get into a job with a very strong culture and a dynamic work environment, not really knowing what they are getting themselves into. Consequently, many correctional officers soon realize that this is not what they had expected, and resign. This results in an extremely high turnover rate in corrections.

Formal Stage

The *formal stage* occurs after an individual has been hired by an organization. *This stage includes the formalized training that immerses the individual into an occupational role.* The formal stage provides the new employee with important job knowledge, but also *reinforces the proper attitudes and behaviors* that the individual started to develop in the anticipatory stage. Also during this stage, a feeling of belonging is created. The emphasis is on the concept of teamwork, ensuring that the new employees realize the importance of working well with others in the organization.

In the police academy, the recruits learn many things necessary to perform their duties, but it is also ingrains in them that they are part of a team, part of a noble and ethical profession, and part of a very unique culture.

Informal Stage

In the *informal stage*, the daily associations with fellow officers, supervisors, and the public shapes the role of the individual as he becomes immersed into the new job and work culture. Very often, the positive values learned in the formal stage can give way to cynicism, alienation, and defensiveness. This is usually caused by other officers saying or doing things that cause the new employee to become disenchanted with the organization and the job.

> **Example:** A new police officer is assigned to a field training officer (FTO) after he has completed the academy. The FTO, who has been on the department for many years, has developed a negative attitude about his job and the department, which is very common with seasoned police officers. What happens next is that the negative attitude of the FTO is not lost on the new officer, who is very impressionable. To him, if the FTO thinks the job and organization is rotten, then it probably is. Very quickly, the new officer has acquired the same attitude as the FTO.

Something unique to the law enforcement profession is that *police officers' social identities are equated with their occupation.* And officers themselves equate their job with their social identity. Because of the nature of the job, many police officers carry guns and badges even when they are off-duty. By doing this, they feel as though they are on duty all the time. So instead of thinking of themselves as just regular people and being a cop is just their job, they see themselves as cops all the time.

The members of the community do this also. People treat police officers differently than they treat other people, even when the officer is off-duty. Because law enforcement is exciting and interesting, when people discover someone is a police officer, they converse with them about their job, and only see this person as a police officer. Hence, the officer's identity is equated with this job. *Because of this, police officers find themselves distancing themselves from the rest of the community because they are constantly reminded that they are unique and different from everyone else.*

Added to this "distancing" distinction, police officers are aware of a great deal of public animosity and criticism of the police, which causes them to feel even more isolated. They withdraw into their group as a defensive measure. This results in the "us versus them" attitude that is prevalent in law enforcement.

> **Personal observation:** Generally, officers take it in stride regarding this realization that they and their comrades are alone in the world against all others, because another characteristic of their profession is the fact that in the course of their duties they experience a constant variety of human tragedies. As an emotional defense, the officers become desensitized, or "emotionally detached," from what they experience. This hardens the officers, and not only does this hardening of their emotions prevent them from feeling upset or disappointed in their alienation from the community, they actually prefer it.

How Police Leadership Can Use the Information about Occupational Socialization

By understanding the anticipatory stage, leaders can structure their selection process to find out if the individual has sufficiently socialized himself to ensure long-term successful employment with the agency.

> **Example:** During oral interviews, police officer candidates are usually asked a question similar to "What have you done to prepare for this position?" The interview board is looking for a response that will indicate to them that the candidate has anticipated entry into the career field sufficiently so that he will not go into culture shock when he is hired, causing him to resign.

In the formal stage, leaders can ensure that proper reinforcement of values and ethics are presented through the formal training process.

> **Example:** In the police academy, officers receive training in ethics and professionalization. During the academy, they are held to a high ethical standard. Deviations result in dismissal from the academy. The value of teamwork is emphasized on an ongoing basis, from the first day of the academy to the graduation ceremony.

In the informal stage, leaders can shield new, impressionable employees from negative values by placing them in assignments or with training officers who will have the least negative impact.

> **Example:** Police FTOs who have negative attitudes can easily pass that attitude on to new, impressionable officers, which

perpetuates the negative attitude throughout the organization. Management must ensure that FTOs are not selected based solely on the criteria of job knowledge and seniority, but rather based on a demonstration of a positive attitude toward their job and the organization.

When the Christopher Commission examined the activities and processes of the Los Angeles Police Department after the riots, the commission made several recommendations. One of these recommendations was that FTOs be selected on criteria that include a demonstration of a positive attitude, so as to prevent the perpetuation of negativity throughout the organization.

A DANGEROUS JOB

The inevitable potential for violence makes police work a dangerous job, which as we have discovered is a dynamic component of police culture. Many studies have been conducted to determine how much this "danger" component affects police culture.

Measuring the danger of police work simply by *measuring the number of officers killed in the line of duty is a poor measure of the real danger*. Per capita, other occupations have a higher death rate, such as construction workers and convenience store clerks.

But, because of good tactics, training, precautions, and backup, police officers reduce their deaths and injury rates despite the danger. Without all these things, the death rates among police officers would be astronomical. Most of the deaths of police officers are a result of "unexpected" danger; something happens that the officer was not prepared for.

> **Example:** Officers respond to a call of a bank robbery in progress. Several officers surround the bank and coordinate responsibilities, such as an arrest team, an entry team, perimeter units, and the like. They are ready for action; they will not be caught off guard by the robbers if they suddenly run out and started shooting. An officer getting out of his car to take a report is shot by an ambusher; the police were just is not prepared for that sort of thing.

Therefore, *assaults more accurately measure the danger of police work.* On average, about 100 police officers are killed in the line of duty in the United States each year. In comparison, 70,000 police officers are injured in the line of duty. Considering that there are approximately 700,000 police officers in the United States, *10 percent* of them are injured *each year* as a result of violence, which is a substantial number. A police officer can be fairly certain that he will be injured in the line of duty because of violence sometime in his career. More likely, he will be injured many times.

Additionally, this 70,000 number is actually underreported. This of itself is a characteristic of police culture. Officers who receive minor injuries during a fight with a suspect are usually not inclined to report it to a supervisor, because it is considered a part of doing business, and it is not viewed as being very masculine to report a scrape or pulled muscle. And, beyond that, this number of injuries does not include police injuries that are not direct assaults.

Many injuries sustained by police officers occur while they are conducting their duties but are not the result of an assault. Officers are often injured in traffic accidents, falls, when climbing walls and fences, by accidental firearm discharges, and a variety of other physical dangers that are unique to the law enforcement profession.

Discussions of danger and police officer safety are not just rhetoric. A big part of police culture is based on the commonsense reactions to real events and experience. All officers have faced violence, and know they will face it again, sometimes alone, and sometimes with fellow officers who will put themselves in harm's way for another officer.

Because of this common denominator of danger in the life of each and every police officer, danger carries what the social scientists call *symbolic weight* in police culture, because it is truly dangerous—it is not just folklore or stories. This symbolic weight is a symbol of the unique character of the job.

The police culture has many symbols, including the gun and badge. The gun is a symbol for violence, and the badge is a symbol for the unique power and authority that police officers have.

It is an understatement to say that danger brings police officers together. *It is the glue of police culture.* "We all go home at the end of the night" is a predominant motto of cops everywhere, one that is drummed into them in briefing sessions by supervisors and reinforced at every hot call that officers respond to.

THREE CORE ELEMENTS OF POLICE CULTURE

Researchers have identified three core elements of police culture that, in essence, explain why the culture is so strong and has such a hold on those who belong to it. These three elements are the perception of violence, solidarity, and social isolation.

Perception of Violence

The perception of violence, which we have already examined, is very real, and is what researchers have referred to as "the seductions of living on the edge." In reality, a lot of police work is boring—driving around looking for trouble that is not there at the moment. But the anticipation, the waiting for the excitement that will eventually come, is a seduction to police officers.

Officers are visibly enthusiastic at the end of a "good" night. The unpredictability of the job and the potential danger around the next corner is a seduction, a part of the unique culture. And, living on the edge is the *good* side of the job.

Cynicism or "dark moods" is the bad part. Some social scientists call this cynicism *realism* because cops see the *realities of life.* What they are saying is that people who are consistently happy and positive are a little clueless to some extent, because they do not understand or perceive the realities of life, other than their own.

Part of what social scientists have attempted to discover about police culture is why anyone would want to do the job, because, in comparison to the rest of the world, the "good" part of the job is very bad in their eyes. And, on top of that, cops do not directly help people, which is generally something that draws people into public service. The police actually do things that hurt people's lives, such as writing citations and making arrests. Indirectly, the police help many people, by taking criminals and violators off the streets and issuing tickets so people drive safer, but there is no immediate satisfaction for the officer; he will not be thanked for his efforts. If someone wants to be thanked for his work and be looked upon as a hero, he should become a firefighter, not a police officer.

> **Example:** After many years in the private sector, an individual decides to pursue his dream of becoming a police officer. He goes to the academy, does well, and is soon working as a cop. He is doing a very good job and shows a lot of promise. After six months he quits. When a supervisor asks him why, he says, "I thought I was going to get to help people."
>
> Obviously, this individual needed the immediate gratification of helping people, which police work rarely does (except for the occasional exception of saving a

drowning child or something similar). Additionally, this clearly shows that this individual missed out on the anticipatory stage of occupational socialization, which should have been identified during the screening and testing process.

The good part (i.e., excitement and anticipation of danger) does not fully describe it. It is participation in a venture from which most people are excluded, doing things that most people just watch on television.

Solidarity

The concept of *solidarity* refers to a *unity of purpose*, a group of individuals united in a cause—them against an opposing force or enemy. This solidarity, the *loyalty between officers*, will always override any differences or disagreements. People do not always get along with everyone else; there will always be personality conflicts and other differences that cause people to not like one another. But in police work, no matter what personal differences there may be, when an officer is in danger and needs help, differences are forgotten and everyone places themselves in harm's way to help the officer who is in danger.

The constant potential for danger, combined with an unsupportive public creates an "us versus them" attitude, which is a core element of police culture. Combined, these two elements create a profound sense of loyalty. According to experts, this solidarity is insulation against danger and rejection.

The insulation against danger provides protection. The insulation against rejection is that they have each other. Cops are rejected by a large portion of society, but they do not really care, because they have each other, which they prefer anyway.

Social Isolation

Police officers believe that they are a distinct occupational group, apart from the rest of society, *which makes it difficult for them to have relationships and interact with members of other groups.* This belief is based on an adversarial relationship with the *public*, the *brass* (i.e., police administration), and the *courts*.

To the police, the enemy is not just the criminals, but the general public, the police administration, and the courts. With regards to the public, the media constantly cast police actions and activities in a negative light. With regard to the brass, higher-ups discipline officers for split-second ambiguous decisions that they make in the field. The courts often view the police as liars, and they are very unsympathetic to their work schedules. For instance, the fact that a police officer has worked all night does not enter into the court's decision to have the officer wait in court all day to testify on a case.

Because of all this, it is very easy for police officers to get into trouble; they often try to be "invisible," lay low. There is a saying that hard-working cops get in trouble, but invisible cops do not. Because of the volatile nature of the job, virtually all police officers receive some sort of discipline during their careers. It is actually perceived by their peers that if they do not get into trouble once in a while they are just lying low, and are not really hard-working cops.

So, officers have to decide if they want to have a reputation as being a *real cop*, and get into trouble once in a while, or a *safe cop*, who hides in the weeds and stays out of trouble, but does not really work as hard as the others. Most cops, because of the strong culture, prefer to be accepted by their peers and get into trouble once in a while. The fact that administrators are quick to hand out discipline in police departments continues to perpetuate the "us versus them" attitude, effectively separating the officers from the leadership. *It is difficult for police leaders to be effective in this adversarial environment.*

Besides feeling isolated from the public, brass, and courts, who are supposed to be on their side, *police officers often feel alienated in social settings.* As has been noted elsewhere in the text, an officer's social identity often is equated with his occupation. Once a civilian learns of the officer's occupation, the officer is talked to differently and treated differently, with conversations focusing on police issues.

So, officers soon view themselves as outsiders to the rest of society. Combined with their feeling of solidarity, this creates a code of silence.

This *code of silence* refers to the unwritten understanding among police officers that they do not report misconduct of other officers. This is a protective measure against all those who seek to find fault and punish them—the public, the brass, and the courts. The police officers believe that they must protect themselves and each other, because no one else is going to.

Police management has a response to the code of silence. They view this as a serious ethical problem, which interferes with disciplinary investigations. To circumvent this strong cultural characteristic, most police departments have a policy or rule that requires that police officers report misconduct of other officers to supervision. Failure to do so will result in discipline for failure to report.

> **Example:** At an incident where several officers are present one officer engages in some sort of misconduct. Once this incident is investigated by Internal Affairs, not only is the violating officer disciplined for the misconduct, but the rest of the officers are disciplined for failing to report the misconduct. Police administration views this as a necessary tool to break down the code of silence and improve the discipline and behavior of the officers.

CONCLUSION

Police work is unique from any other occupation. Because of the unique character of the work, cops stick together. This creates many negative characteristics in police culture that are a byproduct of human beings doing a job that most people would not do. The irony is that most cops would not do anything else.

But, police culture has some very positive characteristics. For example, solidarity provides officers with moral support and reduces physical danger. Because of this bond between police officers, the importance of protecting each other and backing each other up so everyone goes home at the end of the shift prevents many deaths and injuries to officers.

The cynicism, or "dark moods" or realism, that police officers naturally develop as they experience human tragedy provides them with an emotional barrier that helps them to cope with the realities of life, which is much more violent, vicious, and evil than most people will ever realize.

CHAPTER 12

RACIAL PROFILING

Topics

- Management Issues
- Criminal versus Racial Profiling
- The Ethics of Profiling
- Pretext Stops and Racial Profiling
- The Stigma of Profiling
- Management Response

INTRODUCTION

When police agencies throughout the country began to aggressively deal with the increasingly severe gang problem, specialized units as well as patrol operations started developing intelligence information to identify gang members and leaders. By profiling certain characteristics, individuals were interviewed, photographed, and the information placed into databanks. This information enabled gang interdiction units to more effectively investigate gang-related violent crime.

Because the race of the individual was usually a characteristic used by the police to assist in identifying the suspected gang member, it did not take long for civil rights groups to accuse law enforcement of what has become known as *racial profiling*. Unfortunately, this practice has been confused with *criminal profiling*, which is an acceptable and legitimate police strategy.

MANAGEMENT ISSUES

Law enforcement's fundamental responsibility has two components, which are diametrically opposed to each other. One component is the protection of freedom and liberty in a democratic society, and the other is the apprehension and prosecution of offenders. These conflicting goals of protecting personal freedoms versus depriving individuals of their liberty has always been problematic for police managers, as well as a source of tension and conflict between the police and the public.

As sophisticated law enforcement efforts in identifying crime trends and gathering intelligence information became commonplace, instances occurred in which these efforts broached the fine line between civil liberties and the public's demand for effective law enforcement. In law enforcement's zeal to perform their duties diligently, they were accused of crossing the line regarding Constitutional freedoms.

These incidents occurred with sufficient regularity among agencies that lawsuits, injunctions, and legal mandates were brought against these law enforcement organizations that practiced a tactic that became known as racial profiling. This caused police managers to scramble to create policies against racial profiling and to provide training to protect their agencies from liability exposure.

CRIMINAL VERSUS RACIAL PROFILING

It is important to understand that there is a difference between criminal profiling and racial profiling. *Criminal profiling* is a use of quasi-scientific techniques that aid the police in their investigations. This sophisticated law enforcement tactic is used for identifying everything from drunk drivers to serial killers.

True criminal profiling uses a number of variables to assist the police in locating an offender. Race can often be one of the variables, and should not be ignored. The primary variables are the method of operation and patterns of behavior, with physical characteristics included when it is possible to do so. For instance, most serial killers are white males in their 20s. When the police focus their attention on individuals fitting this description, they are not being racist; they are simply using common sense to do their job.

A lot of good police work stems from experienced officers being able to draw on their experience and almost subconsciously analyze a situation and go through a list a variables to determine if someone is worthy of closer scrutiny. Rather than random patrol and contacts, the experienced officer uses a series of demographic and behavioral variables as tools to guide his investigations.

Racial profiling is entirely different, and the similarity in terms has given a negative stigma to criminal profiling. The U.S. General Accounting Office defined racial profiling as "using race as a key factor in making a traffic stop." Another expert labels racial profiling as what occurs when an officer uses a person's race to assess the likelihood of criminal activity. This label, however, does not fully address the definition of racial profiling, because most likely, especially when physical descriptions of offenders are provided, race will certainly be a variable, and should not be ignored. To give physical descriptions to the police that exclude the race of the suspect because it would be politically correct would not only reveal a lack of common sense, but would be of a serious disservice to our society.

> **Personal observation:** It is interesting that many news agencies when providing physical descriptions of dangerous suspects who are on the loose refrain from revealing the race of the suspect. The newspaper or television station asks for the public's support and assistance in locating the suspect, but then fails to provide the viewers with a key piece of information that would assist them should they happen across the suspect.
>
> Withholding that sort of information in a police bulletin or broadcast would be ludicrous, but there are critics of the

police that do not want law enforcement to use race as a variable or descriptor in any form.

A more complete definition of racial profiling is that it is any police action that relies on race or ethnicity rather than behavior or information that leads the police to focus on someone who has been identified as being involved in criminal activity. The key component in this definition that changes criminal profiling to racial profiling is the lack of behavior as a variable.

A combination of demographics (i.e., race, location, gender) and behavior (i.e., suspicious activity, nervousness, furtive movements) is true criminal profiling; an activity demonstrated by good police officers on a daily basis. When race becomes the only factor for a detention by the police, it becomes racial profiling.

The International Association of Chief of Police (IACP) evaluated the tactic of targeting specific locations and individuals based on crime data, known as selective enforcement. During that evaluation, IACP defined racial profiling as "the detention, interdiction, or other disparate treatment of any person on the basis of their racial or ethnic status or characteristics." What is missing from that definition is that the action by the officer is void of consideration of behavioral variables.

What is needed is a definition that combines all essential variables, the behavior of the individual and the physical characteristics of the individual, that, based on previous experience, information, or studies, indicate a likelihood that the individual in question is worthy of closer scrutiny.

THE ETHICS OF PROFILING

Some critics of the police believe that any type of profiling is unethical and should not be tolerated. They will not listen to explanations that legitimate profiling is not racism and is actually respectful of civil rights. If race is a variable in a criminal description, then omitting it from a crime report hinders the investigation, and eventually, the organization will fail to solve many crimes.

Simply put, the race of an offender is an important variable for locating and apprehending the suspect, and as long as other variables are also considered, intelligent people should understand that the police need as much information as possible to carry out their duties. On this topic, Ed Nowicki stated, "It may be borderline incompetence to not use race if intelligence information points to a particular race. Race may be a factor, and it would be ludicrous to ignore the obvious."

However, when officers cross the line of ignoring behavioral variables and focus solely on race, then it becomes racial profiling. An officer who detains or arrests someone solely on the basis of race is in violation of the Fourth Amendment to the Constitution. Major incidents of racial profiling occurred in New Jersey, Maryland, and Colorado that created serious police management problems. This resulted in legislation and policies in 2002 to prevent racial profiling. In addition, many cities began collecting data when making vehicle stops or other detentions to determine if they were guilty of racial profiling.

Two large cities in California, San Diego and San Jose, began such as voluntary collection of data to determine if racial profiling existed in their agencies. However, police managers became concerned that the federal government would interfere and ask for additional information. Additionally, they were concerned that officers asking for additional information regarding race during traffic detentions (already tense situations) would only exacerbate relationships between the police and the community.

The collection of data was wrought with errors and uncontrolled or immeasurable variables. If an officer thought he had stopped too many blacks, he could balance the numbers by stopping a large number of whites. If an officer stopped an abnormally high number of blacks, it could not be determined if he was racially profiling or if he was simply working in an area with a high black population.

PRETEXT STOPS AND RACIAL PROFILING

A common police practice of concern to many law enforcement critics, including the ACLU, is the practice of pretext stops. A *pretext stop*, which has been deemed constitutional, is when an officer wants to detain an individual for further investigation but lacks probable cause to do so. If the individual is driving a vehicle with a minor mechanical violation, such as a burnt out taillight, the officer may make the enforcement stop for the equipment violation, even though he is not concerned about the violation. This gives the officer the opportunity to talk to the driver and possibly develop further information to develop probable cause.

Pretext stops are a valuable law enforcement tool that allows officers to contact suspicious persons that they otherwise would not be allowed to contact.

> **Example:** An officer sees a white male in his 20s leaving a low-rent motel in a known drug sales area at 3:00 a.m. driving an old car. Absent additional information, the officer does not have probable cause to stop the vehicle and detain the driver, even though, based on the officer's experience, he is fairly certain that the driver is in possession or under the influence of drugs.
>
> However, if the vehicle has a minor mechanical violation, the officer may make the stop, because a violation has occurred. The officer is then able to question the driver, and possibly get consent or develop probable cause to search the driver and vehicle for drugs.

The concern that critics have regarding pretext stops is that racism and racial profiling can creep in when making these detentions. One ACLU official argues that with pretext stops being permissible the police can find an excuse to stop anybody. Law enforcement, in contrast, argues that the use of pretext stops is a valuable tool, and is based on probabilities, not prejudice. A pretext stop by an officer on a vehicle containing three black males wearing red bandanas as they cruise slowly through a Hispanic gang area at 2:00 a.m. may result in the arrest of the occupants for weapons violations, and possibly prevent a drive-by shooting. The officer is not being racist, he is simply using his experience to save lives and do his job.

THE STIGMA OF PROFILING

So, there is a distinct difference between criminal profiling and racial profiling. Efforts have been made to make a clear distinction between the two so that true criminal profiling does not receive an unwarranted negative stigma, and the focus for change can be made regarding racial profiling.

Two major law enforcement organizations have attempted to change these labels. The IACP has suggested changing the definition of racial profiling from "disparate treatment on the basis of racial and ethnic status or characteristics" to "disparate treatment because of racial or ethnic status or characteristics."

The Police Executive Research Forum (PERF) conducted an in-depth study of the topic, and changed the term "racial profiling" to "racially-based policing." A recent report by the National Organization of Black Law Enforcement Executives (NOBLE) referred to racial profiling as "bias-based policing." This new identifying label of racially-based policing clarifies the difference between criminal profiling and racism. The definition of racially-based policing, previously known as racial profiling, is "police actions that are based solely on race."

MANAGEMENT RESPONSE

The attention paid to the issue of racially-based policing by various civil rights groups and law enforcement executive organizations is for the purpose of stopping it from continuing, and to prevent its occurrence in the future. With the assistance of much research that has been done in this area, police managers are developing protocols and organizational procedures to eliminate race-based policing from their agencies.

The responsibilities of police management are varied and complex. They can create rules and policies that disallow racially-based policing, but it still is up to the individual officers as to whether they follow the policy. For this reason, police management must do more than make rules; they must create a work environment that ensures that individual rights are routinely protected, not because they have to, but because it is the right thing to do.

Such an environment can be created through proper leadership and an expectation that officers will adhere to the rules and policies of the organization. This is supported through effective training of officers to instill the proper ethics and values that are expected of them. The community must also be trained so that they understand the tactics and practices of the organization, thereby understanding that criminal profiling is not racism. Proper supervision of officers will ensure that their behavior is in the spirit of organizational objectives and ideals. And as technology continues to improve, devices such as video cameras and digital recorders will ensure accountability and adherence to policies.

The American police face a tremendous challenge. They are working harder with fewer resources, but still have been successful in reducing crime over the past several years. With an ever-increasing minority population, the police are more and more often being accused of racism and bias. Many times, as officers target individuals or groups based on a number of variables, and one of those variables happen to be race, the officers are accused of racism, rather than intuitive and fact-based law enforcement.

Police officers are selected only after undergoing exhaustive testing processes, which include background investigations to determine character and integrity, polygraph examinations that confirm moral and legal behavior, and psychological examinations that determine if the candidate has the proper disposition for the demands of the job.

So, the individuals entering law enforcement are usually getting into the field for the right reasons—to protect individual rights and freedoms. If these reasons change, then the blame must be placed on police management and supervision for allowing it to happen. It is incumbent upon them then to follow the suggested guidelines for improving their work environments and creating an atmosphere where officers continue to have the same work ethic that they did when they first entered the field of law enforcement.

Management's biggest challenge, however, is to not run scared because of the politically sensitive nature of racial profiling, causing them to dispense with the success and value of criminal profiling. Criminal profiling is a testament to the intelligence and sophistication of modern law enforcement, and must endure the invalid claims of critics so that heinous and violent criminals are removed from a peaceful society.

By the very nature of the job, there will always be critics of law enforcement activities and practices. Police leaders have always known this. By showing courage from standing their ground to a politically sensitive issue, law enforcement leadership will propel interdiction and investigative efforts into the new millennium with dignity and results.

CHAPTER 13

POLICE MISCONDUCT

Topics

- Types of Misconduct
- Theories of Police Misconduct
- Levels of Corruption
- Citizen Complaints
- Reasons That Complaints Are Made
- Internal Affairs Investigations

INTRODUCTION

An incorruptible person cannot be bought at any price. Cynics say that everyone has a price, a reward that a person would value over his self-respect, his dignity, and his personal moral code. But those in the field of law enforcement know this to be untrue. Fortunately for society, there are several hundred thousand police officers in this country who are not for sale, at any price, ever—don't even try.

How sad for them that they must endure the ridicule and scorn brought against them by the handful of criminals who managed to worm their way into police departments and then use their positions of trust for personal gain or satisfaction. This small percentage of miscreants who became police officers as a means of committing crimes, or who were so weak of character that they succumbed to material temptation, or lacked self-esteem to the point that they sought out a job where they could assault people with immunity, are the embarrassment and scourge of honest and professional police officers whose values and integrity are beyond reproach.

Many positions of public trust have an impact on the lives of citizens, but none more public or immediate than that of a police officer. When a judge or politician commits a corrupt act, it occurs behind closed doors. When a police officer commits one, it occurs in a much more public arena, and even for minor violations he faces discipline from his department, something that most other public officials do not have to face.

> **Example:** If a police officer is involved in a traffic accident that is determined to be his fault, the officer will be disciplined for it. Other public officials do not face discipline for mistakes or accidents.

TYPES OF MISCONDUCT

Police misconduct falls into three categories. Some of these acts of misconduct are the result of flawed personal values, which were shaped prior to entry into law enforcement. Others are the result of changes in one's values after becoming a police officer, and others are simply mistakes or errors in judgment. The three types of misconduct are corruption, abuse of authority, and occupational deviance.

Corruption

Corruption is defined as committing acts through the misuse of police authority for personal gain. The key elements of this type of misconduct are *misuse of authority* and *personal gain*. Corruption differs from other types of misconduct because the others lack the element of personal gain. Police corruption is usually in the form of accepting money from someone involved in illegal activity. The officer is basically being paid to not do his job; that is, to ignore the crimes being committed around him.

> **Example:** A police officer is given money to ignore prostitution or gambling operations on his beat. This can be very easy for an officer weak in moral character to justify to himself, because there is no tangible victim in these types of cases.

A second type of police corruption also has to do with accepting money in exchange for failing to perform one's official duties. Committing one of these acts is much more overt than the latter type. This type of corruption involves an officer committing an act of extortion, in which he forces lawbreakers to pay him off to avoid arrest.

> **Example:** An officer is aware of a drug-dealing operation on his beat. He contacts the dealer and demands money so that he will not arrest them. This is truly a criminal act.

A third type of corruption is just outright stealing. Police officers find themselves in many situations in which they have countless opportunities to take the personal property of another.

> **Example:** Officers respond to a location in response to a burglary alarm. They discover that the business has been burglarized. While waiting for the business owner to respond, the officers load up their vehicles with property from the business. Everyone will just assume that the burglars got away with more property than they actually did.

It is easy for unscrupulous officers to justify these acts also. They know that the business owner's insurance company will cover the loss, so the owner will not actually lose anything as a result of the burglary. Plus, not many people, honest or otherwise, have a whole lot of sympathy for insurance companies.

Abuse of Authority

Abuse of police authority is generally not as outright a crime as corruption is, because there is no personal gain involved. Abuse of authority does not require intent, malice, or motive. It takes the form of injury, denying of rights, or just making someone feel bad. The three types of abuse of authority are physical abuse, psychological abuse, and legal abuse.

Physical Abuse

This type of abuse, of course, involves the physical use of force by a police officer against a suspect. A police officer has a right to use physical force that is *reasonable* to defend himself, make an arrest, or prevent an escape. Anything beyond what is considered reasonable would be an abuse of force.

Additionally, once a suspect appears to be complying (i.e., he reduces his level of resistance), the officer must reduce his level of force. This failure to de-escalate force once the suspect reduces or halts his resistance has gotten many police officers into trouble.

> **Example:** A suspect struggles with an officer to take the officer's gun. In the process, the officer is severely beaten as he tries to maintain control of his weapon. As other officers arrive, the suspect surrenders. Seeing the badly injured officer, these officers commence to beat the suspect.

> **Example:** During a struggle with a suspect, the suspect manages to strike the officer several times. The officer is eventually able to overpower the suspect and handcuff him. Because of the rush of

adrenaline, the officer punches the suspect a couple of times before putting him in the police car.

Psychological Abuse

This type of abuse is much more subtle than physical abuse, and much harder to effectively complain about or to prove. This abuse usually takes the form of a verbal exchange between the officer and citizen.

Some maladjusted officers, who perhaps became police officers to bolster their own lack of self-esteem, commence to demean and demoralize citizens they come into contact with. By doing so, these officers feel superior to these citizens, which feeds their starving egos.

An overly officious tone or an off-handed remark can do a lot of damage. First, it causes psychological harm to the recipient, and second, it causes irreparable harm to the police department.

> **Example:** There are hundreds of things that an officer can say that cause psychological harm and are unnecessary.

- "You people are all the same."
- "Why am I not surprised at this?"
- "I've got better things to do than deal with you."
- "Are you drunk or just plain stupid?"

This is not to say that police officers should be timid little choirboys. Officers should start off being courteous and civil, treating citizens as they would like to be treated by the police. But, as the citizen turns the encounter into a negative one because of his demeanor, language, and insults, the officers will turn the dialogue to one of officiousness and authority so that they maintain physical and psychological control of the situation.

> **Example:** An officer contacts a suspicious person or someone who matches the description of a suspect who just committed a crime. The officer says, "Hi, may I speak to you for a moment, sir?" When the reply is along the lines of "Go to hell, pig," the officer's response will be commensurate with the level of cooperation he is getting. The officer would be justified in saying, "Sit down and shut up, and don't do anything stupid."

Legal Abuse

This type of abuse of authority occurs when a police officer detains, searches, or arrests a person without probable cause to do so. Sometimes legal abuse is intentional—the officer just does not care. But often, the officer believes that he has probable cause according to the law, when in fact he does not. This type of conduct often results in lost cases, but generally does not result in discipline. However, this type of abuse *can* expose the officer and the police department to civil liability due to a violation of civil rights.

This type of abuse does not rise to the serious level of corruption, because there is no element of personal gain. In fact, most of these acts are committed in an effort by the individual officers to help their organization to reach departmental goals and objectives.

> **Example:** An officer is patrolling an area where there has been a great deal of gang-related activity. He sees a person dressed in typical gang attire walking down the street. With no knowledge that this person has committed a crime, the officer detains him to find out who he is and what his business in the area is.

> This is illegal, it is a violation of the person's rights, but the officer is trying to protect the community. This does not excuse the abuse, but it shows that not all acts of legal abuse spawn from an evil heart.

Occupational Deviance

This type of misconduct is different from the other two types in that there is no economic gain, and it is not an overt abuse of official authority. Rather, it is an officer taking advantage of the position he holds. So, it is not job-related misbehavior, but rather a behavior that deviates from acceptable conduct, which may or may not be criminal in nature. This type of misbehavior, which is expressly prohibited in police department rules and regulations, includes such acts as accepting free meals or receiving discounts because of their occupation. Some officers may take advantage of their position even farther.

> **Example:** A male officer sees an attractive female driver. He observes that she is

driving five miles over the speed limit. Normally, he would not even consider stopping the vehicle. But, because of the attractive woman component, he makes a traffic enforcement stop for the sole purpose of trying to get a date.

Technically, this is not an abuse of power since the violation occurred, but the officer is clearly taking advantage of his position as a police officer.

THEORIES OF POLICE MISCONDUCT

A number of theories have been developed with regard to police misconduct. These theories do not oppose one another; rather, they address the different directions in which a police officer succumbs to a personal agenda over a noble one.

Individual Officer Explanation

The most common theory of police misconduct is explained by the "rotten apple" theory, which is perhaps better identified as an explanation stating that one or more individual officers slipped through the recruit process or became tainted later. By identifying them and removing them, the integrity of the organization is preserved.

However, most experts believe that this attitude toward police corruption fails to address the possibility that the organization itself could be a catalyst for misconduct.

Studies have shown that those entering law enforcement do not have weak morals. Apparently, something happened to them later. Also, many agencies are corruption-free, whereas others seem to always have a problem.

Every once in a while a "rotten apple" will be identified in a corruption-free department. Once removed, the agency continues on without problems. This supports the theory, but falls short of explaining more pervasive corruption in other departments.

Even in cases where there were several officers involved in corruption or criminal activity, it has been argued that it was a result of these departments hiring a large number of officers in short time period. This resulted in incomplete background investigations, and a lack of training and supervision, rather than a defect in the organization itself.

As with any theory, there are situations and incidents in which it is applicable, and there are times that it is not. By understanding all the theories related to this distasteful subject, one can begin to understand the complexity involved in what makes a good cop turn bad.

Social Structure Explanation

Although there is supporting evidence for the rotten apple theory, many experts argue that there are structural aspects of the law enforcement profession that provide police officers with unique opportunities to deviate from acceptable conduct without much fear of detection.

Police officers are supervised, but not nearly as closely as those in other occupations involving trust and discretionary decision making. Obviously, a supervisor cannot ride around with each officer for his entire shift. There would have to be as many sergeants as there are officers. Consequently, officers are pretty much on their own in the field, which could be disastrous with a weak-willed officer encountering a tempting situation.

Neighborhood Explanation

Studies have shown that there are more incidents of police corruption by officers who are assigned to areas that have been characterized as "socially disorganized." The types of neighborhoods that appear to foster police corruption have the following characteristics:

- High population turnover
- Poverty
- High unemployment
- High level of foreign-born residents
- High level of lower-educated residents

These are all characteristics of classic slum environments. The lifestyle of a majority of the residents in these areas is less than stellar. It can be expected that there are higher levels of vice crimes, such as drug use and sales, prostitution, and gambling.

It is believed that these "victimless" crimes create more temptation for some officers. Those committing the crimes are willing to pay off officers, which is just a cost of doing business. Additionally, as described earlier, some officers can more easily justify ignoring vice laws because there is no tangible victim, which they translate into the belief that the criminal activity is not harming anyone.

The Nature of Police Work

Some of the characteristics of police work can be a catalyst for police misconduct or corruption. These characteristics are a result of the unique occupational setting of law enforcement.

Opportunities for Corruption

Police officers deal with criminals on a daily basis, which means that there will be many times that a criminal will offer a bribe to avoid arrest. Other occupations simply do not offer this opportunity.

Incidents of police corruption are the highest with officers working vice assignments. These officers are exposed to temptation more often than any other police assignment.

> **Example:** A vice officer is offered bribes by pimps and free sex from prostitutes in exchange for ignoring their activities. A patrol officer does not get these sorts of offers very often. As the vice officer develops familiarity with these offenders, he may succumb to the constant temptation.

Low-Visibility Work

Because police officers work in the field, they have very little direct supervision in comparison to other occupations. So, when faced with temptation, the officer knows that the risk of being caught is very low.

Officer Attitudes

By dealing with criminals and deviates day in and day out, many officers develop cynical attitudes about people in general. It is easier for them to do what everyone else appears to be doing.

The Police Organization

The work environment that an officer works in can affect how he deals with the inevitable temptation of misconduct. In police departments that have developed a culture that deals with misconduct very seriously, there are fewer reported incidents of misconduct than in departments that are more lax with misconduct incidents.

If an officer perceives that he will be severely disciplined for misconduct, it is more likely that he will not succumb to temptation than an officer in a department where it is perceived that discipline for misconduct will be dealt with less harshly.

It is the responsibility of the leadership of the agency to create the proper culture and to lead by example.

> **Example:** A police captain had a reputation as a patrol officer of having free sex with prostitutes while on duty as a vice officer. This led to an attitude by other officers that this sort of activity is acceptable, and the captain is not in a very good position to put a stop to it.

The Police Subculture

The police subculture is possibly the strongest of all occupational subcultures. There is a great deal of loyalty and solidarity among police officers. They rely on one other in life-and-death situations, and this reliance can reach beyond normal work activities.

The code of silence, in which employees do not report misconduct of other employees, is strongest among police officers. There has been a great deal of research on this concept, which shows very little change over the years. This means that if an officer engages in some sort of misconduct, he knows that it is highly unlikely that a witnessing officer will report it to supervision.

Additionally, as new officers are immersed into this powerful subculture, they will likely take on the attitudes and beliefs of their fellow officers. If these attitudes and beliefs include certain types of misconduct, these new officers will probably absorb these as their own.

> **Example:** An officer fresh out of the academy understands the concept of reasonable force, and has not even considered using more force than is reasonable and necessary to protect himself and make an arrest. However, because of the unique culture of this department (which could be much different than a neighboring department), he observes repeated incidents of excessive force by other officers. Over time, as this new officer absorbs the cultural norms of the department, he also

takes on this "street justice" attitude, and begins to use excessive force on suspects.

LEVELS OF CORRUPTION

Levels of corruption vary in some departments. It may involve an isolated incident with a single officer, whereas in another department corruption may be widespread.

Level One: Rotten Apples and Rotten Pockets

At this level, a single officer engages in a corrupt act. In this case the department has a rotten apple. In other instances, it may involve a small, cohesive group, such as a team of vice officers, who are involved in corruption—a "pocket" of officers, who become a "rotten pocket."

At this level, this corruption is an aberration, an anomaly inconsistent with the norms of other officers.

Level Two: Pervasive Unorganized Corruption

This level is much more serious than level one, because more officers are committing acts of corruption. However, at this level, the officers involved are acting independently of one another. There is no organized effort.

> **Example:** The majority of officers in patrol accept bribes from traffic violators to avoid a citation. Each officer is acting on

his own; there is no collusion or conspiracy with other officers.

This level of misconduct would be a sign that the subculture of this agency is seriously flawed, which should be addressed by the leadership of the organization.

Level Three: Pervasive Organized Corruption

This is the most serious level of police corruption. In the 1970s, Frank Serpico, a vice officer, reported this type of corruption in the New York Police Department, resulting in the Knapp Commission being formed to investigate the pervasiveness of corruption in the department. Corruption was in the form of organized payoffs that reached high levels of the organization.

CITIZEN COMPLAINTS

The majority of police misconduct incidents come to the attention of police management as a result of citizens who report the misconduct to the police department. These complaints cover a wide range of allegations, such as illegal searches, illegal detentions, poor demeanor, and excessive use of force.

> **Personal observation:** Most of citizen complaints come from individuals who are angry that they have been issued a citation or who have been arrested or have had a friend or family member arrested. The bulk of their complaint rests on

allegations of an uncaring or uncompassionate attitude by the officer, which they are unable to articulate into objective facts, which is needed to justify disciplinary action. Many complainants withdraw their complaints once they have calmed down and the actions of the officer or the procedures of the department have been explained to them.

Citizen Characteristics

Some citizens are more predisposed than others to make formal complaints about an officer. Studies show that minorities, especially African Americans, make the majority of complaints. It is believed that this is due to the high level of tension between the police and minorities, who feel they are being singled out by the police.

It could be argued that the reason that minorities make a disproportionately high number of complaints against the police is because they are disproportionately abused by the police. Although there may be a basis for this thinking, studies show that minorities' definition of police brutality and misconduct is much broader than that of whites. Many minority complaints allege "police brutality" for an allegation of rude or abusive language.

Any use of force by the police will more likely be perceived as excessive or brutal by minorities than by whites, even when the level of force was reasonable for the level of resistance encountered. And the argument that the perception of excessive force by minorities is justified because they are more often the target of it was discounted by a survey conducted after the Rodney King incident. The results of this survey showed that 92 percent of African Americans believed that the police used excessive force, while only 72 percent of whites believed the force to be excessive.

Officer Characteristics

A number of studies have been conducted to determine if there are differences between male and female police officers when it comes to a variety of job performance measurements. The results of many of these are inconclusive because of inconsistent results. However, statistics show that female officers proportionally receive fewer citizen complaints than male officers. They are also involved in fewer use-of-force incidents, and fewer deadly force incidents.

When the Christopher Commission examined the Los Angeles Police Department after the Los Angeles riots, it identified 120 officers who had the highest number of citizen complaints for excessive use of force. None of the officers were female.

More complaints are made against minority officers by minority citizens than against white officers. It is speculated that minority citizens are more confident that minority officers will not be protected by the department as much as white officers would be. But speculation is the best that the experts can do, because all the research is based on reported incidents, rather than the actual number that occur.

In addition to gender and race, the age and education of officers have also been found to affect the potential for generating citizen complaints. Younger police officers tend to be more aggressive regarding work productivity. They also usually have less experience than older officers, which causes them to make more mistakes, which can include conduct that generates complaints.

Additionally, new officers make more public contacts than experienced officers. Experienced officers know what cars to stop and which pedestrians to question. Rookie officers do not, so they stop everything that moves. Consequently, they make more contacts than experienced officers, which could lead to more negative encounters that generate complaints.

Higher education levels also tend to reduce the number of complaints made against an officer. The belief is that higher education increases tolerance and understanding of minorities.

REASONS THAT COMPLAINTS ARE MADE

People have many reasons for filing a citizen's complaint, and many of them have nothing to do with the conduct or actions of the officer involved. Some people get angry because they received a traffic ticket or were arrested. Their goal of making a complaint is to either get even with the officer or to help them win their case in court. Many criminal defense attorneys advise their clients to make a complaint against the arresting officer.

Some people are ignorant regarding the law or police procedure. Because on a television show two detectives came to a victim's home, people will complain that they only got one. Or, if their crime was not solved, they complain that the detective is incompetent. (These are not fictional exaggerations, they are actual complaints that were made and investigated.)

Some people think that any use of force is excessive force and will complain even when others commend the officers for their restraint. An arrested person will complain that he was handcuffed, even after he told the officer that he would not try to escape.

Many people complain that when they received a ticket the officer was rude to them. They rarely, if ever, can articulate anything that the officer said or did that would support their allegation. What is typical in this type of situation is that the officer was professional and impersonal in his demeanor, which was then perceived by an angry motorist as rude. If the officer had been friendly, the complainant would probably complain that the officer enjoyed issuing the ticket too much.

INTERNAL AFFAIRS INVESTIGATIONS

The unfortunate thing about citizen complaints as it pertains to the officers is that the law requires that the police take any complaint they receive and conduct an internal affairs investigation, no matter how ludicrous or ridiculous the complaint may be. If a motorist complained that the officer's handwriting on a ticket was poor, the police would actually have to take the complaint and investigate it.

Another unfortunate thing about citizen complaints as it pertains to the officers is that all complaints, no matter the outcome, become part of the officers' permanent personnel files. And when it comes to allegations of excessive use of force, this can be especially damaging to an officer's reputation. If an arrested person was charged with assault against the officer, this person's attorney can make a motion with the court to have the arresting officer's personnel file reviewed for previous allegations of excessive force. The purpose of this is to create a self-defense issue at trial. And if an officer is sued for an excessive force claim, even prior complaints in which the officer was cleared for wrongdoing can be admitted.

Only 10 percent of all allegations of police misconduct are found to be true, but 100 percent of them become part of an officer's personnel file. A unique characteristic of police work is that a high percentage of the population does not like the police in general. Even supporters of the police will complain just to get back at an officer who wrote them a ticket or arrested them for drunk driving. The citizen complaint procedure truly is an effective method for disgruntled citizens to get their pound of flesh.

After an internal affairs investigation is completed, the investigator can assign one of four possible dispositions to report his findings: exonerated, unfounded, not sustained, or sustained.

- **Exonerated:** The conduct or actions by the officer did in fact occur, but the conduct or actions were proper, legal, and justified.
- **Unfounded:** Based upon the information provided in the allegation, the conduct or actions of the officer did not occur. In essence, the investigator proved that the complainant lied or was mistaken.

- **Not sustained:** The investigator was unable to obtain sufficient evidence to prove that the allegation occurred; that is, the investigator could not prove or disprove what happened, which means that the officer may be guilty, but it cannot be proven. This disposition will not result in disciplinary action, but it certainly casts suspicion on the officer.
- **Sustained:** When an allegation of misconduct is sustained, it means that there is sufficient evidence to prove that the misconduct occurred. When this is the disposition, the officer will face disciplinary action.

Management can choose from several levels of disciplinary options. The choice that they make will be based on many factors:

- **Severity of the offense.** This will be the primary factor in determining the severity of the discipline.
- **Repeat violations.** If the officer has been disciplined in the past for similar misconduct, the concept of *progressive discipline*, in which discipline becomes increasingly more severe as misconduct continues, will be employed.
- **Pattern of behavior.** If the officer has a history of misconduct, even if not for like violations, the discipline will be more severe.
- **Impact on the organization.** If discipline is too light, others in the organization will believe that this particular type of misconduct is insignificant. If the discipline is too severe, it will have a demoralizing effect on the other officers.

The following is a list of disciplinary measures, in order of severity, starting with the least severe. This is discipline that is dispensed either as a result of a sustained citizen's complaint or because of misconduct observed by supervision or management.

- **Counseling:** This level of discipline is nothing more than a conversation between the officer and his immediate supervisor. This level of discipline, which is for very minor violations, is considered nothing more than additional training, with no formal documentation, unless it is a result of a citizen's complaint.
- **Documented counseling:** This is the first step of progressive discipline. The documentation begins a history of the behavior that, if repeated, will result in progressively more severe discipline. This discipline is also for relatively minor violations and does not become a part of the officer's permanent record unless it is a result of a citizen's complaint.
- **Letter of reprimand:** This stage of discipline starts an official record, which is actually the first level of actual discipline. The previous two levels are considered training issues. However, when an official reprimand is issued, it is the start of potentially more severe discipline if violations continue.
- **Suspension:** This is considered a severe form of discipline in which the officer is relieved of duty without pay, which can range from one day to several months, depending on the seriousness of the violations and/or repeat violations.

- **Transfer:** Many police departments transfer officers out of desirable assignments as part of the disciplinary process. The justification is that due to the misconduct, the officer needs to be placed in an assignment in which supervision has greater control over the officer's activities. Most officers would gladly take a suspension over a transfer, because getting transferred back into the assignment may not ever be possible again.
- **Demotion:** This is an extremely severe form of discipline, in which an employee is taken out of a supervisory or management position and placed into a lower-ranking and lower-paid position. This will occur when the employee has committed an act of misconduct that demonstrates that he is not suited for the responsibilities of the higher position. A demotion can also occur if the employee has performed poorly in the higher position. This level of discipline can have an extremely demoralizing effect on the employee, as he must now work with peers who were his subordinates and must work for supervisors who were his peers.
- **Termination:** This is obviously the most severe form of discipline that can be administered. Termination is the last resort and occurs after a long history of misconduct or when the officer's misconduct is so grievous that retaining the officer as an employee is not an option. This is usually the case when an officer commits a crime or has in some way lost credibility, which

would make him ineffective as a police officer, such as an act of moral turpitude.

CONCLUSION

With all this talk about police misconduct and police corruption, it could cause one to believe that this sort of deviant behavior is widespread, and a grave threat to society.

Well, it is not widespread, not in the least. In fact, it is quite rare—the corruption part anyway. Almost every hard-working, conscientious police officer will make a mistake or error in judgment from time to time, resulting in disciplinary action. In such a volatile, dynamic, and ever-changing work environment, it is virtually impossible to avoid criticism that results in negative consequences to the officer.

In some agencies, an officer getting into trouble for the first time enters a right-of passage of sorts, in which the officer exits the fairy-tale world of helping others and saving lives, and enters the real world of real cops, which is covering their asses and protecting their partners. And only once the new, idealistic officer gets chopped off at the knees for the first time, causing his altruistic attitude to evolve into a realistic understanding that he has to look out for himself and his fellow officers, will he be able to understand what being a cop is all about, and that part of it is looking out for other cops. Because not only does everyone else not try to look out for them, they are looking out to get them.

This is the attitude of cops, like it or not, brought on by a powerful subculture that no one but other cops understand. This culture is a defense mechanism to protect its members from those who do not understand or appreciate what it is that cops do, which is everyone else but other cops.

Okay, back to corrupt cops. The people who hate corrupt cops the most are all the other cops—the professional, dedicated, honest, fair, and courageous men and women who must take all the flak for the very, very few bad apples who once wore a police uniform. They were not cops; they were criminals disguised as police officers. Fortunately for the profession, they have been identified and removed from the profession, but not without a cost. The cost is the tainted reputation that besmirches the integrity of the vast majority of police officers who would never even consider committing a corrupt act.

CHAPTER 14

THE FUTURE OF POLICING

Topics

- Environmental Scanning
- Scenario Writing
- Changes in Police Leadership in the Future

INTRODUCTION

Predicting the future is very difficult, because sometimes dramatic events that cannot be foreseen can cause broad changes in society, such as the changes in the world after 9/11. Major events such as this can alter predictions made by experts; experts can never anticipate unforeseeable incidents, because they rely on trends and history to assist them in their predictions.

A prediction is not the same as foretelling the future, which is a claim a fortune-teller would make. An expert in the social sciences bases his opinions and predictions on a combination of historical facts, current trends, and an educated guess as to how this will all come together in the future.

For 10,000 years, agriculture was the primary source of wealth. It was only 100 years ago that this was replaced by mass production, now giving way to today's information society. Back when our founding fathers developed the Constitution, they had no concept of how much the country would change in the next 200 years, but we still follow the Constitution, which even its authors would probably maintain is outdated because the world has changed more than they could have ever imagined.

However, in today's world, experts have a little more history to help them with their predictions. They acknowledge that the potential for technological advances is much more unlimited that it was viewed 100 years ago. Because of this, they can predict that it may be incomprehensible, rather than not even realizing the potential.

(Simply put, our founding fathers were oblivious to what the future held in comparison to what social experts now believe could happen. And because of this, predictions will probably be more accurate than in the past, but they are not so confident in their opinions that they will limit them, especially in the area of technology.)

ENVIRONMENTAL SCANNING

Experts try to predict the future through what is called *environmental scanning*. They examine several factors, and with the aid of history, predict what will change.

With environmental scanning, three categories of variables are used to predict changes in crime. These variables are referred to by social scientists as *drivers*, those variables likely to *drive* the environment, resulting in change.

Social and Economic Conditions

The first variable is the *social and economic conditions* that the country will face in the future. The conditions that the experts examine that can have an effect on crime are the size and age of the population, immigration patterns and employment, and lifestyle characteristics.

Size and Age of the Population

Demographic changes will occur in the future. The baby boomer generation, which is a large portion of the population, is aging. Because of changing demographics, experts believe that there could be an *increase in crimes against the elderly*, because there will be many more of them, and therefore more potential victims. Older adults typically are not common victims of violent crimes, but an increase in other types of crimes, such as frauds and con schemes, will likely increase, especially with advancements in technology, which will aid sophisticated criminals in obtaining personal and financial information from their target victims.

And, as the baby boomers get older, the younger generation will also get older. The age group that commits the most crimes, 18 to 24 year olds, will get older, and will not be committing as much crime. *This may result in a decrease in juvenile and gang crime,* because there will be a fewer individuals in this age group in the very near future. In the previous decade, juvenile and gang crime was up, and this was due to the increased number of people in this age group of potential offenders.

What the police tried to do to stem the tide of juvenile crime in the past was to *change children's values* before they reached an age where they were committing crimes. Experts say that children must be reached by the time they are in third grade: their values and principles are developed by that time, and successful reversal by others is unlikely.

This fact was instrumental in ushering in the many *intervention strategies and police programs designed to prevent children from becoming future criminals* such as the D.A.R.E. program, which was designed to educate students in the dangers of drug abuse. (Note that programs such as this may not be as much of a priority in the future, when the demographics change again, and because there is evidence that D.A.R.E. is a failure.)

It is not the responsibility of law enforcement to cure all of society's ills, but the police are in a unique position to intervene in many instances by supporting and being involved in programs that change or modify juvenile's behavior before they commit serious crimes. When the demographics change again, and kids are committing most of the crime, the police will again have to focus on this age group, by being prepared with new intervention programs and enforcement tactics, such as gang interdiction units.

Immigration Patterns and Employment

Changes in immigration laws will have an effect on crime. If immigration into the country increases, it will not necessarily cause an increase in crime committed by immigrants. There are more native-born Americans than immigrants in prisons. What will occur is an increase in *immigration victimization*, because immigrants are more prone to being victimized than native-born Americans.

The potential increase in immigration will create unique problems for law enforcement:

- More *bilingual police officers* will be needed for improved efficiency and effectiveness.
- This will also help the police in another challenge they will have to face, which is to *develop an environment of trust* between the police and the immigrants, who traditionally come from an environment in which the police are brutal and corrupt.
- This trust issue will likely be impossible for the police to build up if the current trend of involving local law enforcement with the *enforcement of immigration laws* continues. Not that the police should not be doing this, perhaps they should, but legislators and police administrators must take this trust issue into consideration when making these future decisions, and decide what their priorities should be.

Besides the immigrant victimization issue, as immigrant groups cluster into low-income areas the police become more involved because of the increase in crime that usually accompanies dense, low-income areas.

Also, as lower-income jobs become scarcer due to increased immigration, it could lead to unrest and violence in these groups. This will result in an additional burden to law enforcement, adding to their every growing responsibility as well as increasing calls for service and a probable increase in the crime rate.

Historically, *when the poverty level is high, property crimes also increase.* So, if there is a marked increase in unemployment, it will predictably lead to an increase in property crimes. Because of this, future employment levels will have to be continually monitored to assist experts in predicting an increase or decrease in property crimes.

Another social factor that could have an effect on the poverty level, and thereby cause an increase in crime, has to do with technology and education. With the workforce becoming much more technologically oriented, there is a higher demand for educated workers. *This may cause a shrinking of the middle class.* The good jobs (i.e., the high-tech and public service jobs) will go to the educated workers, leaving the uneducated out of the high-paying job market. The educated middle class with get richer, and the uneducated will become poorer.

Lifestyle Characteristics

Society has gone back and forth on drug-related issues. If drug use is decriminalized (such as decriminalization of marijuana in the 1970s), it may reduce drug-related crimes. If someone can buy cocaine at the drug store, there will be fewer "bad drug deal" homicides and robberies, but it is unknown how it will affect other crimes.

For instance, historically, a large number of crimes are committed by drug users who need the money to buy drugs. But if drugs are cheap and easy to buy, it may result in fewer crimes being committed by drug users needing the money for a fix. On the flip side, many violent crimes and traffic accidents are caused by individuals who are under the influence of drugs. (Statistics show that almost 4 out of 10 violent crimes involve the use of alcohol.) If drug use becomes acceptable behavior, there could be an increase in crimes caused by people being impaired.

The divorce rate in the country is well over 50 percent. It is believed that this trend will continue. If it does, this factor alone could have an effect on the crime rate. *Studies show that children from one-parent homes commit a disproportionate amount of crime.* As divorce rates increase, so will the level of crime by juveniles. So, even though the change in demographics will result in fewer potential juvenile offenders, more of the kids in this demographic category will become actual offenders.

Statistics show that 90 percent of homeless children and runaways come from one-parent families. Seventy percent of juveniles who are incarcerated come from fatherless home as well, 75 percent of kids in drug abuse institutions are also from single-parent homes.

Shifts in the Amount and Type of Crime

Technological advancements have occurred at a breathtaking pace over the past 20 years. This has resulted in new types of crimes that the police must deal with. Identification theft and other computer-assisted crimes have replaced the more mundane and less-challenging theft cases. As criminals begin to catch on to more ingenious ways to commit crime, the police will have to keep pace with them, and develop ways to identify and apprehend them.

For instance, when cellular telephones first became popular, criminals devised a way to steal the electronic identifier of other telephones, and then implant them into another telephone. They then sold the telephone to someone who used the telephone for a month or so until the victim discovered the crime and had the service cancelled. (This was when cellular telephone usage was very expensive.)

The police had to devise ways to identify whether or not a telephone had been "cloned" or not. Eventually, technology caught up with the criminals, and cloning of cellular telephones is no longer a crime problem.

Developments in the Criminal Justice System

Three areas will have a significant impact on the criminal justice system in the future: technology, community policing, and attitudes about incarceration and rehabilitation.

Technology

The information systems used by police agencies are not as sophisticated as they could be. Each police department has a computer system that is independent of those of other police departments. (This does not include state and federal information systems that all agencies have access to.) If a detective wants to find out about any contacts that a suspect has had with the police, he would need to contact the various police departments that the detective believes the suspect may have had contact with.

Steps have been made in this area, however. Some police agencies are being invited to join voluntary integrated systems in which member agencies will have access to other agencies' computer systems. Eventually, when police departments can afford to upgrade, this impediment will soon be a thing of the past.

Advances in technology are certainly going to help law enforcement, but it is also going to hurt it.

How technology is going to *help* law enforcement:

- **Integration and improvement of information systems:** The ability of the police to solve crimes is greatly dependent upon their ability to get information quickly. As these systems improve, it will likely improve their ability to identify and apprehend offenders.
- **DNA testing:** Identification of offenders through their DNA has had a tremendous effect on the effectiveness of the criminal justice system. Convicted felons of certain crimes are required

to submit their DNA to a data bank. As the range of offenders is increased, which will increase the size of the data bank, the number of offenders being identified will also increase. If this process ever gets to the point that it currently is with fingerprints, then DNA technology will be responsible for a great number of solved crimes.

- **Video and audio recording devices:** Many police agencies are taking advantage of this technology for assisting them in recording criminal activity, obtaining incriminating statements and actions, as well as providing protection from liability exposure. As technology continues to improve, many more agencies will take advantage of it, which will likely result in stronger criminal cases.

- **Red light cameras:** Technology has helped the police enforce traffic laws, which are meant to reduce traffic collisions and the resultant injuries. Camera systems have also been used to enforce speed laws and are being installed in high-crime areas to monitor and record criminal activity. As this trend continues, and technology improves, this type of patrol could revolutionize the concept of police patrol. In the future, the use of satellites for police surveillance and patrol could make traditional police patrol obsolete.

How technology is going to *hurt* law enforcement:

- **Increased sophistication of criminals:** As law enforcement has already seen, criminals are becoming more sophisticated as they learn to commit crimes with the use of computers and the Internet. The risk of apprehension in committing these crimes versus the higher payoff is drawing a high number of criminals to this new trend in criminal activity.
- **Speed of change:** It is often a case of the police playing "catch up" with new types of crimes that are being committed. In fact, with the dramatic improvements in technology the law cannot keep pace with the changes. Several years ago, there were no Internet sexual predator laws because until Internet usage became widespread, these activities were not occurring. When they did begin to occur, and quite rapidly increase, law enforcement had to scurry to create laws to protect children from sexual predators prowling the Internet for victims.

Community-Oriented Policing

If community-oriented policing works, the police will continue to use it and remain as an open system by sharing responsibility of crime control with the communities they serve. But, if it does not work, the police will revert back to their traditional form, one that has worked for them for many years.

the removal of layers of management and supervision in the formal organizational structure.

This organizational restructuring simply has not happened. It is unlikely that managers will be willing to give up their positions and power. Such a radical departure from tradition is so counterintuitive to what the police accept and are comfortable with that it is highly unlikely that it will ever occur.

Attitudes Regarding Incarceration and Rehabilitation

If society reverts back to a *rehabilitation approach* to corrections, it will result in the early release of convicts, which will cause the crime rate to increase. When correctional systems are required to use this approach, convicts are released when it appears that they have changed and are ready to lead crime-free lives. However, the recidivism rate is extremely high, and most offenders who have done time in prison become repeat offenders.

Currently, crime continues to decrease in no small part because of the *incarceration approach* to corrections. Offenders are being required to serve a higher portion of their sentences than they were in the past. When convicts are in prison, as opposed to in society, they are unable to commit new crimes. Consequently, there are fewer criminals running free and committing crimes.

SCENARIO WRITING

Based on the variables that the experts think may have an effect on crime in the future, the next step in their analysis is to use *scenario writing* by applying these drivers (variables likely to drive the environment) to three primary situations: the amount of crime, the tolerance of crime, and the ability of the criminal justice system to deal with crime.

- **The amount of crime:** Obviously, one of the goals of the experts is to predict how much crime there will be based on the social and economic conditions, shifts in crime, and developments in the criminal justice system.
- **Tolerance of crime:** The futurists will also attempt to predict what will be a crime in the future, and what will not be a crime based on lifestyle characteristics of the future. For instance, efforts have been made to decriminalize some offenses that are considered "disorderly activity," which as we already know, is marginal criminal activity that in itself is not a huge danger to society but can lead to more significant criminal activity if it is not kept under control. Besides these marginal offenses, which are laws primarily meant to maintain public order, efforts have been made to decriminalize some drug offenses, arguing that addiction is a disease, not a lifestyle choice.

  Example: In May 2006, Mexican officials announced that citizens could possess small amounts of various illegal drugs for personal use. It is only because of heavy pressure by the United States that Mexico amended its plans.

- **The ability of the criminal justice system to deal with crime:** When analyzing this situation, experts predict how effective the system will be based on changes in technology, community support, and budgetary issues.

The futurist experts bring these together the environmental scanning variables and the three scenarios and provide a variety of possible predictions, which are based on each driver being high or low. For instance, they make a prediction on how the *social and economic conditions* will affect the criminal justice system if the *amount of crime* is low, and if it is high. Then they will make a prediction on how the *social and economic conditions* will affect the criminal justice system if the *tolerance of crime* is low, and if it is high.

So, these futurists do not actually predict what will happen in the future—oh, that they could. They simply offer a variety of possibilities based on uncontrollable variables.

CHANGES IN POLICE LEADERSHIP IN THE FUTURE

If community-oriented policing continues, and it is taken seriously, it will mean a *flattening of the hierarchy*, which means fewer layers of police management, and more responsibility and authority usually reserved for these positions conferred upon those who are ultimately responsible for reducing crime—the police officers on the street.

As mentioned earlier in this chapter, little evidence suggests that major organizational changes such as this will actually occur, because in the decades that community policing has been implemented by hundreds of police agencies there have been virtually no significant organizational changes to reflect this fundamental tenet of community policing—decentralization of power, evidenced by the removal of management positions.

And if community-oriented policing does actually continue, and is genuine, *it will require a major change in the leadership style* that police administrators use. Traditionally, police managers use an autocratic style, in which they give orders, and subordinates carry them out without question. This style simply will not work in a true community-oriented policing approach. Police administrators will have to *change their style from one of power and control to one of power sharing.*

Police administrators will have many other issues to deal with as well. With the increased complexity of society, it has placed many more responsibilities on the shoulders of law enforcement, without additional resources to address them. To compound the problem, police agencies will continue to deal with *reduced budgets,* which will inhibit their ability to meet their goals and objectives. The bottom line is this: they will have to learn to do more with less.

But some experts believe that rather than the police having to do more with less, they will have to do less with less. That is, police management is going to have to develop priorities for police service with the community and may have to consider *reducing some services* not directly related to law enforcement.

> **Example:** Many police agencies have discontinued investigating noninjury traffic collisions on private property, because most traffic laws do not apply on

private property, and therefore, are not
police business. This has been expanded
by many agencies to include noninjury
collisions on roadways as well.

Any decisions about the reduction of services, however,
will be based on the individual needs, expectations, and
organizational philosophies as to the priorities of the
agency and the community.

As police departments continue to deal with reduced
budgets and higher demands for service, administrators
will have to consider the issue of *user fees*. Currently,
citizens are charged for some of the services that the
police provide, such as public fingerprinting, background
checks, collision investigation reports, and false alarm
responses.

These fees have become common practice, and it is
expected to continue. Currently, most user fees are not
accurately calculated to reflect the true cost of a service.
Many administrative costs and overhead costs are not
factored in, resulting in a much lower fee than would be
appropriate. Consequently, as the realities of true costs
are realized by agencies, costs commensurate with the
services will likely be the result.

Example: When someone is involved in a
traffic accident, it costs about $10 to get a
copy of the report. If all the overhead
costs of the investigation are factored in,
such as the salary of the officer, a portion
of his training and equipment, dispatch
salaries, administrative, and facility

overhead costs, the $10 report would actually cost several hundred.

Example: Because of the high number of false burglary alarms, many cities have enacted ordinances that call for fines when there are too many false activations. For example, after three false alarms in a year, the property owner will be required to pay $25. This sum is not even a fraction of the cost that has been spent by the police department to respond to these false alarms. If all the costs were taken into account, the fines would be in the hundreds, if not thousands, of dollars.

Because of the reduced budgets, law enforcement agencies will continue to be faced with *downsizing*, resulting in fewer positions in the agency and *fewer promotions* being available to those who wish to promote within the agency. In police departments, when positions are eliminated because of budgetary shortfalls, the decision makers know better than to eliminate the essential positions, those at the line level who deliver the services of the agency to the community.

Rather, they cut the fat, the supervisory and management positions that are important but not critical for the organization to function. Additionally, if management does continue with community policing, which means eliminating supervisory and management positions, it will mean even fewer positions will be available for officers who want to promote.

If these traditional rewards will not be available, police managers are going to have to devise some other way to provide for an adequate reward system for officers. They will have to develop methods to *enrich and enlarge* the jobs of the officers so that the officers still have a high level of job satisfaction, and their morale and motivation levels are not negatively affected:

- **Job enrichment:** Management can enrich an officer's job by giving him additional responsibility beyond the level of competency that he is currently required to demonstrate. This can provide for a feeling of accomplishment and job satisfaction that may satisfy the officer's desire to seek the traditional goal of promotion to achieve this feeling. Again, if community policing is taken seriously, and management does all the things they are supposed to do regarding the flattening of the hierarchy and decentralization of power, then job enrichment in police organizations may be possible. Job enrichment is management's attempt at making the jobs more challenging.

- **Job enlargement:** Management can enlarge the scope of a police officer's job by giving them additional responsibilities, but at a level commensurate with the level of competency that they are currently required to demonstrate. In other words, the officers would have much more variety in their jobs, but it would not be responsibility beyond their normal job descriptions. With the high level of specialization in law enforcement, this is difficult to accomplish. But, if community policing is successful, it might be possible to provide officers with a higher level of job enlargement, because community policing gives officers additional duties and responsibilities to their current assignments. Job enlargement is management's attempt to make the jobs more interesting.

Besides all of these challenges, police leaders must realize that they will be encountering a *different workforce culture* than they have in the past. As we learned in chapter 9, because of the affluent and peaceful era that they grew up in, the people entering the law enforcement workforce have a higher concern for higher salaries and recreation time. And because they are less likely to submit to an autocratic management style, officers will require some involvement in work decisions.

CONCLUSION

Obviously, the future is uncertain—for society in general, and for law enforcement as well. The terrorist attacks of 9/11 attest to the fact that the course of human events can move from a predictable one to one which causes the imagination to reel. The unimaginable of today can be tomorrow's reality in the blink of an eye.

But monumental and catastrophic events aside, many predictable variables allow experts to formulate a number of possible scenarios for what we can expect see in the future. Community policing takes center stage here. If law enforcement efforts are successful in reducing crime using this approach, then the era of community policing will continue to thrive. However, if crime rates increase, it is very likely that the police will abandon the warm and fuzzy philosophy of community policing and revert back to what has worked in the past—making arrests and preventing crime through a strong and intimidating presence. And since in the past, this approach was only marginally successful, the police will have to step it up a notch; that is, become more authoritarian and militaristic than they have ever been, and much more than they want to be.

Let's face it, the police do not want a police state any more than anyone else; they have to live here, too. But if the alternative is to live in constant fear of crime and violence, the police will relinquish to reason that what they have to offer is the lesser of two evils.

How's that for a job description? "The lesser of two evils." As stated earlier in this book, police officers are American citizens who have chosen to do society's dirty work for them. Believe it or not, police officers are society's most staunch supporters of individual liberties and personal dignity. They are the defenders of the American dream, which is to live freely and unmolested in a civilized and just environment.

Whatever the future holds for this country, Americans can rest assured that their police officers will rise to the occasion and take on the monumental task bestowed upon them: to protect and to serve the public, placing themselves in harms' way to preserve the lifestyle that has become the envy of the world, the lifestyle of a free American.

Anecdotal evidence of the success of community-oriented policing exists, but there have also been many failures, which obviously do not make it into the professional journals and publications. Community policing is expensive and difficult to maintain, primarily because of the required public involvement. Consequently, many police agencies have shifted toward problem-oriented policing, which is a modern approach to traditional policing—solving crime problems—but doing it intelligently and ingeniously.

One group of experts has an interesting prediction about the future of police operations. They state that rather than continuing with community policing, they predict *a move toward a more militaristic approach to policing*. To them, community policing is turning into more of a fancy public relations campaign rather than an effective solution to crime control. Problem-oriented policing, on the other hand, is an effective and modern tactic that works well with the traditional policing approach.

So, if the crime problem gets worse, and the rhetoric and fluff of community policing does not work, the police will likely revert back to what has worked for them in the past. In support of this belief is a study that shows that even with community-oriented policing police structures have remained relatively unchanged. This supports the notion that community policing is all talk to most agencies, and nothing more than an expensive public relations program. True community policing calls for a *decentralization of power* so that the majority of authority is relinquished to patrol officers, rather than to managers and supervisors Acceptance of this tenet of community policing would require a *flattening of the hierarchy*; that is,

Appendix A

Typical Bureaucratic Organizational Chart

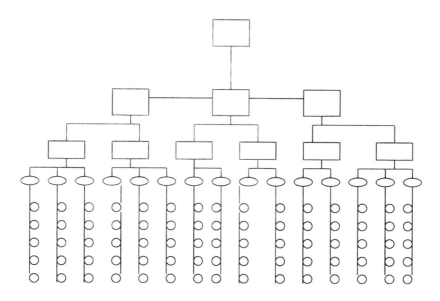

This chart shows five hierarchical levels in the organization.

These levels, in descending order are:

Chief Executive Officer	(Chief of Police)
Upper Manager	(Captain)
Mid Manager	(Lieutenant)
Supervisor	(Sergeant)
Line Level Employee	(Police Officer)

Appendix B

Maslow's Hierarchy of Human Needs

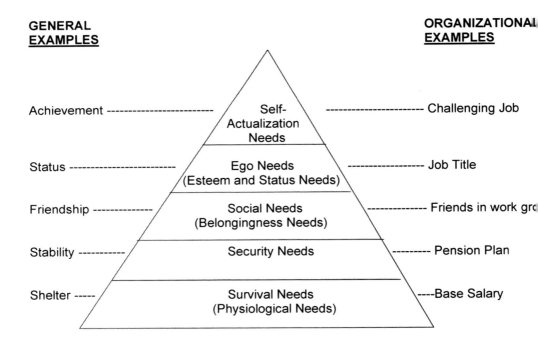

GENERAL EXAMPLES

ORGANIZATIONAL EXAMPLES

Achievement ------------------------- Self-Actualization Needs ----------------------- Challenging Job

Status ------------------------ Ego Needs (Esteem and Status Needs) ------------------ Job Title

Friendship -------------- Social Needs (Belongingness Needs) -------------- Friends in work gro

Stability ----------- Security Needs --------- Pension Plan

Shelter ----- Survival Needs (Physiological Needs) ----Base Salary

Appendix C

Criminal Justice System

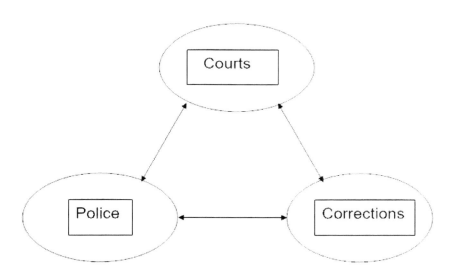

BIBLIOGRAPHY

Bennett, Wayne W., and Karen M. Hess. *Management and Supervision in Law Enforcement*. Belmont, CA: Thompson Wadsworth, 2004.

Bock, Wally. "Recruitment, New Kids on the Beat." *The Police Chief* (December 1990).

Brown, Gary E. "What You Always Wanted to Know about Assessment Centers but Were Afraid to Ask." *The Police Chief* (June 1978).

Cohen, Stephen L. "Pre-Package vs. Tailor Made: The Assessment Center Debate." *Personnel Journal* (December 1980).

Crank, John P. *Understanding Police Culture*. Cincinnati: Anderson Publishing, 1998.

Delattre, Edwin J. *Character and Cops*. 4th ed. Washington, D.C.: AEI Press, 2002.

Flynn, John T., and Barbara E. Anderson. "The Development of Reliable Oral Interview Procedures for Promotional Candidates." *Journal of Police Science and Administration* (1985).

385

Fridell, Lorie, Robert Lunney, Drew Diamond, and Bruce Kuba. *Racially Biased Policing: A Principled Response.* Washington, D.C.: Police Executive Research Forum, 2001.

Gaines, Larry K., and Victor E. Kappeler. *Policing in America.* 5th ed. Cincinnati: Anderson Publishing, 2005.

Graham, Gordon. "Civil Liability for Public Sector Organizations." Seminar, 1996.

Gilbert, James N. *Criminal Investigation.* 5th ed. Upper Saddle River, NJ: Prentice Hall, 2001.

Hess, Karen M., and Henry M. Wrobleski. *Police Operations, Theory and Practice.* 3rd ed. Toronto: Wadsworth/Thompson Publishing, 2003.

Holmes, Robert R., and Jerald R. Vaught. "Structured Oral Promotional Examinations." *The Police Chief* (January 1980).

Hunter, Ronald D., Thomas Barker, and Pamela D. Mayhall. *Police–Community Relations and the Administration of Justice.* 6th ed. Upper Saddle River, NJ: Prentice Hall, 2004.

International Association of Chiefs of Police. "Sample Professional Traffic Stop Policy and Procedure." Alexandria, VA: IACP, p. 2.

Joiner, Dennis A. "Assessment Center in the Public Sector: A Practical Approach." *Public Personnel Management Journal* (1984).

Klofas, John, Stan Stojkovic, and David Kalinich. *Criminal Justice Organizations: Administration and Management.* Belmont, CA: Thompson/Wadsworth Publishing, 1990./

Lyman, Michael D. *Criminal Investigation: The Art and the Science.* 2nd ed. Upper Saddle River, NJ: Prentice Hall, 1999.

Lungren, Daniel E. C.O.P.P.S., Community Oriented Policing and Problem Solving: Definitions and Principles. California Department of Justice, Attorney General's Office, 1995.

Murray, Charles, Tetsuro Motoyama, and W. V. Rouse. *The Link Between Crime and the Built Environment: The Current State of Knowledge.* Volume I. Washington, D.C.: U.S. Department of Justice, National Institute of Justice, 1980.

More, Harry W. *Special Topics in Policing.* 2nd ed. Cincinnati: Anderson Publishing, 1998.

More, Harry W., and W. Fred Wegener. *Behavioral Police Management.* New York: Macmillan, 1992.

National Center for Women and Policing. *Equality Denied: The Status of Women in Policing.* Los Angeles: National Center for Women in Policing, 1998.

Nowicki, Ed. "Racial Profiling Problems and Solutions." *Law and Order* (October 2002): 16–18.

Peak, Kenneth J. *Policing America: Methods, Issues, Challenges.* 2nd ed. Upper Saddle River, NJ: Prentice Hall, 1997.

Peak, Kenneth J. *Policing America: Methods, Issues, Challenges.* 4th ed. Upper Saddle River, NJ: Prentice Hall, 2003.

Schott, Richard. G. "The Role of Race in Law Enforcement: Racial Profiling or Legitimate Use?" *FBI Law Enforcement Bulletin* (November 2001): 24–32.

Souryal, Sam S. *Police Organization and Administration.* 2nd ed. Cincinnati: Anderson Publishing, 1995.

Stojkovic, Stan, David Kalinich, and John Klofas. *Criminal Justice Organizations: Administration and Management.* Belmont, CA: Thompson/Wadsworth Publishing, 2003.

Thibault, Edward A., Lawrence M. Lynch, and R. Bruce McBride. *Proactive Police Management.* 6th ed. Upper Saddle River, NJ: Prentice Hall, 2004.

Thurman, Quint C., and Jihong Zhao. *Contemporary Policing: Controversies, Challenges, and Solutions.* Los Angeles, CA: Roxbury Publishing, 2004.

Walker, Samuel, and Charles M. Katz. *The Police in America: An Introduction.* 5th ed. Boston: McGraw-Hill, 2005.

Wallace, Harvey, Cliff Roberson, and Craig Stechler. *Fundamentals of Police Administration.* Upper Saddle River, NJ: Prentice Hall, 1995.

Weston, Paul B., and Kenneth M. Wells. *Criminal Investigation: Basic Perspectives.* 7th ed. Upper Saddle River, NJ: Prentice Hall, 1997.

Whisenand, Paul M., and R. Fred Ferguson. *The Managing of Police Organizations*. 4th ed. Upper Saddle River, NJ: Prentice Hall, 1996.

White, Michael D. *Current Issues and Controversies in Policing*. Boston: Pearson Education, 2007.

Wilson, James Q., and George L. Kelling. "Broken Windows: The Police and Neighborhood Safety." *The Atlantic Monthly* 249 (March 1982): 29–38.

CPSIA information can be obtained
at www.ICGtesting.com
Printed in the USA
LVOW10s0447160817
545127LV00008B/22/P

9 781516 522965